Finger Lakes
Bicyclist's Tour Guide

2nd Edition

Harvey Botzman

Finger

Lakes

Bicyclist's

Tour

Guide

2nd Edition

Harvey Botzman

Cyclotour Guide Books
Rochester, New York

2006, Revised 2008

Finger Lakes Bicyclist's Tour Guide, 2nd Edition
© Harvey Botzman, 1998, 2005, 2006, 2008.
Cyclotour Guide Books
PO Box 10585
Rochester, New York 14610, USA
www.cyclotour.com
cyclotour@cyclotour.com

Other books by the author:
Long Distance Bicycle Touring Primer
'Round Lake Ontario: A Bicyclist's Tour Guide
'Round Lake Erie: A Bicyclist's Tour Guide
'Round Lake Huron: A Bicyclist's Tour Guide
'Round Lake Michigan: A Bicyclist's Tour Guide
'Round Lake Superior: A Bicyclist's Tour Guide
Erie Canal Bicyclist and Hiker Tour Guide
Please use the order form at the end of this book.

Disclaimers:

The author, publisher, wholesale and retail purveyor or library owner of this book and its contents are not responsible for your bicycle riding habits or bicycle. They encourage users of this *Guide* to wear a helmet; use a bicycle which is in mechanically sound condition; use reflectors; use lights; wear clothing which is readily visible to motorists, pedestrians and others; watch for other vehicles and pedestrians; position yourself and your bicycle correctly on a roadway; and obey all traffic laws, rules and regulations.

Road and trail conditions change. The routes suggested herein may be altered due to road and trail construction, surface conditions; your need to explore; and factors beyond the control of the author, purveyors and library owner of this *Tour Guide*. Every effort has been made to provide accurate information.

LCCN: 2005903285

ISBN: 9781889602332 (ISBN: 1-889602-22-7)

10 9 8 7 6 5

To Adventurers

*Adventure is
discovering the
unlimited potential
of oneself in unfamiliar
environments and situations.*

Finger Lakes Bicyclist's Tour Guide, 2nd Edition

Harvey Botzman

Preface	9
Route Segments and Distances	11
Tour Preparation	17
Information Sources	37
How to Read the Entries	39
Getting to the Starting Point	43
Cyclists! Start Your Pedals Rotating	51
Of Ice and Water	71
Ice Covers the Earth	81
Debris	95
Hills and Routes	113
Size and Depth	163
Hey, These Aren't Finger Lakes	183
Moo and Yum	191
Politics	215
Conquest and Settlement	235
Water	241
Women	245
Pristine and Not So Pristine	257
Bibliography	261
Appendix	263
Index	277

I

Preface

Bicycle tour guides are strange books to write. There is almost always another way to go from point A to point B. The routes chosen in this *Guide* were particularly fraught with alternatives. A steeper direct route verses a rolling hills indirect route. A view of a lake from an *on high* route verses a view from a shore line route.

The route choices were made with the non-resident cyclotourist in mind. To the bicyclist familiar with the Finger Lakes a few magnificent vistas might be missing; a few unbelievably challenging roads avoided. All to accommodate the folks who come to the Finger Lakes Region to bicycle, meet kindred spirits and most likely have a limited amount of time to tour the area.

Each Lake has a circumnavigation route. Each of the eleven major Finger Lakes has at least two connecting routes between the Lake to the East and to the West of it.

The common perception is that the North-South route along each Finger Lake is a level roadway (OK, with a few rolling hills). Such is not necessarily the case. Thanks to glaciation the northern end of each Lake is at a higher elevation than the southern end of each Lake. Thanks to erosion the route along the lake shore sometimes is relatively level.

Have no fear, there are level routes among the challenging hill laden routes particularly at the northern ends of the Lakes. The areas between each Lake and at the southern ends of the larger Lakes have challenging ascents and descents which should be treated with respect.

These inclines and declines will make your ride around a specific Lake longer both in distance and time. Allow extra time and energy to account for climbing the *hill*.

Have fun.

Route Segments

Segment	Page	Mi.	Km.
Syracuse to Otisco Lake	51	24.6	39.6
Rochester to Conesus Lake	57	25.5	41.0
Rochester to Hemlock, Honeoye & Canandaigua Lakes	67	33.4	53.7
Otisco Lake Circumnavigation	72	16.9	27.2
Otisco Lake to Skaneateles Lake Northern Direct Connecting Routes	75	7.4	11.9
Otisco Lake to Skaneateles Lake Northern Scenic Connecting Route	76	7.1	11.4
Otisco Lake to Skaneateles Lake Middle Connecting Route	77	2.0	3.2
Otisco Lake to Skaneateles Lake Southern Connecting Route	78	7.2	11.6
Skaneateles Lake Circumnavigation	82	35.9	57.8
Skaneateles Lake to Owasco Lake Northern Connecting Route	89	10.6	17.1
Skaneateles Lake to Owasco Lake Middle Connecting Route	90	5.3	8.5
Skaneateles Lake to Owasco Lake Southern Connecting Routes	91	13.0	20.9
Owasco Lake Circumnavigation	96	35.0	56.3
Owasco Lake to Cayuga Lake Northern Connecting Route	101	17.4	26.0
Owasco Lake to Cayuga Lake Middle Connecting Route	102	10.2	16.4
Owasco Lake to Cayuga Lake Southern Scenic Connecting Route	103	28.0	45.1
Owasco Lake to Cayuga Lake Southern Direct Connecting Route	107	18.7	30.1
Cayuga Lake Circumnavigation	113	81.9	131.8
Cayuga Lake Circumnavigation Triphammer Alternate Route	125	42.3	68.1
Cayuga Lake Circumnavigation Remington Road Route	129	18.1	29.1

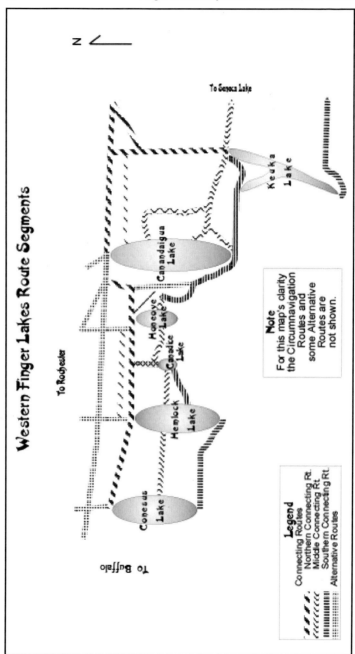

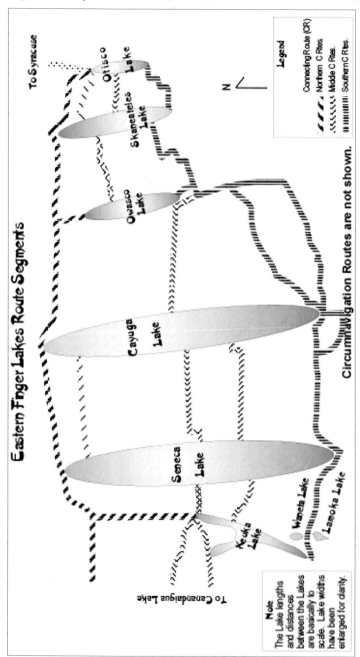

Eastern Finger Lakes Route Segments

To Syracuse

Otisco Lake

Skaneateles Lake

Owasco Lake

Cayuga Lake

Seneca Lake

Keuka Lake

Waneta Lake

Lamoka Lake

To Canandaigua Lake

N

Legend

Connecting Route (CR)

Northern C Rtes.

Middle C Rtes.

Southern C Rtes.

Circumnavigation Routes are not shown.

Note
The Lake lengths
and distances
between the Lakes
are basically to
scale. Lake widths
have been
enlarged for clarity.

Route Segments

Segment	Page	Mi.	Km.
Cayuga Lake Circumnavigation Rt. 96 Projectile Route	132	18.1	29.1
Cayuga Lake Circumnavigation Rt. 89 West Side Route	140	42.3	68.1
Cayuga Lake Circumnavigation Rt. 96 Trajectory Route	143	18.1	29.1
Cayuga Lake to Seneca Lake: Northern Direct Connecting Route	149	9.6	15.4
Cayuga Lake to Seneca Lake: Northern Scenic Connecting Route	151	8.1	13.0
Cayuga Lake to Seneca Lake: Middle Connecting Route	152	6.3	10.0
Cayuga Lake to Seneca Lake: Interlaken - Lodi Connecting Route	154	7.8	12.6
Cayuga Lake to Seneca Lake: Southern Connecting Route	156	25.2	40.6
Cayuga Lake to Seneca Lake: Enfield Loop	160	19.0	30.6
Seneca Lake Circumnavigation	163	78.0	125.5
Seneca Lake Circumnavigation: National Forest Parallel Route	169	11.6	18.7
Seneca Lake to Keuka Lake: Northern Connecting Route	177	20.6	33.2
Seneca Lake to Keuka Lake: Outlet Trail Connecting Route	179	5.0	8.0
Seneca Lake to Keuka Lake: Middle Connecting Route	180	11.0	17.7

Waneta Lake-Lamoka Lake Figure 8
  Waneta Lake Circumnavigation
  Lamoka Lake Circumnavigation
	183
	185
		10.7
		12.1
			17.2
			19.5

Seneca Lake to Keuka Lake: Southern Connecting Route	187	21.5	34.6
Keuka Lake Circumnavigation	191	44.6	71.8
Keuka Lake Circumnavigation: Bath Road Ramble Parallel Route	194	15.0	24.1
Keuka Lake Circumnavigation: V of the Y	202	18.7	30.1

Route Segments

Segment	Page	Mi.	Km.
Keuka Lake to Canandaigua Lake: Rollin' Hills (North) Connecting Route	205	26.5	42.6
Keuka Lake to Canandaigua Lake: Middle Connecting Route	207	35.3	56.8
Keuka Lake to Canandaigua Lake: Southern Connecting Route	210	22.9	36.9
Canandaigua Lake Circumnavigation	215	51.8	83.4
Canandaigua Lake Circumnavigation: Gannett Hill Route	221	10.0	16.1
Canandaigua Lake to Honeoye Lake: Northern Connecting Route	225	19.8	31.9
Canandaigua Lake to Honeoye Lake: Middle Connecting Route	226	19.4	31.2
Canandaigua Lake to Honeoye Lake: Cross Country Connecting Route	228	10.5	16.9
Canandaigua Lake to Honeoye Lake: Southern Connecting Route	230	17.9	28.8
Honeoye Lake Circumnavigation	233	19.4	31.2
Honeoye Lake to Canadice Lake: Northern Connecting Route	237	7.8	12.6
Honeoye Lake to Canadice Lake: Middle Connecting Route	239	2.4	3.9
Canadice Lake Circumnavigation	240	12.2	19.6
Canadice Lake to Hemlock Lake: Northern Connecting Route	242	5.1	8.2
Hemlock Lake Circumnavigation	245	29.7	47.8
Hemlock Lake to Conesus Lake: Northern Connecting Route	253	9.1	14.6
Hemlock Lake to Conesus Lake: Middle Connecting Route	254	10.7	17.2
Hemlock Lake to Conesus Lake: Southern Connecting Route	255	9.0	14.5
Conesus Lake Circumnavigation	257	18.6	29.9
Total Distance for All Listed Routes		1181.9	1902.1

Tour Preparation

Tour Preparation Contents

Types of Bicycle Touring 17
Friends, Family & the Passionate Cyclist 19
Breakdown Cruise 20
Equipment 20
Bicycles 21
Mt. Bikes 22
Tires 23
Gearing 24
Other Bits and Pieces 24
Equipment Lists 25
Climate 25
Food for Body and Mind 26
Carrying Food 28
Repairs of Bike and Body 29
Tools 29
Personal Health and Safety 30
People 30
Lodging 31
Public Transit 31
How to Box Your Bike 33
Maps 34
Postal Addresses 35

Types of Bicycle Touring

I travel as a self-contained bicycle tourist. I cyclotour in this manner in order to intimately view the world where I'm traveling as well as for economic reasons. The philosophical concept of self-reliance has a direct bearing on my mode of travel.

Other people cyclotour with only a credit card, an emergency repair kit, some snacks, and a few pieces of clothing. Some people travel alone others with family or friends. Still others travel with a sag wagon containing all their equipment, friends or family members. Many folks prefer to cyclotour with commercial or non-profit organized tours.

It really doesn't matter why or how you define your form of cyclotouring. You made a choice to travel by bicycle rather than by auto or public transportation. You will meet people who state, "...since I rode my first bicycle I've always wanted to bicycle tour." You're doing it!

In American society we tend to define and classify what we do. In my mind bicycle touring is cyclotouring is bicycle touring. For others the following definitions of cyclotouring can help to sort out the type of touring which best meets your needs and wants. Self-contained (self-reliant) Cyclotouring is when the bicyclist, (alone or with others) carries sufficient equipment to maintain the bicyclist(s) for the entire tour period. The equipment includes but is not limited to camping gear, clothing, personal gear, tools, and food. Obviously, consumables (food, *etc.*) will be replenished as the tour progresses. Self-contained Small Group Cyclotouring is simply a group of people traveling together. The group can include one experienced bicycle tourist who's object is to teach the other group members touring skills. Partially Loaded Cyclotouring is when the bicyclist carries emergency sleeping/camping equipment, basic repair equipment, a limited amount of clothing and personal items, snacks, or food for one meal. Any combination of commercial lodging and preparing one's own food or camping and eating in restaurants all can be considered as partially loaded cyclotouring. Credit Card Cyclotouring is for bicyclists who want to be least encumbered with *stuff!* A credit card or debit card is necessary! Travelers checks will suffice! Only small panniers are needed. The panniers contain the minimum amount of clothing; a small repair kit; snacks (lunch?); a lock; a wallet with credit cards; and a small amount of cash! Meals are eaten in restaurants. Lodging is at motels, b&bs or hostels. The cyclotourist travels by charging everything to the credit card or paying cash (obtained via credit card at ATMs). Hopefully the tourist doesn't forget to pay the bills! Day Tripping is when an individual or a group travel for one day on a round trip tour of a specific area. Usually these travelers carry the bare minimum amount of equipment, eat in restaurants or carry a sandwich. Sometimes a day trip includes an overnight stay at commercial lodging. Personal Sag Wagon Cyclotouring is a touring mode in which the food, camping and bicycle specific equipment is carried in a sag wagon. A spouse or friend functions as the sag wagon driver. The bicyclist(s) carries the minimum amount of snacks, water, repair equipment, and some rain gear. Many times lodging for sag wagon bicycle tourists is at motels or b&bs rather than campsites. The bicyclist(s) and sag wagon can meet at predetermined places for food, sightseeing, fun, and lodging. Segment Cyclotouring is completing a long distance tour over a period of time with breaks to return home. The bicyclist starts each segment at the point where the previous segment was completed. Thus instead of bicycling the entire Finger Lake Region as one continuous cyclotour, the bicyclist might circumnavigate Honeoye Lake one weekend; a few weeks later circumnavigate Cayuga Lake; and on another weekend several weeks later circumnavigate Owasco Lake.

Arranged Cyclotouring is when all long distance touring arrangements (with or without sag wagon support) are made by a non-profit or commercial bicycle tour company. Cyclotourists who have participated in arranged touring have had memorable experiences less the hassles associated with making all the arrangements themselves. They have enjoyed meeting and interacting with people who have similar interests.

Bikepacking is off road cyclotouring. Usually the object is to establish a camping spot and Mt. bike on single track trails from that spot.

Guerrilla Camping is finding a beautiful secluded place, off the road and using it as your camp site. The guerrilla camper makes every effort to obtain permission to camp if there is an indication that the site is on private property.

This *Tour Guide* is designed for bicyclists no matter how they define their mode of cyclotouring.

Friends, Family and the Passionate Cyclotourist

How to convince your non-cycling family members or friends to help you exercise your cyclotouring fantasy without breaking up the relationship!

1. Make certain all family/friends have bicycles.

2. Plan your tour so that the first few overnight stops are 20-30 miles apart. This will allow you to spend time with your loved ones or friends while you tour.

3. The *passionate cyclotourist* bicycles to each overnight stop. At the overnight stopping point, the dedicated cyclist joins the other members of the touring group for an hour or two of recreational bicycling. Enjoy your vacation!

4. The passionate cyclist suggests to the other vacationers that one non-passionate bicyclist accompanies him/her on a portion of the next day's ride between overnight stops.

5. The sag wagon meets you and the co-rider at an intermediate point; picks up the co-rider who normally would not want to bicycle the entire distance between stops. You, the experienced cyclotourist, continues riding the entire distance to the next overnight stop.

6. Continue doing this for a few days and your family and friends will start enjoying *total* bicycle touring with you.

7. Alternatively, purchase a tandem!

Breakdown Cruise

At least two weeks before you plan to leave take a short trial tour. Pack everything you *intend* to take on your long distance cyclotour. Include, in your panniers, what you *think* might be needed on your cyclotour. Ride twenty or thirty miles to a nearby campground. Stay overnight. Make notes on how you and your bike traveled.

When you return home, toss out everything which was superfluous on your weekend trip. Be vicious! Be heartless! *"Less is more,"* Mies Van der Rohr said. Truer words were never stated in regard to cyclotouring. The less you load into your panniers the lighter your bike will be! And the more enjoyable your tour will be!

Equipment

Frequently I'm asked what I take on a tour.   There are many bicyclists with more miles under their toes than me who easily carry more equipment than I do. My needs are very basic while cyclotouring. Your needs are different.

One bicycle (kind of essential and I use an old one) - 18 speed, triple crank (24/40/52 x 13/34). In 2004, I purchased a new used bicycle with 21 gears instead of 18. I'm still getting used to this bike.

The panniers are packed as follows:

Right Rear Pannier	Left Rear Pannier
Tent	Stove inside a 1 qt. pan
Tent Poles	Fuel Bottle
Mattress Pad	First Aid Kit
Tools & Lights	Maps, misc. papers
Personal Items	Personal Items
1/2 "U" lock	1/2 "U" lock

Sleeping bag on top of the rear rack.

Right Front Pannier	Left Front Pannier
Clothing	Food

Total weight = ~37 lb./17 kg. including panniers.

For aerodynamic and theft reasons, I try to have very few items *blowin' in the wind*!

The load is balanced, left and right sides, front and rear. I shift items between panniers to better balance the load. Rarely is a handlebar bag on my bike.

I use both sets of panniers because I'm small and light weight. In reality all my *stuff* will fit into a set of rear panniers, but if all the weight is on the rear wheels I lose some steering control.

This pannier set up changes when I do not use front panniers. Then the rear panniers are balanced by a handlebar bag containing a limited number of heavy items: "U" lock, camera, snacks (fruit weights a lot), rain wear, towel, and bathing suit.

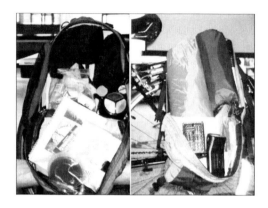

Ready?

Bicycles

Your Bike vs. a Touring Bike

Many cyclotourists, including the author, use traditional road or touring bikes. These are fine bikes to cyclotour in the Finger Lakes area.

For most cyclotourists their tried and true bike will suffice for this set of tours. The limited number of dirt roads (*e. g.*, Honeoye Lake) which must be traversed to 'round a Lake are relatively smooth and solidly packed. If you are riding a knobby tired hybrid or mountain bicycle then change the tires; put some racks and panniers on your bike; and start pedaling!

It is the *fit* not the type or brand of bicycle which is important for successful cyclotouring or any type of bicycling. An improper fit of your body to a bicycle will make riding a horror. A proper fit of your body to a bicycle will make riding a joy.

You can use any type of bike, with some modifications, for this or any other cyclotour. You can place racks, panniers, lights, fenders, different tires, and change the gearing on a standard hybrid, sport tourer, Mt. bike or even a racing bike and still successfully tour! Yes, touring purists! People do successfully tour on department and discount store bicycles.

Traditional touring bicycles with long chain stays and a full range of gears are a rare sight in American or Canadian bike shops.

Approximately ten mass bicycle manufacturers make touring bikes. An additional fifteen or so custom builders make touring bikes. If you think you really need one, have your local bike shop order it.

The primary differences between a touring bicycle and a recreational bike or Mt. bike are in the chain stay length; head tube angle; frame flex; having sufficient frame strength to carry a load; and having sufficient busses for attaching racks, water bottles, *etc.* A touring bike usually has chainstays which are ~18 in./45.7 cm. or more in length. The head tube angle on a touring bike tends to be ~73°.

Yes, all these technical specifications do make for a more comfortable long distance ride.

Bicycle manufacturers put all sorts of *do dads* on recreational bikes to make them appear as touring bicycles. The fact of the matter is that frame strength and flex; chain stay length, head tube angle and gearing are what really determine if a bicycle is a true touring bike not the *do dads!*

Mt. Bikes

A Mt. bike makes a fine touring machine! Traditional touring bike riders may scoff but they do! True, a few modifications are necessary to make a Mt. bike a more efficient touring bike. None the less, they make comfortable touring bikes.

A Mt. bike with a front suspension fork generally can not use front panniers. This means that all the weight of your *stuff* will be on the rear wheel. Use a handle bar bag and place some of the weightier items (U lock) in it to help balance the load.

Or change the front fork! If you do this, make certain that the new suspension fork has busses for attaching front racks. Several manufacturers now make special MTB front forks specifically designed for attaching front racks. Front panniers are not really necessary if you limit the amount of *stuff* you take on your cyclotour! "Less is More!"

A number of rack manufacturers now make special Mt. bike front and rear racks which can be used with front and rear suspended frames. Look through bicycle magazines and check with your local bike shop for these special racks.

Mt. bikes with short chain stays may present a problem with rear panniers. Your heels may continually strike the rear panniers as you pedal. If this occurs on your bike, move the panniers a few centimeters or inches rearward and carefully pack your rear panniers with the heaviest items centered over the axle.

Mt. bike handle bars and handle bar mounted shifters are designed for constant shifting on difficult terrain. Generally cyclotourists do not shift often but need to change their hand positions often to relieve numbness.

Don't go out and purchase a new set of shifters or handlebars! A simple and inexpensive Mt. bike modification is to add bar ends to a Mt. bike handlebar. The bar ends will allow you to use your current shifters and provide additional hand positions to relieve numbness. One type of Mt. bike bar end has the traditional dropped curved section. A number of cyclotourists use bolt on aero bars to provide even more hand positions.

Tires

Many of the roads on which you will be traveling are two lane chip sealed county highways. These roads usually have a small (~2 ft./.6 m.) gravel or mowed grass shoulder. Standard road tires are fine for these roads.

New York State highways are smooth asphalt. These roads usually have a striped paved shoulder of at least 4 ft./1.2 m.

A set of the multipurpose touring tires or hybrid tires will be perfect for the Mt. biker, racer and cyclotourist in the Finger Lakes. Multipurpose touring tires are efficient at negotiating smooth asphalt and will allow you to successfully explore rural dirt roads which strike your fancy along the way.

Slick, no tread tires, are not suitable for touring even if you plan to race around each Lake! Occasionally you might have to go off the roadway onto the gravel or grass shoulder. Slicks, on such surfaces, will provide you with a greater chance to wipe out!

A set of fairly wide, > 28 mm./1⅛ in. wide touring or hybrid tires with a well defined (but not knobby) tread pattern will be well worth their premium price. The well defined tread pattern on either side of the central smooth section will provide excellent traction to slough off roadway and shoulder irregularities. The smooth central road tread area will provide low rolling resistance.

Although Mt. bikes make fine touring machines for this tour, knobby treaded Mt. bike tires are not useful for traveling on asphalt or chip seal. Knobby tires have too much rolling resistance and tend to wear out very out fast on asphalt/chip seal road surfaces touring with a loaded bicycle.

I dislike making endorsements (and I have not received any freebies) and the tire models listed are to provide you with ideas of tread patterns which are most suitable for touring. Continental Top Touring 2000, Continental Town & Country, Michelin Touring, Michelin Wild Gripper, Specialized Nimbus and tires with similar tread patterns allow any cyclotourist, regardless of their type of bicycle (touring, Mt. bike, hybrid, etc.), to efficiently ride on the roads encountered on this cyclotour. These types of tires can also allow you to go occasionally on an off road trail with ease.

Gearing!

A triple chain ring with a relatively small inner chain ring is will be extremely useful cyclotouring around and between the Finger Lakes. There are many significant inclines and many rolling hill sections of the route where you will be unable to gain significant momentum to easily conquer the next hill. A triple will make your bicycling more pleasurable.

Ummmmmm! Mt. bike gearing usually provides a full range of choices for street and off road use. Mt. bikers might find that the higher gears used for road travel are needed for their specific riding style. One relatively easy way to obtain a more suitable gear configuration is to change the chain rings. Simply bolt on a large chain ring with more teeth. Don't forget to remove the current chain ring! You might have wider steps between some gear stops. Keep the small chain ring, you'll need it for the hills!

Given the chain rings on newer bikes (road and mountain), this might not be such a simple modification. Check with an experienced bicycle mechanic at a good bike shop before replacing the chain rings or the freewheel.

Jonathan Perez

"...since my first pedal stroke, I've always wanted to tour"

Other Bits & Pieces

A first aid kit is a necessity.

Rain gear for the inevitable rain shower is a must.

Warm clothing for chilly mornings/evenings and after a rain shower will help prevent hypothermia. Do not take too much clothing, Laundromats are available in both small and big towns. Clothing is bulky and, surprisingly, weighs a lot.

H_2O must be carried. Dehydration is the prime malady of bicyclists. Drink at least 8-12 fl. oz. (235-355 ml.) of water per half or three quarters of an hour. You can add those high energy/electrolyte replacement substances/drinks to your water bottle but good old H_2O and some fruit will be just as effective for the majority of cyclotourists.

Equipment Lists

Do not take too much! *Less is more!* Excess weight due to excess equipment, clothing, tools, and food make a bicycle tour a drudgery rather than a pleasure. There are sufficient supply depots along the way. The US Postal Service & UPS are always available to send *stuff* home!

The *Equipment Lists* can help you plan and choose the items you need on your tour. The *Lists* are simply provided. **You** make the decision what to pack in your panniers. Base your equipment decisions on the type of cyclotouring you are doing—fully loaded to credit card—and your need for *stuff*. You will be able to purchase *stuff* along your route. You will be able to send home anything which is superfluous to your tour if you pack too much *stuff* in your panniers.

Balance your load, front and rear; right and left sides. Do not overload your bicycle.

Climate

Wind: The bane of cyclists! Each Finger Lake is a relatively very large body of water which alters the climate of the surrounding land. Powerful winds suddenly can come off a Finger Lake. These instantaneous winds might last for a few hours at best. The winds can be very strong one day but most likely the next day will be relatively calm, allowing you to travel in splendor. The winds coming off a Lake should not present any significant delays to your travels. Generally the wind blows from the Northwest or West.

Lake Effect: A climate factor called, *lake effect* influences the land mass surrounding large lakes creating a micro-climate area bordering a lake. Lake effect areas have a different climate than a location one or two miles away from the large body of water. You might notice these micro climates as the route verges away from the Lake. Lake effect also contributes to the betterment of man/woman kind by creating ideal conditions for growing wine grapes and certain fruits like apricots.

Altitude: Although the Finger Lakes Region is not at a particularly high elevation, altitude changes will affect the climate where you are riding. There may be sun near a Lake but drizzle or rain on the ridge between two Lakes. Thus be prepared for this slight change and have rain gear readily at hand.

Rain and Temperature: In April and May the day time temperature range is from 50-70°F (10-21°C) with rain a few days week. Rarely does it rain all day. Days during June, July and August are sunny and clear with temperatures in the 73-85°F (23-30°C) range. It rains during the summer about once a week but rarely for more than an hour or two. Evenings in late August can drop the temperature to the high 50s° F (teens° C). Early September days usually are warm with clear cloudless skies.

In late September the day time temperatures begin to descend to the 60-70°F (12-21°C) range. Mid-October brings precipitation similar to September with slightly chillier day time temperatures. The added bonus of fantastic Fall foliage in late September and early October makes the Finger Lakes Region a prime cycling destination for both the locals and visitors from afar.

Snow is not unknown but is a rare occurrence in March and November. Don't think snow hinders bicyclists from using the routes bordering the Lakes. Road cyclists switch to Mt. bikes with knobby tires or simply use tires with a more defined tread pattern. All area bicyclists layer their clothing to ride all year long. Mt. bikers claim that snow is like mud except colder.

Fuel for Body and Mind

I carry very little food. Some pasta, dehydrated sauce mixes, cereal, snacks, fresh fruit, and two bottles of water. Food can be obtained readily in this area.

Along the described route there are very few days when you will not pass at least one small local grocery or convenience store. The routes around Honeoye, Canadice and Hemlock Lakes have few or no stores along their shores.

Perishable products such as meat, cheese, milk or ice cream (the exception is yogurt) do not travel well on a bicycle. It is best to buy perishable products on a daily basis and only within a half hour of stopping to cook and eat them. Salmonella and other gastro-intestinal diseases can turn a delightful tour into a miserable experience. With a little common sense and care you should have few problems.

Without preaching, eating is important. Bicycle touring is a strenuous activity when you are touring everyday for a few weeks. Food and the correct foods to refuel and rebuild your depleted carbohydrate and protein supplies is of utmost importance.

I tend to eat more vegetables and carbohydrates (primarily pasta and rice) and less meat on my tours. These foods are relatively simple to store and prepare on the backpacking stove I use. I do eat my requisite beef, fish and chicken protein sources and they seem to taste even better mixed with farm fresh veggies. Very fresh vegetables and fruit can be bought at the roadside stands. Bananas and most citrus fruit, which tend to be staples of bicyclists, might have to be bought at groceries in towns and cities. You will be missing a vital and satisfying culinary experience if you do not purchase and eat fresh fruit and vegetables from the many stands along the way.

Take your fishing pole! Yup! There are fish in the Finger Lakes. Happy fish. On each Lake's shore you will encounter fisherpersons. And they eat the fish they catch!

If you are planning to catch your meal, check with the New York State Department of Environmental Conservation about eating certain species of fish. Oh! Make certain you have a current fishing license.

Take a chance eating at what appears to be a non-imposing restaurant or tavern. In most cases, you will be pleasantly surprised with a fine, hearty meal and a friendly atmosphere. Similarly, the village bakeries (real bakeries, not the supermarket variety) have superb local delights!

A notation is made in the text of grocery stores, convenience stores, gas stations, and the more permanent farm stands along the route. In urban and suburban areas only the last supply depots before entering a relatively long stretch of road devoid of stores are they noted.

Many State and private campgrounds have small stores which cater to campers. Usually, their selection is limited. Bear in mind that the concessionaires try to stock what is needed most by the campers in a given park. If the park has a large number of RV campers then there will be fewer groceries. Most RV campers come to the park prepared and have little need for purchasing groceries. Make life easy for yourself, plan ahead, stop at a grocery which is within a half hour of your next meal. Use the *Food List* to help plan your needs.

Cookin"

Keep everything light. Try not to buy canned goods. Use dehydrated sauces and fresh foods which will be consumed in a day or two. Price will rarely be a factor for small quantities. A short paragraph about dehydrated food. You are not going to be traveling in an area which is totally isolated from civilization. Only a few 50 mi./80 km. stretches of road are relatively devoid of humanity (trees, grains, fruits, deer and cows being the dominant inhabitants). Expensive backpacker type dehydrated food packets are unnecessary. Search your grocery store for items like packets of sauces, veggie burgers in dehydrated form and pasta. Dehydrated foods—both those specifically designed for backpackers and those off the shelf in a grocery store— should be bought prior to the trip and tested for taste and preparation ease. There is nothing worse than looking forward to an easily prepared meal, making it and then discarding it for its foul taste.

You might find that pasta with locally made cheese is just as easy to prepare as an expensive box of macaroni and cheese. It probably will taste better, too!

Carrying food

Plastic freezer bags are the simplest and easiest way to carry foods. Purchase freezer rather than normal plastic bags, they hold up better. You'll probably need a few different size bags.

Sauces make meals interesting. Instead of carrying bottles or cans of pasta sauce use packets of different varieties of dehydrated sauce mixes (marinara, pesto, alfredo, Thai noodle, sweet and sour, etc.). These are found in almost any grocery store. The dry sauce can be sprinkled on top of a sandwich's interior items as a condiment. A packet of dehydrated sauce can be used for two or three meals! Simply roll over the packet top and place it in a small plastic bag to store them.

Sauce Mixes: Most commercial sauce mixes contain too much salt for my taste. I make my own dehydrated mixes and carry two or three different mixes in different containers. Bulk spices can be found in many grocery stores and natural food stores. You'll only need about .02 oz./.5g of these bulk spices for five days of touring!

Watch your calories; your carbohydrate, fat, and protein balance! Drink sufficient water! Eat enough carbohydrates to refuel your bod. Do not BONK!

Repairs of Bike and Body
Tools

I'm a fanatic about tools. I probably bring too many. After being stuck in some desolate places without a nut or screw of the right size or thread I try to be prepared for almost anything.

In truth there are only two sections of this route where you will be more than 50 mi./80 km. from a bike shop. The Post Office, UPS or a friendly motorist can easily transport a vital item to your campsite or lodging.

Although bicycle shops are located in major cities and towns, hardware stores and general stores abound. Most of these *substitute* bike shops will have something you can use for an emergency repair.

See the *Tool List* and make your own selection. Tools weigh a lot! A real lot! Use discretion. The newer multiple use tools are great, provided they meet your needs. Test the way your tools work before loading them into your panniers.   Combine tools. Unscrew or cut off parts of tools you don't think you'll need. A patch kit, pump, one tube, hex wrenches, and screw drivers are the bare minimum. A spare tire is unnecessary on this trip. If your tire degenerates to the point of no return, simply call the nearest bike shop and have them mail or UPS you a new one.

All and more than is necessary.

Personal Health & Safety

First Aid supplies are absolutely essential on a long distance tour. You can purchase ready made kits or you can assemble your own first aid supplies. Large and small adhesive gauze pads, a general bacterial agent, sun screen, general headache and muscle ache pills, adhesive tape, and a triangular bandage are the basic items. At some time on a tour you will probably use all of these items. It may take two or three years before you do, but you will use them!

Be familiar with the danger signs associated with heat and muscle exhaustion, dehydration, hypothermia, and just being plain tired. Rest. Take care of yourself. Stop riding. If necessary go to a physician or hospital for treatment.

Helmet! Helmet! Helmet! Always wear one! Even on rural roads and urban bikeways. If you have something to protect, your brains, wear a helmet.

In New York State bicycles must be equipped with a rear red reflector (a flashing red rear light is OK if it also is a passive red rear reflector); a front reflector <u>and</u> a front light; aural warning device; and other basic safety equipment.

During the day, the red flashing rear light should be on. It helps to make you more visible to motorists. The red flashing rear light marks you as an experienced safety conscious bicyclist.

During dawn, dusk and night a bright white front light of at least 12w is preferred. You will be traveling on rural roads and highways. As such there will be no street lights. Visibility to motorists and mammals, such as deer, is the key to safe bicycling during dawn, dusk and night.

Wear clothing which is very visible to motorists. When riding into the sun, wear clothing with dark stripes or a patterned shirt. When riding with the sun at your back wear a shirt or which will make you stand out from the scenery and sky. Use lots of reflective clothing during dusk, dawn and at night.

These safety items could save your life.

People

Meeting people and speaking with them is part of the joy and accessibility of cyclotouring.

A touring bicyclist with panniers is generally a rare sight around the Finger Lakes. There are plenty of local bicyclists. I'm sure you'll meet them and have a chat.

The always friendly folks in the Finger Lakes will ask about your trip when you stop for a breather. People will offer help. Answer their queries with delight! Provide stories. Weave tales which will make them jealous.

Loaded cyclotourist's lodging

Lodging

All known bed & breakfasts and campgrounds are listed in the text
with their complete address and telephone numbers. There may
be some recently established lodgings which are not listed.
Conversely, there may be some listed lodgings which no longer
are in operation. These changes are the bane of tour guide
writers and are unavoidable.

Consult the local tourist information office for a current
accommodations list if you have any questions. Lodgings are
not rated.

Public Transit to Your Starting Point

A very efficient and enjoyable way to start your cyclotour is to travel
to the Finger Lakes Region via Amtrak, airline or an intercity
bus. Of course if you live near by just ride to a Lake. This *Guide*
is designed so that a cyclotourist can begin and end at any point
along each of the Finger Lakes. Directions to and from the
major train stations, airports and bus terminals are provided in
the text.

Before you start on your cyclotour, take pictures of your bicycle, with
and without panniers. Open the panniers and take some
pictures of the contents of the panniers. If any damage occurs in
transit you might need these pictures to assert your claim.

Each carrier—airlines, bus companies and Amtrak—have specific
rules regarding the transport of bicycles. All carriers specify that
bicycles must be boxed and shipped as baggage. Amtrak and
the airlines will sell you a box at the terminal. Bus companies do
not have boxes for sale at their terminals.

If you are traveling to the Finger Lakes Region by Amtrak or via an
airline purchase the carrier's box. These boxes are designed so
that you simply have to turn the handlebars and remove the

pedals to fit a bicycle into the box. Very simple! You must have your own tools. A cone wrench is usually needed for pedal removal. On recently manufactured bicycles, a special type of hex wrench will be needed for both the pedals and stem. Make certain that you have the proper type and size wrenches or special tools for the pedals and handlebar stem. No "common" carrier has bicycle tools at any station or terminal. Using the carrier's bike box assures that the carrier can not claim your box was too weak for holding a bicycle. Amtrak's bicycle boxes cost ~US$10.00; the airlines charge US$15.00+. Most commuter airlines do not have facilities for the transport of bike boxes.

Unless you have a folding bicycle or use a Japanese *rinko bukuro* (a bicycle bag, 2m.x 2 m. (6 ft.x6 ft.). Amtrak only carries bicycles in baggage cars. This is significant! Not all Amtrak stations have baggage facilities! Make certain that both your originating and terminating station have baggage facilities for the train which will be transporting both you and your bike. Otherwise your bike will be at one station and you at another.

Fortunately for the cyclotourist coming to the Finger Lakes Region, Amtrak terminals in Rochester, Syracuse and Buffalo have baggage car facilities. Unfortunately, only one train (in each direction), The Lake Shore Limited, has a baggage car. Four trains a day in each direction traverse New York State.

Bus travel presents a different problem. Bus line offices do not stock bicycle boxes. You will have to do one of the following:

1. Obtain a bicycle box from a bike shop;
2. Go to Amtrak or an airline and obtain a box from those carriers;
3. Construct your own box from two or more smaller boxes;
4. Put your (unboxed) bike into the baggage compartment when the driver's back is turned. Many drivers suddenly disappear with the implication that you should do this heinous crime!

Canadian bus companies, most notably, Ontario Northern, use a most efficient method of carrying bicycles. Very large plastic bags can be purchased at major bus terminals for a very moderate charge. The bike is then inserted into the bag and placed in the baggage compartment. Passenger luggage is not damaged by bike grease/oil and the bikes travel just fine on their side.

Ah! To be back traveling in Africa (Peace Corps '66-'69) where bikes are simply placed on top of the bus or lashed to the wall of the train's baggage car. How simple! And rarely were the bikes damaged.

The bike goes into the box and to the Finger Lakes you go!

How to Box Your Bike

The first time I boxed my bike I did it at home. I carefully inserted extra cardboard into the box to reinforce its long sides. I double sealed all edges using reinforced packing tape. I loaded the bike filled box into my station wagon and brought it to the terminal the day before my departure date. It took an interminably long time to do all this >3 hours. What a chore! Make life simple for yourself. Pack the box at the terminal. Allow an extra 30 minutes to pack the box. I'm down to 15-20 minutes *bike into box* packing time now! Last summer with only 20 minutes until the train arrived in Syracuse I packed the bike box at the Amtrak station in in 10 minutes. This rapid packing allowed the baggage agent plenty of time to process the bike box.

1. Bring the following tools:
   Cone wrench (pedals)
   Hex wrenchs (stem bolt)
   Roll of 2" wide reinforced packing tape
   Cord (for tying the handlebars & a crank arm to a chain stay)
   Black felt tipped marker
2. Obtain a bicycle box.
   Clearly mark, with a black permanent felt tipped marker, on at least four sides of the bike box the following information:
   Destination:
   Departure date:
   Train or Flight number:
   Ticket number:
   Your name:
   ↑ pointing to the top of the box
3. Remove both pedals using a cone or hex wrench. Tape or tie one crank to a chain stay. Put your pedals into a pannier.
4. Loosen the brake cables; loosen the stem; turn the stem or

34   Finger Lakes Bicyclist's Tour Guide, 2nd Edition

remove it so as to align the handlebars parallel to the top tube. Wrap or tie the handlebars to the top tube or front rack.
5. Wheel the bike into the bike box.
6. Secure the bike by wedging your sleeping bag/1 pannier between the bike and the box sides. Do not overload the box with heavy panniers. The other panniers go with you as carry on bags.
7. Seal the box with the 2" reinforced packing tape.
8. Bring the filled bike box to the baggage room and obtain a baggage claim check. Keep the claim check with you. You will not be able to claim your bike without this claim check.
Time needed to disassemble your bike and pack the bike box = 20-45 minutes.

At your destination:
Claim your bicycle!
I have to preface this discussion of damage claims with the fact that my bike has never been damaged traveling via Amtrak and only once on a plane trip. Amtrak stores bikes in an upright position in its baggage cars. Airlines and bus lines store bikes on their side in baggage holds. Thus there is a greater chance of damage occurring on airplanes and buses.
Check the bicycle box for possible in transit damage. If you see any damage to the exterior of the bike box, immediately take a picture of the damage and show the damage to the baggage personnel before you open the box.
Open the bike box, check your bike for any damage or missing items. If damage occurred, immediately show it to the baggage personnel and complete the checked baggage damage claim form.
After assembling your bike, take a short ride in the terminal to make certain there was no non-visible damage to the gearing, frame, wheels, etc. If you determine that there is some damage, take a picture of the damage and immediately show it to the baggage personnel. Ask for and complete the checked baggage damage claim form.
Find a local bicycle shop. Purchase the part, etc. Copy the receipt and make copies of your completed claim form. Send a copy of the receipt with the original claim form to the carrier. Mail home, the original receipt and one copy of the claim form. It takes 2-6 weeks for most airlines, bus lines or Amtrak to begin to settle baggage damage claims. Enjoy your cyclotour.

Maps
The maps in this book provide more than sufficient information for you to cyclotour the Finger Lakes circumnavigation and connecting routes. Most of the county tourist agencies will send you a map of their county free of charge.

You can purchase a large sheet map of the entire Finger Lakes Region at most grocery or bookstores along the route. Maps and other paper can be waterproofed by coating them with *Map Seal*.

Postal Addresses

These USPS postal conventions are primarily for visitors from other nations.

The proper form of addressing letters is important for your mail to arrive at its destination. The U. S. Postal Service is very efficient. There are Post Offices in small hamlets and cities throughout the Finger Lakes Region. Letters and weighed packages can be given to any postal worker in a delivery vehicle which you encounter on your tour.

All addresses in this book are in New York State. Thus the postal abbreviation for New York—NY—has not been included. The Zip Codes are included wherever possible.

U. S. Addresses:

Zip codes should be on all mail addressed to the U. S. A.

   USA Zip Codes (postal codes) consist of five or nine numbers:
      NNNNN or NNNNN-NNNN

Addresses should be printed in capital letters without punctuation.
   Use two or three letters to abbreviate roadways.
      street = ST; avenue = AVE; road = RD; drive = DR; *etc.*
      New York = NY.

A return address is placed in the upper left corner of the envelope.
   The stamp goes in the upper right corner.

The addressee's address is centered on the envelope with a .5 in. (2 cm.) blank space at the bottom of the envelope.

RETURN NAME   1st Class
ADDRESS   Postage
CITY ST NNNNN

                        NAME
                        ORGANIZATION
                        STREET
                        CITY ST NNNNN
                        NATION

Information Sources

Glossy tourist brochures with all sorts of information and discount coupons will be joyfully supplied by tourist information bureaus. I suggest that you write for them. A post card will be sufficient. I have had to search, dig and cajole regional and local planners; transportation agencies; county and municipal officials for valid bicycling route information. I've biked around each Lake in both directions; biked between each Lake; and car/bike checked the routes. A very time consuming and expensive endeavor. Exactly why you purchased this book! You can simply cyclotour to your heart's mighty beat!

You should request bicycling information and a bicycling map if only to make tourism officials aware that people do want to bicycle in their locality. Mention that you obtained their address/phone number/web site from *Finger Lakes Bicyclist's Tour Guide* by Harvey Botzman. It helps!

New York State is in the process of developing a full fledged bicycling packet. The State Bicycle Coordinator will send you a number of goodies, unobtainable elsewhere.

As you progress from Lake to Lake you will pass through 9 Counties. A 5 additional counties are included in the list because they are considered as part of the Finger Lakes tourism region or due to their position as originating/terminating points for you tour of the Finger Lakes Region. Each County and regional convention and visitors bureau (CVB), Chamber of Commerce (CofC) or tourism office (TO) is listed below. The information sources are divided into 2 groups, regional and county sources. Then listed alphabetically. The text notes when you cross a County border. Municipal (city and town) information sources are listed in the text.

Do be careful as you cross a county border. The authorities may be hiding behind a billboard and if you're speeding, a ticket will be proffered. A piece of paper to be cherished! Passports are not needed when crossing county borders!

State & Regional Information Sources
Finger Lakes Tourism Alliance, 309 Lake St., Penn Yan 14527, 800 548-4386/315 536-7488, www.fingerlakes.org
New York Wine & Grape Foundation, 350 Elm St., Penn Yan 14527, 315 536-7442, Web site: www.newyorkwines.org
NYS Div. of Tourism, 30 S. Pearl St., Albany NY 12245, 800 225-5697/518 474-4116, www.iloveny.com
Cayuga Wine Trail, PO Box 123, Fayette NY 13065, 800 684-5217/ 607-869-4281, www.cayugawinetrail.com

Keuka Lake Wine Trail, 2375 Route 14A, Penn Yan NY 14527, 800 440-4898/315 536-3791, www.keukawinetrail.com
Seneca Lake Winery Assn., 2 N. Franklin St., Ste. 320, Watkins Glen NY 14891, 877 536-2717, www.senecalakewine.com
NYS Rt. 90 Assn., PO Box 587, Union Springs, NY 13160, 800 889-5836

County Information Sources

Cayuga County Tourism, 131 Genesee St., Auburn, NY 13021, 800 499-9615/315 255-1658, www.tourcayuga.com
Chemung Co. CofC, 400 E. Church St., Elmira NY 14901, 800 627-5892/607 734-5137, www.chemungchamber.org
Cortland County CVB, 37 Church St., Cortland NY 13045, 800 859-2227/607 753-8463, www.cortlandtourism.com
Livingston County Tourism, 4560 Millennium Dr., Geneseo NY 14454, 800 538-7365/585 243-2222, www.fingerlakeswest.com.
Monroe County/Greater Rochester Visitors Association, 45 East Ave., Rochester NY 14604, 800 677-7282/585 546-3070, www.visitrochester.com
Onondaga County Greater Syracuse CVB, 572 Salina St., Syracuse, NY 13202, 800 234-4797/315 470-1910, www.visitsyracuse.org
Ontario County/Finger Lakes Visitors Connection, 25 Gorham St., Canandaigua, NY 14424, 800 654-9798/585 394-3915, www.visitfingerlakes.com
Schuyler County CofC, 100 N. Franklin St., Watkins Glen NY 14891, 800 607-4552/607 535-4300, www.schuylerny.com
Seneca County Tourism, 1 DiPronio Dr., Waterloo NY 13165, 800 732-1848, www.visitsenecany.net
Steuben County CVB, 1 W. Market St., Corning NY 14830, 866 946-3386/607 936-8544, www.corningfingerlakes.com
Tioga County Tourism, 188 Front St., Owego NY 13827, 800 671-7772/607 687-7440, www.visittioga.com
Tompkins County/Ithaca CVB, 904 E. Shore Dr., Ithaca NY 14850, 800 284-8422/315 272-1313, www.visitithaca.com
Wayne County Tourism, 9 Pearl St., Lyons NY 14489, 800 527-6510, www.waynecountytourism.com
Yates County Visitor Ctr., 2375 Rt. 14A, Penn Yan, NY 14527, 800 686-9283/315 536-3111, www.yatesny.com

How to Read the Route Entries

It's really easy! The entire route is broken down into 64 circumnavigation or connecting route segments.

The circumnavigation routes are written as if you are 'rounding a Lake in a clockwise manner starting at the North end of the Lake. That is, with the Lake on your right hand side.

The connecting routes are written as if proceeding from the eastern Lake to the western Lake.

With the exception of the three largest Lakes, each Finger Lake can be circumnavigated in one day. Use care when planning your overnight sojourns. Some villages and hamlets along the way simply do not have formal places to sleep. Guerrilla campers have a distinct advantage in this regard.

At the beginning and end of each circumnavigation and connecting route section you will see, besides normal chapter titles, a barred route heading:

Clockwise & Westbound travelers read the mileage on the <u>left</u> side of the page downwards from the top of the page.

↘

Clockwise	**CANANDAIGUA LAKE**	Counterclockwise
[E to W]	**CIRCUMNAVIGATION**	[W to E]
mi. (km.) Read ↓		mi. (km.) Read ↑

↖

Counterclockwise & Eastbound travelers read the mileage on the <u>right</u> side of the page upwards from the bottom of the page.

The **first line** of an entry gives the cumulative distance in miles and kilometers (in parentheses) in either direction and a location intersection. Usually it is in the form of:

13.0 (20.9)   N. Vine Valley Rd. @ E. Lake Rd.   38.8 (62.4)

Every effort has been made to be accurate in the distances noted. Mistakes might occur! If so, please send me a post card noting the error.

The distances are cumulative. You will have to do the subtraction to find the distances between entries.

The **second line** of each entry usually gives directions: Turn,

Continue, Stop, Look, *etc.* And where to go: *e. g.*, Turn South on to Rt. 31. Cardinal compass directions are used as if proceeding **clockwise** around a Lake or from **East to West when going between two Lakes.** Left and right directions are rarely used.

Turn East on to Co. Rd. 10/N. Vine Valley Rd.

Special Instructions
Counterclockwise and West to East Travelers
Travelers proceeding Counterclockwise and West to East must *reverse* the direction provided in a text entry.

Turn East
should be read as:
Turn **West**.
by ounterclockwise and eest to east travelers

This only becomes a problem if you have absolutely no sense of direction. Counterclockwise/west to east travelers rapidly get used to reading the mileage/kilometage [*sic*] upwards on the right side of the page and mentally reversing the directions. Use builds expertise!

Getting lost has always been a treat for me. I've discovered new and interesting routes, places and most importantly people. Think of it as part of the adventure of traveling.

Information Entries
The entries for cities, towns or villages with specific services appears like this:

NAPLES
Information:
Cycling & Hiking Information:
Services & Facilities:
Accommodations:
Attractions:

If there is no or limited cycling specific information then this category does not appear, likewise with the other parts of this entry.

Bed & Breakfast and camping accommodations are listed with addresses, telephone numbers and sometimes a notation of how far the B&B or campground is from the route.

Chain and local motels are noted simply as *motel* without a name, address or telephone number unless the entry is in a particularly isolated section of the route. For motel accommodations you will have to use a telephone book or write to the information source provided.

Restaurants are only listed as, restaurant without a name.

Symbols
Throughout the text various symbols are used to highlight
   intersecting routes
      ↻ Clockwise Circumnavigation Route
      ↺ Counterclockwise Circumnavigation Route
      ⇔ Connecting Route
      ꜛꜜ Alternative Route

Why things are not in this tour guide.
If every bit and piece of information in my files was listed in this
   Guide, it would be more than 600 pages long and weigh over
   1¾ lb. (68 kg.). Thus a bit of research before you depart will
   allow you to follow the *Less is More* rule! Of course you could
   be a *wanderlust* cyclotourist and let your front wheel lead you to
   wherever!
If you think I should include something in the second edition or in the
   other Tour Guides please complete the Comment and
   SurveyForms and send your suggestions to me.

A Family Outing.

Getting to the Starting Point

For many United States citizens as well as visitors from other nations, New York is New York *City*. For these folks, New York is all skyscrapers and busy people rushing around. Television, radio and the print media just avoid the rest of the State as if it really does not exist. There really is a vast expanse of land between New York City and the Canadian border. It is populated with real people; as well as with farm and wild animals; developed and undeveloped land; and it is crisscrossed with roads, lakes, hills and valleys.

New York Cityites, with their provincial attitude of *nothing exists West of the Hudson River or North of Westchester County*, simply defines their lack of sophistication. The six million of us who live outside the *New York City* metropolitan area realize that for *Cityites* it is a longer distance to go from New York City to the Finger Lakes than it is to go from the Finger Lakes to New York City.

And so be it. "Those 'foreigners' with their strange [downstate] accents just move too fast. They ought to slow down and enjoy life. Smell the wild flowers and view the beauty. It's clean up here and we look after each other." A life long resident of the most rural part of Livingston County once said to me. "I haven't left the County in 30 years. I've never been further from home than Corning, Albany, Niagara Falls, or Rochester. Oh! I once did go to New York City."

Then with a sweep of his hand on that beautiful blue sky morning as a deer was prancing through his field and the birds were singing in his ear, he said, "Why leave all of this!"

For New York Cityites and others from afar who are having a hard time locating the Finger Lakes Region on a map these directions should help you.

Suggestions for traveling by bicycle to the Finger Lakes area follow the Auto section.

Auto

Limited Access Highways

Essentially the Finger Lakes are encased by three limited access Interstate highways and one limited access State highway:

      North: I 90, New York State Thruway
      East: I 81
      West: I 390
      South: NY Route 17/I 86, Southern Tier Expressway

Use any of these roadways to go to the Region's major cities and towns. In some cases you might be as far as 50 mi. (80 km.) from a Lake when you exit the limited access highway. None of these limited access highways have parallel bikeways on their right of ways!

State Highways

Parallel to these Interstate highways are major State highways which bicyclists, both local and touring use:

North:	NY Rt. 5/US Rt. 20
East:	NY Rt. 174
West:	NY Rt. 15
South:	NY Rt. 17

NY Rt. 5 or US 20 traverse and connect the northern tip of each Lake. When Rt. 5 and US 20 junction they are usually pronounced as one single word, *5&20*. Rarely said with *Route* and rapidly spoken.

NY Rt. 15 is the nearest major road between the two western most Finger Lakes. The State highways linking the southern tips of each Lake are numbered differently and many do not go directly from Lake to Lake.

New York State maintained highways have at least a 6 ft. (1.8 m.) shoulder. As State highways are reconstructed their shoulders are widened to this minimum and in many cases to 10 ft. (3 m.). State highways usually have a 6 ft. (1.8 m.) mowed grass shoulder bordering the asphalt shoulder and most trees closer than 12 ft. (3.6 m.) to the roadway edge have been removed. Thus there is usually very little shade on State Highways except early in the morning or late in the afternoon.

Bicycle Routes to the Finger Lakes

For the bicyclist, highways maintained by the New York State Department of Transportation are smooth asphalt.

Directions from Rochester and Syracuse for bicyclists and automobile travelers immediately follow this wordy explanation of transportation modes to the Region.

Bicyclists coming to the Finger Lakes from Boston via Albany, *i. e.*, the East, should follow the Erie Canal route to Syracuse. This route is described in *Erie Canal Bicyclist and Hiker Tour Guide.*

Bicyclists traveling from the West, Chicago/Cleveland, or North from Toronto and entering New York State at Buffalo/Niagara Falls can use the Erie Canal route or the routes described in *'Round Lake Ontario: A Bicyclist's Tour Guide.* The cyclotourist need only turn South from Rochester or Oswego (using the Oswego Canal Route to Syracuse) to enter the Finger Lakes Region. Routes from the West and North leading to Buffalo/Niagara Falls are descibed in *'Round Lake Erie: A Bicyclist's Tour Guide*; *'Round Lake Huron: A Bicyclist's Tour Guide* and *'Round*

Lake Ontario.

Montréal cyclotourists can go South on the Chambly Canal bikeway. From the New York border they would follow the Champlain Canal and the Hudson River to Waterford and the Erie Canal. The *Erie Canal Bicyclist and Hiker Tour Guide* includes these routes from Montréal.

New York Cityites can take the IRT subway to the Bronx Park East or 241st St. & White Plains Rd. stops. Then use to the Bronx River Parkway and its parallel path. The Bronx River Parkway links with the Taconic State Parkway. At the Parkway's terminus, East of Albany, it is a 25 mi. (40 km.) ride to Albany and the beginning of the Erie Canal at Waterford. Alternatively, folks bicycling North from New York City can use New York Bike Route 9 which actually begins in New Jersey at the George Washington Bridge. This is the least hilly of the road options leading from New York City but it does go through many towns. The aforementioned *Erie Canal Bicyclist & Hiker Tour Guide* contains the valid bicycle tour routes along both sides of the Hudson River from New York City to Albany.

On the West side of the Hudson River, Rt. 9W can be used to go to Suffern and Old Rt. 17/Rt. 17C which basically parallels Rt. 17, Southern Tier Expressway. There is a NY Bike Route 17 which goes from the Hudson River to Lake Erie. Folks coming from the the New York City/New Jersey megalopolis should read the next few paragraphs too. Megalopolites do live Southwest of the Finger Lakes!

Those of you who are traveling from the South, even as far South as Florida, can simply use US Rt. 15. Yup, its the same US 15 that hugs the Western edge of the Finger Lakes Region. You will have to traverse some massive hills in WV and Penn. but it is possible to come to the Finger Lakes region via US 15.

From the border of Pennsylvania and New York a cyclotourist can travel North on US 15 to Presho where 15 becomes a limited access highway. From there, parallel local roads take the rider to Painted Post/Corning. Following NY 414 North from Corning brings the bicyclist to Watkins Glen and the southern end of Seneca Lake.

An alternative route North from Waverly on NY Bike Route 17 (NY St. Rtes. 17C & 427 at this point on Bike Rt. 17) using NY Rtes. 34 and 96/96B allows the bicycle tourist to go directly to Ithaca and Cayuga Lake.

From Owego (NY Rtes. 17C & 434 on Bike Rt. 17) near the New York - Pennsylvania border a cyclotourist can travel North on NY Rt. 38 to Moravia and the southern end of Owasco Lake.

Airplane

There are major airports in Rochester, Syracuse and Buffalo (not technically in the Finger Lakes Region). To transport your bicycle on a plane it must be boxed. For instructions on boxing a bicycle refer to the Tour Preparation Chapter. A number of smaller cities in the Region have commuter airline service. Most commuter aircraft do not have a large baggage compartment. Thus bicycles are rarely transported by commuter airlines.

For those of you who have your own airplanes as well as bicycles, you're in luck! Each County in the Finger Lakes region has a general aviation field. A number of towns have air fields (paved and grass). Search your general aviation air field directories for one nearest the Finger Lakes.

The easy way to climb severe hills!

Lake you want to bicycle around! What a way to come here!

Train

Amtrak's Empire Service operates across New York State. As of 2005 there are four trains a day in each direction traversing the region. Bicycles can be carried on Amtrak. Bicycles must be boxed and carried in the baggage car. Only one of the four trains—The Lake Shore Limited has a baggage car. The Lake Shore Limited goes from New York City to Chicago. This train has full baggage car service in both directions. At Albany it connects with Boston and Montréal trains (which sometimes do and sometimes don't transport boxed bicycles in their a baggage cars. Both the Rochester and Syracuse Amtrak stations have checked baggage service.

Cyclotourists with their bicycles coming from Toronto or Windsor can take VIA Rail and GO commuter trains to Niagara Falls. From the Falls, it's a ~90 mi. (~145 km.) to the western most Finger Lake. Amtrak's Maple Leaf and Niagara Rainbow trains do not have baggage service across the border. Weird!

An alternative way for Canadian cyclists to come to the Finger Lakes is to take VIARail/GO trains to Toronto and then cross Lake Ontario using the Toronto-Rochester ferry.

Amtrak is working with the NYS Department of Transportation and local bicycle clubs to make provisions for all of its Empire State Service trains to transport both boxed and unboxed bicycles. When this will be a reality is a giant twisted spoke!

Personally, I use the train to go to New York City, Erie, Cleveland and Chicago with my bicycle. It's the most hassle free way to travel in the Great Lakes region. Certain types of Amtrak fares allow you to disembark and embark at several stops along a route.

Bus
Intercity Bus Service
Intercity bus service in the Finger Lakes Region is primarily operated by New York/Adirondack Trailways, Greyhound and Shortline. There are several other companies which operate in the area. Usually these other companies provide bus service between specific cities, e. g., Cortland and Syracuse. Trailways and Greyhound will get you to the Finger Lakes Region from anyplace in the United States, Canada and Mexico.

You will have to box your bicycle (see the Tour Preparation Chapter.) To emphasize a caveat concerning transporting your bicycle on Intercity buses, no bus terminals have bike boxes.

Local Bus Service
Three cities—Rochester, Ithaca and Syracuse have bicycle racks on all local and suburban buses. Quite a feat! This is all due to the persistence of local bicycle clubs and their members badgering local transportation planning agencies and the NYSDOT to use the ISTEA/TEA21 (Intermodal Surface Transportation Enhancement Act) federal highway funds for the purpose of placing bicycle racks on local buses.

This has been a very beneficial and successful program. In the program's first year, during the period Oct., 1997-March, 1998 (the winter) over 2600 bicyclists transported their bikes at least one way in Rochester. In 2000, the Rochester Transit Service estimated that it gained between 500 and 1000 riders per month directly attributable to equipping all its buses with bike racks. Please note that a number of the CENTRO (Syracuse based) and RTS (Rochester based) suburban route buses do not have exterior bike racks. These buses do carry bikes in their baggage holds. The bus driver will stop for a bicyclist and will allow your bicycle to be placed in the baggage hold. This particulary applies on Syracuse to Auburn/Skaneateles or Oswego routes; and the Rochester to Lyons or Avon routes.

For the cyclotourist coming to the Finger Lakes this means that you are able to go from airport terminal, bus station or train station directly to the nearest Finger Lake via a local bus. Just remember that the nearest Finger Lake to Rochester or Syracuse is on a suburban/exuban bus route and that the buses may only operate during weekday rush hours.

Many of the other counties (Wayne, Ontario, Seneca, Schuyler, Livingston) in the Finger Lakes region do have limited local bus service. However none of these county bus systems have buses which are equipped with bike racks.

You can help local cyclists to achieve one of their intermodal transportation goals by writing to the county tourism agencies, on the *Information Source* pages, about the need for bicycle racks/ carriage faciles on local buses and on Amtrak trains.

Notes

Syracuse to Otisco Lake

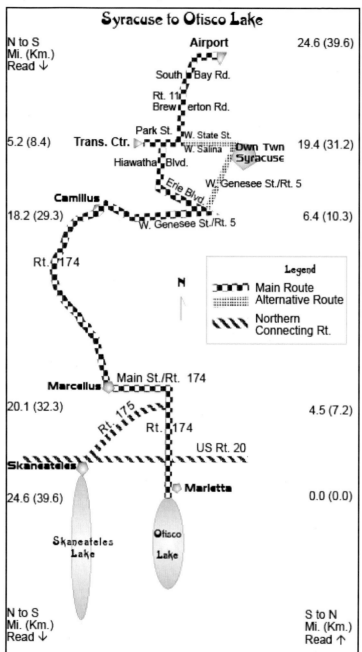

N to S
Mi. (Km.)
Read ↓

Airport   24.6 (39.6)

South Bay Rd.

Rt. 11
Brew erton Rd.

Park St.   W. State St.
5.2 (8.4)   Trans. Ctr.   W. Salina   Dwn Twn   19.4 (31.2)
         Hiawatha Blvd.   Syracuse

             Erie Blvd.   W. Genesee St./Rt. 5

Camillus
18.2 (29.3)   6.4 (10.3)
             W. Genesee St./Rt. 5

Rt. 174

N

Legend
━━ Main Route
▦▦ Alternative Route
〜〜 Northern Connecting Rt.

Main St./Rt. 174
Marcellus
20.1 (32.3)   4.5 (7.2)
Rt. 175
       Rt. 174

US Rt. 20
Skaneateles

24.6 (39.6)   Marietta   0.0 (0.0)

Skaneateles   Otisco
Lake   Lake

N to S   S to N
Mi. (Km.)   Mi. (Km.)
Read ↓   Read ↑

Cyclists! Start Your Pedals Rotating!

SYRACUSE

Information: Greater Syracuse CVB, 572 S. Salina St., Syracuse, NY 13202, 315 470-1910. Request: Onondaga Bicycle Map & the Onondaga Lake Park Map. Area code: 315. Zip: various

Cycling & Hiking Information: Onondaga Cycling Club, Inc., PO Box 6307, Teall Station, Syracuse, NY 13217, regular weekend and Wednesday night rides throughout the season. There are many bicycle shops in Syracuse and its suburbs. Check the telephone book for a shop closest to your location.

Services & Facilities: All. Retail stores and banks abound in and around Syracuse. General shopping is primarily in suburban shopping malls. Several hospitals.

Accommodations: Motels galore! Syracuse AYH Hostel, 535 Oak St., Syracuse 13203, 315 472-5788. B&Bs: Giddings Garden, 290 W Seneca Tpk., 492-6389; Wellington, 707 Danforth St., 474-3641; Dickenson House on James, 1504 James St., 423-4777; Moonstruck Manor, 3009 W. Genesee St., 488-1224; Ophelia's Garden, 400 South Avery Ave., 488-3621. B&Bs in suburbs: Beard Morgan House, 126 E. Genesee St., 637-4234, Fayetteville; High Meadows B&B, 3740 Eager Rd., 492-3517, Jamesville; Ancestors Inn at the Bassett House, 215 Sycamore St., 461-1226, Liverpool. Camping: Green Lakes St. Pk., 7900 Green Lakes Rd., 637-6111, Fayetteville; Sunset Park Cpgd, 547 Sprague Rd., 635-6450, Memphis.

Attractions: New York State Fair (August). Sports: Chiefs baseball, Skates soccer, Crunch hockey, Syracuse University sports. Neighborhood festivals throughout the summer.

Music & Drama: Jazz Festival, 475-7979; Syracuse Symphony Orchestra, 411 Montgomery St.,424-8222; Syracuse Opera, PO Box 6904, zip: 13217, 475-5915; Rock/Country concerts are held at the Carrier Dome, Syracuse University, 443-4534; SummerFest Drama Festival, Mulroy Civic Center (& other locations) 411 Montgomery St., 435-2121.

Museums: Erie Canal Mus., 318 Erie Blvd. East, 471-0593; Everson Mus. of Art, 401 Harrison St.; Onondaga Historical Mus., 321 Montgomery St., 428-1864; Mus., of Science & Technology, 500 S. Franklin St., 425-0747; Salt Mus., Onondaga Lake Pkwy., Liverpool, 453-6715; Sainte Marie Among the Indians, Rt. 370, Liverpool, 453-6767; Burnet Park Zoo, 1 Conservation Place, 435-8511.

Public Transportation:
Regional Transportation Center: Public terminals for local and

intercity bus lines; commuter light rail; and Amtrak trains are centralized at the Carousel Transportation Center behind the P&C Stadium near the Carousel Mall. The SYRACUSE TO OTISCO & SKANEATELES LAKES route takes you from the Airport to the Regional Transportation Center.

Local Bus & Rail: CNY Centro, 200 Cortland Ave., PO Box 820, Syracuse NY 13205, 315 442-3400, has an extensive system of routes including Skaneateles and Auburn suburban routes from downtown Syracuse and the Regional Transportation Center.

Bike Racks On Buses: All Syracuse City bus routes have bike racks. Bike racks or baggage holds are for bicyclist's use on suburban, Oswego, Auburn (Owasco Lake), Skaneateles and other Finger Lakes bound buses. Bicycles can be transported, unboxed and during non-rush hours, on the OnRail light rail trains.

Intercity Bus: Syracuse is a major transfer point for intercity buses. Greyhound, Trailways and Shortline have routes which go in all directions from Syracuse. All intercity buses arrive and depart from the Regional Transportation Center.

Train: Amtrak has baggage car service to Syracuse.

Airplane: Hancock Airport is in North Syracuse. The SYRACUSE TO OTISCO & SKANEATELES LAKES ROUTE provides directions from the Airport to the Regional Transportation Center and on to the Lakes.

E to W/N to S	**SYRACUSE TO**	W to E/S to N
Read ↓	**OTISCO LAKE & SKANEATELES LAKE**	Read up ↑

00.0 (00.)   Main Airport Terminal   24.6 (39.6)
@ Airport Access Rd.
Follow the Airport Access Rd. to South Bay Rd.

1.7 (2.6)   South Bay Rd. @ Airport Access Rd.   22.9 (36.9)
Turn South on to South Bay Rd.

2.3 (3.7)   Brewerton Rd./Rt. 11   22.3 (35.9)
Jct. South Bay Rd.
Continue traveling South on Brewerton Rd./Rt. 11
Somewhere along Brewerton Rd./Rt. 11 it changes its
name to Wolf St./Rt. 11. Just travel South!

5.1 (8.3)   Park St. @ Wolf St./Rt. 11   19.5 (31.4)
Turn West on to Park St.

5.2 (8.4)   Park St. @ Hiawatha Blvd.   19.4 (31.2
Turn South on to Hiawatha Blvd. to go to Otisco &
Skaneateles Lakes.
Regional Transportation Center; P&C Stadium; Carousel
Mall.
Continue traveling West on Park St. to enter the Regional
Transportation Center. All local and intercity buses, OnRail
commuter trains, and Amtrak trains will board and
disembark at the Regional Transportation Center.
🚲 Park St. links with Old Liverpool Rd. and Onondaga
Lake Pkwy. Use these roads to take a counterclockwise
ride around Onondaga Lake. Onondaga County's
Onondaga Lake Park brochure provides a map of the route
around Onondaga Lake.

5.3 (8.5)   N. Salina St. @ Hiawatha Blvd. W.   19.3 (31.1)
Continue traveling South on Hiawatha Blvd. W. to go to
Otisco & Skaneateles Lakes.
⇔ If you have a yearning to go on a side trip, use the
TRAIN STATION TO TRANSPORTATION CTR. ROUTE to
go to Old Erie Canal State Pk. and Green Lakes St. Pk.
(camping).

6.6 (10.6)   Erie Blvd. W. @ Hiawatha Blvd. W.   18.0 (29.0)
Turn East on to Erie Blvd. W. to go to the Otisco &
Skaneateles Lakes.
Turn West on to Erie Blvd. W. to go clockwise around
Onondaga Lake.

6.9 (11.1)   W. Genesee St./Rt. 5   17.7 (28.5)
@ Erie Blvd. W.
Turn West on to W. Genesee St./Rt. 5.
During rush hours this is a busy street and you will have to
use caution. Off hours it isn't too bad.

9.2 (14.8)   W. Genesee St. Jct. Rt. 5   15.4 (24.8)
Continue traveling West on W. Genesee St. Do not follow
the Rt. 5 signs. Most of the motor vehicle traffic goes
on the limited access hwy. Rt. 5 at this point.

13.2 (21.2)   Munro Rd.@ W. Genesee St.   11.4 (18.3)
Follow the W. Genesee St. signs. W. Genesee St. makes a
northward turn and becomes just plain Genesee St. as it
enters Camillus Village.

13.4 (21.6)   Milton Ave. @ Genesee St.   11.2 (18.0)
Travel westward on Genesee St.

CAMILLUS

Info.: Camillus Town Hall, 400 W. Genesee St., Syracuse
NY 13219. AC: 315. ZC: 13219.
Bike Info.: 8 mi. (12.9) trail, Old Erie Canal Tow Path.
Services: Restaurants, hardware stores, grocery.
Lodging: Motels. **Attractions:** Camillus Erie Canal Pk,
5250 DeVoe Rd., 672-5110/448-3409; Wilcox Octagon
House, 5420 W. Genesee St.

Jealous drivers wait as bicyclists breeze through!

13.8 (22.2)   Genesee St. @ Elm St./Rt. 174   10.8 (17.4)
Bear Southwest on to Elm St./Rt. 174.

18.2 (29.3)   Rt. 174/North St.   6.4 10.3)
@ Rt. 174/E. Main St.
Turn East on to Rt. 174/E. Main St. Follow the Rt. 174 signs.

MARCELLUS

Services: Restaurants, hardware store, & grocery. Area code: 315. Zip code: 13108
Accommodations: Motels. B&Bs: Debevic Homestead, 2527 W. Seneca Tpk., 673-9447; Baltimore Woods Historic Land Use Ctr., Bishop Hill Rd., 673-1350; Blakeslee House, 3708 South St. Rd., 673-2881; Slate Hill Meadow, 3651 Slate Hill Rd., 673-1283.

18.7 (30.1)   Rt. 174/E. Main St.   5.9 (9.5)
@ Rt. 174/Lee/Mulroy Rd.
Turn South on to Rt. 174/Lee-Mulroy Rd.
Rt. 175 junctions here with Rt. 174.

20.1 (32.3)   Rt. 175 Jct. Rt. 174   4.5 (7.2)
Continue traveling South on Rt. 174 to go to Otisco Lake.
⇔ Travel Southwest on Rt. 175 to by pass Otisco Lake and go directly to Skaneateles Lake. At the intersection, US 20 @ Rt. 175, 3.5 mi. (5.7 km.) Southwest of this point, turn West on US 20 for 2 mi. (3.2 km.) and you'll be in Skaneateles.

22.8 (36.7)   US 20 Jct. Rt. 174   1.8 (2.9)
Turn West on to Rtes. 174/20.

23.0 (37.0)   Rt. 174 Jct. US 20   1.6 (2.6)
Turn South on Rt. 174 to go to Otisco Lake.
⇔ Travel West on US 20 to go to Skaneateles Lake. It is 5.5 mi. (8.9 km.) to Skaneateles.

24.6 (39.6)   Marietta Village @ Rt. 174   0.0 (0.0)
↻ ↺ The OTISCO LAKE CIRCUMNAVIGATION route at this intersection.

Read ↓   **OTISCO LAKE & SKANEATELES LAKE**   Read up ↑
E to W / N to S   **TO SYRACUSE**   W to E / S to N

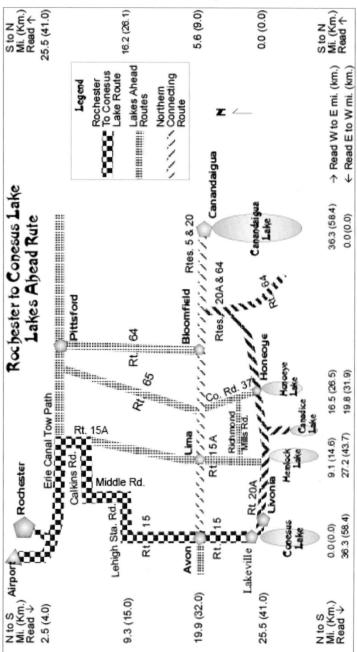

Rochester to Conesus Lake
Lakes Ahead Route

ROCHESTER

Info.: Greater Rochester Convention & Visitors Center, 45 East Ave. Rochester, NY 14614, 585 546-3070. Don't forget to request bicycle and bus maps! Area code: 585. Zip code: various.

Biking Info.:

Bike Rochester, www.bikerochester.com, an information, not a sales web site, sponsored by the independent bicycle shops of the greater Rochester area united as the Genesee Valley Bicycle Dealers Association. There are over 12 bike shops in Rochester and its suburbs. If you need repairs or equipment, determine where you located and then consult a phone book or a passing cyclist for directions to the nearest bike store. There are camping equipment stores in the suburban shopping malls.

Rochester Bicycling Club, PO Box 10100, Rochester NY 14610, 888-857-8198, ~300 rides scheduled during the season. www. rochesterbicyclingclub.org. Visitors are welcome to ride with the club.

Genesee Valley Cyclilng Club (racing), http://gvcc.11net.com/ visitors are welcome to participate in training rides.

Other formal & informal clubs: Tuesday Night Urban Assault, http://home.rochester.rr.com/scarey/TNUA; Rochester Area Recumbent Enthusiasts, http://home.rochester.rr.com/rare/. Ride calendar & info sources on line. Greater Rochester Eating and Tandeming Society (GREATS), http://managan.home.isp-direct. com/greats/. Ultra cycling (see Rochester Bicycling Club).

The *Greater Rochester Area Bicycling Map* is available, free of charge, from the Genesee Transportation Council, 55 W. Main St.., Rochester 14614, 585 232-6240.

Genesee Greenway, a multi-use dirt & stone dust trail, going South for 90 mi. (145 km) is under construction but usable. Friends of the Genesee Greenway, P.O. Box 42, Mt. Morris NY 14510, Phone: (585) 658-2569, www.fogvg.org.

Erie Canal Tow Path: A multi-use asphalt/stone dust path extending 100 mi. (160 km.) West to Lockport & Tonawanda and 35 mi. (56 km.) East to Clyde. Refer to the *Erie Canal Bicyclist's & Hiker's Tour Guide* for information on the Canal routes.

Services: All. Hospitals. Most retail stores are in suburban shopping malls. Banks and specialty shopping venues are in the city itself. There are a number of natural foods stores.

Lodging: Motels and hotels vary in price from $40.00-$135.00. The least expensive motels are in the suburbs or around the Airport although there are at least 2 clean, well run and safe motels in downtown Rochester. Motel locations are noted on the ROCHESTER TO CONESUS LAKE ROUTE. There is no hostel and the colleges do not rent to non-students. B&Bs: Dartmouth

House, 215 Dartmouth St., 271-7872. B&B at 428 Mt. Vernon, 428 Mt. Vernon Ave., 271-0792; Edward Harris House Inn, 35 Argyle St., 473-9752; Reen's, 44 Magee Ave., 458-9306; Marigold Gardens, 16 Country Club Rd., East Rochester 586-8664. There are additional B&Bs in the suburbs, contact the CVB.

Camping: You must plan to camp South of Rochester. There are no campgrounds in Rochester or within 15 miles of the City.

Attractions: Museums: George Eastman House/International Museum of Photography, 271-3361; Strong Museum, 454-7639; Strassenburgh Planetarium & Rochester Museum and Science Center, 271-1880; Susan B. Anthony House National Historic Landmark, 235-6124; Memorial Art Gallery, Mt. Hope Cemetery, Erie Canal, Lake Ontario, 18th & 19th cent. Buildings.

Music, Theater & Dance: Rochester Philharmonic, GEVA Theater, 232-4382; Garth Fagan Dance Co.

Other: Seneca Park Zoo, 467-9453, High Falls Urban Cultural Park; Lake Ontario beaches; summer neighborhood festivals.

Architecture (including a Frank Lloyd Wright house), Landmark Society, 133 South Fitzhugh St., 14608, 716 546-7029, has a complete list/booklet of the architecturally significant buildings.

Gardens: Garden Center of Rochester, Highland Park, 5 Castle Park, 473-5130/5138 has a brochure detailing all significant gardens in the Rochester & Finger Lakes area.

Sports: Rhinos soccer; Red Wings baseball, Nighthawks lacrosse, Amerks hockey. Rochester Twilight Criterium (August).

Cruises: Canal: Colonial Belle Canal Tour & Dinner Boat, 377-4600, Fairport Lady, 223-1930; Mid-Lakes Navigation 800 545-4318/315 545-4318; Sam Patch, 262-5661. Lake Ontario: Harbor Town Belle, 342-1810.

Public Transportation: Local Bus: Regional Transit Service (RTS), (mailing address: 1372 East Main St., Rochester 14610), 654-0200. All RTS buses have bike racks (accommodating 2 bicycles) or baggage holds in which bicycles can be carried. During the morning or evening rush hours, you can use a RTS bus (# 91) & its bike rack to go to the Lakeville Park & Ride Stop near (~3 mi./7 km.) the northern end of Conesus Lake. Park & Ride buses only operate during weekday rush hours. This bus, No. 91, also is routed through Lima & Honeoye Falls which may be closer to Hemlock Lake than the Lakeville Park & Ride.

Airplane: The airport is on the western edge of the City along the Erie Canal, use the AIRPORT TO EIRE CANAL & RIVERVIEW TRAIL & the ROCHESTER TO CONESUS LAKE ROUTE to go to the Finger Lakes themselves.

Intercity Buses: Trailways and Greyhound have routes which go in all directions from Rochester. The intercity bus station is downtown. If you are arriving/departing from Rochester use the

ROCHESTER TO CONESUS LAKE ROUTE after following the directions to the Riverview Trail Head from the bus terminal.

Train: Amtrak has 4 trains which stop in Rochester. Unfortunately only one train has full baggage car service, The Lake Shore Limited. You will arrive in downtown Rochester. Use the directions to the Riverview Trail Head from the train station and then follow the ROCHESTER TO CONESUS LAKE ROUTE to go to the Finger Lakes. It is possible to obtain a special Amtrak fare which allows you to embark from Rochester or Syracuse, bicycle the Finger Lakes and return to your originating station from the other Amtrak station.

Ferry: Bay Ferries Ltd., operates the "Cat" ferry across Lake Ontario between Rochester and Toronto. This is a car-passenger-bicycle ferry. As of the publication of this book (May, 2005) information on the ferry's operation is not entirely available. Please refer to the visit Rochester web site or the City of Rochester web site or a travel agent for more information. It is about a 10 mi. (16 km.) ride from Lake Ontario to downtown Rochester. There is a bus with bike racks that goes from downtown to Lake Ontario. Only part of the route is an off road trail. Use either Lake Ave. or St. Paul St./Blvd. to go downtown.

TRAVELER'S NOTE

ROCHESTER TO CONESUS LAKE ROUTE: The most efficient and safest way to go from intercity bus terminal & train station in downtown Rochester to the western most Finger Lake, Conesus Lake, 25 mi. (40 km.) due south of Rochester] is to use the Riverview Trail, Erie Canal Tow Path, and NY 15A/15. Directions from each terminal to the Riverview Trail Head and Erie Canal Tow Path and on to Conesus Lake immediately follow the AIRPORT TO GENESEE RIVER ROUTE.

LAKES AHEAD ROUTE. I was at a Regional Transportation Planning Council Bicycle/Pedestrian Action Committee meeting and the other citizen members chastised me for not providing a Route to the other near by Finger Lakes - Hemlock, Honeoye and Canadaigua Lakes. The Lakes Ahead Route follows the Rochester To Conesus Lake Route.

W to E/N to S Read ↓	**ROCHESTER AIRPORT TO** **ERIE CANAL & RIVERVIEW TRAIL**	E to W/S to N Read up ↑

00.0 (00.0)   Airport Exit @ Brooks Ave./NY 204   2.3 (3.7)
Turn East (left) on to Brooks Ave./NY204.

0.5 (0.8)   Brooks Ave.   1.8 (2.9)
                  @ Holiday Inn @ Canal Tow Path (CTP)
Just to the East of the Holiday Inn's driveway is the
entrance to the Erie Canal Tow Path. Enter the Canal Tow
Path access ramp. You will be traveling South on to the
Canal Tow Path, continue traveling South.
To the Airport: Exit the Canal Tow Path after the Brooks
Ave. underpass and use the *Path's clover leaf* to exit on to
Brooks Ave. westbound. Ride .5 mi. (.8 km) to Buell Rd.
(stop light at this intersection). Cross Brooks Ave. and use
the sidewalk to enter the Airport. Bike straight through the
parking garage to the terminal.   Using these directions
you'll avoid going up a steep hill to the departure terminal.

Cruisin' & bikin'! A natural fit!

1.8 (2.9)   Genesee River @ CTP   0.5 (0.8)
                   Viaduct/Arched Bridge @ CTP
Turn North and follow the Trail.
The Trail makes a sharp northward turn at an overhead
viaduct (arched bridge) as it meets the Genesee River.
If you continue South on the Trail, going under the viaduct,
you'll be on the Genesee Greenway Trail. The Greenway
goes all the way to the NY—PA border. Info.: Friends of the
Genesee Greenway, P.O. Box 42, Mt. Morris NY 14510,
Phone: (585) 658-2569, www.fogvg.org.
From the Bridge over the Canal on the West side of the
River, looking East, you can see the intersection of the
Canal and the Genesee River. Hopefully a canoe or boat
will be on the water to enhance your photo.

2.0 (3.2)   Pedestrian Bridge (W. bank)   0.3 (0.5)
                   @ Canal Tow Path (CTP)
Turn East on to the Pedestrian Bridge over the Genesee
River!
Do not go any further North on the West bank.

2.3 (3.7)   Pedestrian bridge (E. bank)   0.0 (0.0
                   @ Canal Tow Path & Riverview Trail
Go straight East! Well! You'll have to make a tiny curve
southeastward, but essentially go straight on the Canal
Tow Path.
Do not completely traverse any of the small bridges which
go over the Canal from the CTP. They are dead ends and
populated with *characters*. You can go to the center of
these small bridges for a picture.
⇔ ROCHESTER TO CONESUS LAKE ROUTE. From this
intersection begin to follow the .
⇔ RIVERVIEW TRAIL TO DOWNTOWN ROCHESTER.
⇔ LAKES AHEAD ROUTE. Continues along the Erie
Canal Tow Path following the Rochester to Conesus Lake
Route.

| W to E/N to S | **RIVERVIEW TRAIL & ERIE CANAL** | W to E/S to N |
| Read ↓ | **TO ROCHESTER AIRPORT** | Read up ↑ |

N to S	**ROCHESTER BUS TERMINAL**	S to N
W to E	**& TRAIN STATION TO**	E to W
Read ↓	**RIVERVIEW TRAIL HEAD**	Read up ↑

TRAVELER'S NOTE

The nearest bike shops to the bus terminal and the train Station is Blue Moon Vista, 180 St. Paul St., 546-4030; Towner's, 271-4553, on University Ave. near Culver Rd.

Bus Terminal to Trail Head:
Face the large black Xerox building opposite the Bus Terminal
Walk East, an infinitesimally small distance, to Chestnut St.
Mount your bike and ride South on Chestnut St.
Ride 1 block to Woodbury Blvd. Landmark: Strong Museum.
Turn West on to Woodbury Blvd., *i. e.*, away from the Museum.
Ride three blocks West to South Ave.
Carefully cross South Ave.
The Riverview Trail Head is at your front wheel on the Genesee River side of South Ave.
⇔ Use the ROCHESTER TO CONESUS LAKE ROUTE from the Riverview Trail Head.

Train Station to Trail Head:
Ride down the sweeping Amtrak driveway to Central Ave.
Turn Right (West) on to Central Ave.
Make a quick South bound (left) turn on to Clinton Ave.
Ride over the Inner Loop towards the YWCA. Use the sidewalk in front of the Y because Clinton Ave.
Ride South on Clinton Ave. for 1 block to Andrews St. Landmark: Red Front restaurant.
Turn West (right) on to Andrews St.
Travel one block to St. Paul St.
Turn South (left) on to St. Paul St./South Ave.
Ride to Court St. Landmark: Public Library.
Just South of Court St., on the Genesee River side of South Ave. is the Riverview Trail Head.
⇔ Use the ROCHESTER TO CONESUS LAKE ROUTE from the Riverview Trail Head.

N to S	**RIVERVIEW TRAIL HEAD TO**	S to N
W to E	**ROCHESTER TRAIN STATION**	E to W
Read ↓	**& BUS STATION**	Read up ↑

| N to S | **ROCHESTER RIVERVIEW TRAIL HEAD** | S to N |
| Read ↓ | **TO CONESUS LAKE** | Read up ↑ |

TRAVELER'S NOTE

From downtown Rochester to the Erie Canal you will be riding parallel to the Genesee River on the Riverview Trail. I caution you to stay on the East bank of the Genesee River. Ride on the paved Riverview Trail; under a complicated highway interchange, past the University of Rochester, until you come to the second pedestrian bridge over the Genesee River, where the Erie Canal Trail meets the Riverview Trail.

00.00   Riverview Trail Head   25.5 (41.0)
               @ South Avenue & Woodbury Blvd.
Turn South on to the Trail.
⇔ RIVERVIEW TRAIL HEAD TO ROCHESTER TRAIN STATION & BUS STATION.

.9 (1.4)   Ford St. Bridge @ Riverview Trail   24.6 (39.6)
Trail goes under this bridge. Landmark: housing project.

1.5 (2.4)   University of Rochester   24.0 (38.6)
               @ Riverview Trail
Pedestrian bridge. Do not cross the River at this pedestrian bridge. The path goes down to the River here. Ride along the River bank, it's a delightful ride.

2.0 (3.2)   Elmwood Ave. @ Riverview Trail   23.5 (37.8)
Underpass leading into Genesee Valley Park.

2.5 (4.0)   Pedestrian Bridge   23.0 (37.0)
               @ Erie Canal Tow Path (CTP)
               Jct. Riverview Trail
Travel East on the Canal Tow Path (CTP}, that is, travel away from the Genesee River.
Do not be tempted to cross any of the small bridges you see going over the Canal. They lead to dead ends with *characters*. You can go to the center of these bridges for a picture.
⇔ Airport arrivees/departees using the AIRPORT TO ERIE CANAL AND RIVERVIEW TRAIL join/leave us here.

3.8 (6.1)   E. Henrietta Rd./NY 15A   21.7 (34.9)
               @ Canal Tow Path
Exit the Canal Tow Path on to East Henrietta Rd.
There may be a sign on the Trail which states "East

Henrietta Rd." and then again there may not be a sign. Interestingly there are no discernible landmarks. The best I can tell you is that this is the Trail exit after W. Henrietta Rd. and before Clinton Ave. If you reach Lock 33, 2.6 mi. (4.2 km.) eastward on the Trail, then you've definitely gone too far! Turn South on to East Henrietta Rd. Use care, E. Henrietta Rd./NY 15A between the Canal and I 390 is a heavily trafficked road. E. Henrietta Rd. is a wide 4 lane road. Motorists are used to bicyclists going to the Community College. There is a bike shop, 473-3724, at W. Henrietta Rd. near the Canal approximately 3 blocks north. Another bike shop is in the shopping plaza near Wegmans grocery, on NY 383 (Jefferson Rd.) 427-2110.

⇔ LAKES AHEAD ROUTE: Continue traveling West on the Erie Canal Tow Path to go directly to Hemlock, Honeyoe or Canandaigua Lakes. The Lakes Ahead Route immediately follows this Rochester Riverview Trail Head to Conesus Lake Route.

5.5 (8.9)   Jefferson Rd/NY 283   20.0 (32.2)
                 @ E. Henrietta Rd./NY 15A
Continue traveling South on E. Henrietta Rd. Motels nearby.

6.8 (10.9)   Calkins Rd.   18.7 (30.1)
                 @. E. Henrietta Rd./NY 15A
Turn West on to Calkins Rd.
On E. Henrietta Rd./NY 15A, near the big liquor store just before this intersection is bike shop, 334-1083.
                    Route Information
ᛋᚱ Uh! Oh! You had a change of mind and really want to go to Hemlock or Honeoye or Canandaigua Lakes instead of Conesus Lake. Well you're in luck! Simply go South on NY 15A and you be at Hemlock Lake in about 22 mi. (35 km.). As for Honeoye or Canandaigua Lakes read the Route Information entry at: 19.9 (32.0) Rtes. 5&20 @ NY 15 5.6 (9.0) below.

8.0 (12.9)   Middle Rd. @ Calkins Rd.   17.5 (28.2)
Turn South on to Middle Rd.
Middle Rd. is slightly obscure. It is just before the I 390 overpass.

8.7 (14.0)   Lehigh Station Rd. @ Middle Rd. 16.8 (27.0)
Turn West on to Lehigh Station Rd.

9.3 (15.0)   W. Henrietta Rd./NY 15   16.2 (26.1)
                    @ Lehigh Station Rd.
Turn South on to W. Henrietta Rd./NY 15. Motels on NY 15.

19.9 (32.0)   Rtes. 5&20 @ NY 15   5.6 (9.0)
Continue traveling South on NY 15.
EAST AVON: Convenience store/gas station, toilets; restaurants, grocery on Rtes. 5&20 westbound.
Route Information:
🚲 Rtes. 5 or 20 essentially connect the northern ends of the Finger Lakes.
If you prefer to go to Hemlock, Honeoye or Canandaigua Lakes from this intersection, then turn East here and follow Rtes. 5&20.
🚲 Honoeye & Hemlock Lakes: Turn East on to Rtes. 5&20. At West Bloomfield, turn South on to Co. Rd. 37/South Rd. Then use the HONEOYE LAKE TO HEMLOCK LAKE NORTHERN CONNECTING ROUTE directions from the intersection of Co. Rd. 37 @ NY 15A. It is approximately 22 mi. (35 km.) to Honeoye Lake from this intersection.
🚲 Canandaigua Lake: Turn East on to Rtes. 5&20. You'll be at Canandaigua Lake in Canandaigua about 28 mi. (45 km.) down the road.

22.2 (36.1)   I 390 @ NY 15   3.3 (5.3)
Automobile travelers using I 390 would exit here on to NY 15 to begin their cyclotour.

Reclining

23.2 (37.3)   NY 256 @ NY 15   2.3 (3.7)
Continue traveling South on NY 15 to go to Lakeville/Livonia and circumnavigate Conesus Lake clockwise.
Turn South on to NY 256 to go around Conesus Lake xounterclockwise.

24.7 (39.8)   NY 20A/Big Tree Rd. @ NY 15   0.8 (1.3)
Turn East on to NY 20A/Big Tree Rd.
LAKEVILLE: Restaurants, convenience stores, hardware store, cottage rentals, gas station. Rochester Transit Service Park & Ride Stop. This is the closest Park & Ride stop to Conesus Lake and the Finger Lakes from Rochester. The Conesus Lake Circumnavigation Route has more details concerning Lakeville. The nearest bike store is ~10 mi. (16 km.) West on NY 20A in Geneseo.

25.5 (41.0)   East Lake Rd./Co. Rd. 6   0.0 (0.0)
                   @ Rtes. 15/20A /Big Tree Rd.
↻ You're here! Turn South on to East Lake Rd./Co. Rd. 6 & follow the CONESUS LAKE CIRCUMNAVIGATION ROUTE.
I suggest that you go to Livonia to obtain groceries and other items before you begin your trek. Livonia is only .5 mi. (.8 km.) westward on Rtes. 15/20A. There are a few convenience type stores along the shore but they have a very limited selection of goods. See the Conesus Lake Circumnavigation Route for more details concerning Livonia.
⇔ If you desire to go directly to Hemlock Lake from this intersection use the HEMLOCK LAKE TO CONESUS LAKE: NORTHERN CONNECTING ROUTE.

N to S   **CONESUS LAKE TO**   S to N
Read ↓   **RIVERVIEW TRAIL HEAD & ROCHESTER**   Read up ↑

0.0 (0.0)   E. Henrietta Rd./NY 15A   33.4 (53.7)
                   @ Canal Tow Path
Continue to travel East on the Erie Canal Tow Path.
⇔ CONESUS LAKE TO RIVER VIEW TRAIL ROUTE.
South to North Travelers: Continue traveling West on the
Erie Canal Tow Path. It is 3.8 mi. (6.1) to the Riverview
Trail and Genesee River.

2.6 (4.2)   Lock 33 @ Canal Tow Path   30.8 (49.6)
Continue to travel East on the Tow Path.
Watch the Lock work!

3.9 (6.3)   Lock 32 @ Canal Tow Path   29.5 (47.5)
Continue eastward on the Tow Path.
Use the portage steps and ramp. Do not cross Culver Rd.
(the street at the Lock's entrance) at the street level. This is
a very busy street and it has blind sight lines for drivers at
the Lock entrance.
Be real careful just before the next Tow Path access point
(Monroe Ave.). You will be descending a steep grade and
there is a fence at the end of the grade.

5.0 (8.0)   E. Park St. @ Canal Path   28.4 (45.7)
                   Monroe Ave. @ Canal Path
Turn Right on to E. Park St. Then, turn Right again at the
end of the buildings, you'll see the Canal, go towards it!.
Finally, turn Left to return to the Canal.
If you find yourself on a 4 lane major street, make a U turn
and go back to the Canal.

5.5 (8.9)   Main St./NY 96 @ Canal Tow Path   27.9 (44.9)
Exit the Canal Tow Path on to Main St. Turn South on to
Main St. Don't use the underpass almost in front of your
wheel. Go up to the Street Level
PITTSFORD: Bike shop, 381-2808; & other stores.

6.0 ((9.7)   NY 64/Mendon Ctr. Rd.   27.4 (44.1)
                   @ Main St. NY 96
Travel straight on to NY 64 South. NY 64 begins here.

12.5 (20.1)   NY 251 @ NY 64   20.9 (33.6)
Continue traveling South on NY 64.
MENDON: Convenience store & gas station.

20.3 (32.7)   Rtes. 5&20 @ NY 64   13.1 (21.1)
HEMLOCK & HONEOYE LAKES: Turn West on to Rtes.
5&20.
ﾁ CANANDAIGUA LAKE: Turn East on to Rtes. 5&20 and
travel for 8.4 mi.(13.5 km.) to arrive at the northern end of
Canandaigua Lake.

24.0 (38.6)   Co. Rd. 37/South Rd. @ Rtes. 5&20   9.4 (15.1)
Turn South on to Co. Rd. 37/South Rd.

29.7 (47.8)   Co. Rd. 15/Richmond Hill Rd.   3.7 (5.9)
                  @ Co. Rd. 37/South Rd.
To go to Honeoye Lake continue traveling South on Co.
Rd. 37/ South Rd.
ﾁ HEMLOCK LAKE: To go to Hemlock Lake, turn West on
to Co. Rd. 15/Richmond Mills Rd. Travel 4.2 mi. (6.7 km.)
to Rtes. 15A/20A and Turn South on NY 15A. 2.5 mi. (4.0
km.) South on NY 15A is Rix Hill Rd. and the northern end
of Hemlock Lake.

32.4 (52.1)   NY 20A @ Co. Rd. 37/South Rd.   1.0 (1.6)
Turn East on to NY 20A.

33.4 (53.7)   Co. Rd. 36 @ NY 20A   0.0 (0.0)
HONEOYE: Refer to the Honeoye Lake Circumnavigation
Route for information.
↻ ↺ HONEOYE LAKE CIRCUMNAVIGATION Route.
⇔ HONEOYE LAKE TO CANANDAIGUA LAKE
CONNECTING ROUTES
⇔ HONEOYE LAKE TO HEMLOCK LAKE CONNECTING
ROUTES

N to S   **LAKES AHEAD ROUTE**   S to N
HONEOYE, HEMLOCK & CANANDAIGUA LAKES TO
Read ↓   **ROCHESTER**   Read up ↑

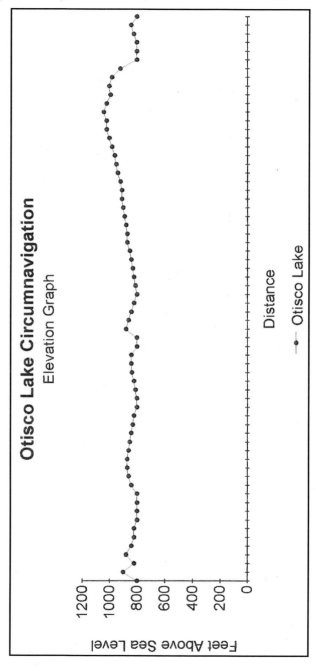

Otisco Lake Circumnavigation

Elevation Graph

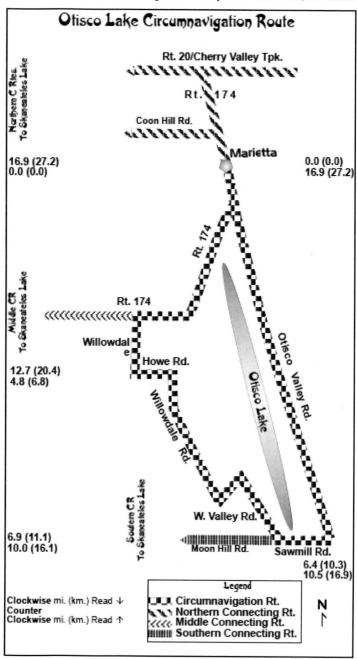

Otisco Lake Circumnavigation Route

Rt. 20/Cherry Valley Tpk.

Rt. 174

Coon Hill Rd.

Marietta

0.0 (0.0)
16.9 (27.2)

16.9 (27.2)
0.0 (0.0)

Northern C Rts.
To Skaneateles Lake

Rt. 174

Rt. 174

Otisco Valley Rd.

Otisco Lake

Middle CR
To Skaneateles Lake

Willowdale

Howe Rd.

12.7 (20.4)
4.8 (6.8)

Willowdale Rd.

W. Valley Rd.

Soudern CR
To Skaneateles Lake

6.9 (11.1)
10.0 (16.1)

Moon Hill Rd.

Sawmill Rd.

6.4 (10.3)
10.5 (16.9)

Legend

Clockwise mi. (km.) Read ↓
Counter
Clockwise mi. (km.) Read ↑

Circumnavigation Rt.
Northern Connecting Rt.
Middle Connecting Rt.
Southern Connecting Rt.

N

Of Ice and Water

The scope of this Tour Guide can not possibly fully discuss the geologic formation of the Finger Lakes. At best it can provide a precís of the books listed in the bibliography. During the Pleistocene (ice age) era a series of glaciers covered a good portion of North America and altered the existing land forms. The pre Pleistocene era Finger Lakes Region dominate land form was a peneplain which had been up lifted. It is this combination of sedimentary rock layers on a pre-glacial lake bed being uplifted and then eroded by glacial action and weathering which created the Finger Lakes, surrounding uplands, escarpments, valleys, gorges, and waterfalls.
It is theorized that well before the Pleistocene era, the North American land mass as well as the other continents drifted apart from being one somewhat unified land mass. This continental drift formed the basis of elevation changes on the land masses themselves. Tectonic (forces involved in changing the earth's crust) during the most active drifting events created the basic elevation and depression characteristics of the continents. In turn, these depressions and elevations became channels for water to flow from the higher to lower elevations. The water eroded softer stone and other materials as it flowed along its course from high points to lower points. Carrying and depositing the suspended *dirt* along the stream banks and into enlarged low areas on the continents. The enlarged catchment areas for water became what we now call lakes.
What makes the Finger Lakes region unique is the original basic nature of the land form when the continents separated. Rather than having severely uplifted land forming a vast essentially flat sloping plain was formed. Over time, hundreds of millions of years, the North American land mass was uplifted and depressed by additional tectonic forces forming what we now call the Adirondack, Teconic, and Appalachian ranges of mountains as well as the Allegheny plateau; and the great depressed land area from the Great Lakes were formed.
It is thought that at the beginning of the Ice Age the basic land forms of the Finger Lakes region were already established - a plain (relatively flat land mass) at ~1800 ft. (~550 m.), the Great Lakes, escarpments, mountains and weathering land forms most notably, streams and rivers. The plain itself sloped downward from North to South. A sloping plain at such an altitude is termed a peneplain. The underlying rocks of the peneplain had themselves been formed by vulcanization,

tectonicization and subsequent erosion and layering of mineral deposits carried by water into the vast Lake Iroquois (Lakes Huron, Erie and Ontario).
Now that I've horrified geologists with this very simplified version of the geologic formation of the area, go bicycle around Otisco Lake. It's more fun to see the land and water, flora and fauna than reading about it. The continuing story of land, water and ice will greet begin to traverse Skaneateles Lake. The effects of glaciation awaits your pedal strokes as you ride between the Lakes.

Clockwise Read ↓	**OTISCO LAKE CIRCUMNAVIGATION**	Counterclockwise Read up ↑

TRAVELER NOTE
There are no services on the route around Otisco Lake. Make certain that you have sufficient H_2O, snacks and repair supplies.

0.0 (0.0)   NY 174 @ Marietta Village   16.9 (27.2)
Travel South on NY 174.
Lodging: Otisco Lake Cpgd., 1544 Otisco Valley Rd., Marietta NY 13150, 315 636-9925.
⇔ OTISCO LAKE TO SKANEATELES LAKE: NORTHERN DIRECT CONNECTING ROUTE
⇔ OTISCO LAKE TO SKANEATELES LAKE: NORTHERN SCENIC CONNECTING ROUTE.

0.5 (0.8)   NY 174 @ Otisco Valley Rd.   16.4 (26.4)
Turn East on to Otisco Valley Rd.

1.6 (2.6)   Amber @ Otisco Valley Rd.   15.3 (24.6)
Continue South on Otisco Valley Rd.

4.7 (7.6)   Otisco Rd. @ Otisco Valley Rd.   12.2 (19.6)
Continue South on Otisco Valley Rd.

6.4 (10.3)   Sawmill Rd. @ Otisco Valley Rd.   10.5 (16.9)
Turn West on to Sawmill Rd.

6.9 (11.1)   W. Valley Rd./Moon Hill Rd.   10.0 (16.1)
                    @ Sawmill Rd.
Turn North on to W. Valley Rd.
⇔ OTISCO LAKE TO SKANEATELES LAKE: SOUTHERN CONNECTING ROUTE.

8.8 (14.2)	W. Valley Rd. hairpin turn.	8.1 (13.0)
Turn Southward 'round the hairpin turn.		
9.3 (15.0)	Willowdale Rd. @ W. Valley Rd.	7.6 (12.2)
Turn North on to Willowdale Rd.		
12.0 (19.3)	Willowdale bears North.	4.9 (7.9)
Follow Willowdale Rd. northwards		
12.7 (20.4)	Howe Rd. @ Willowdale Rd.	4.2 (6.8)
Turn East on to Howe Rd.		
13.3 (21.4)	Willowdale Hill Rd. @ Howe Rd.	3.6 (5.8)
Turn North on to Willowdale Hill Rd.		
13.8 (22.2)	NY 174 @ Willowdale Hill Rd.	3.1 (5.0)
Turn East on to NY 174.		

⇔ OTISCO LAKE TO SKANEATELES LAKE: MIDDLE CONNECTING ROUTE begins here.

16.9 (27.2)   Otisco Valley Rd. @ NY 174   0.0(0.0)
⇔ OTISCO LAKE TO SKANEATELES LAKE: NORTHERN DIRECT CONNECTING ROUTE
⇔ OTISCO LAKE TO SKANEATELES LAKE: NORTHERN SCENIC CONNECTING ROUTE.
You've rounded Otisco Lake and deserve 3 cheers. Take a break and look around. Smell the clean air and view the flora and fauna. Cyclotouring is magnificent!

TRAVELER NOTE
There are no services on the Route around Otisco Lake. Make certain that you have sufficient H_2O, snacks and repair supplies.

Clockwise	**OTISCO LAKE**	Counterclockwise
Read ↓	**CIRCUMNAVIGATION**	Read up ↑

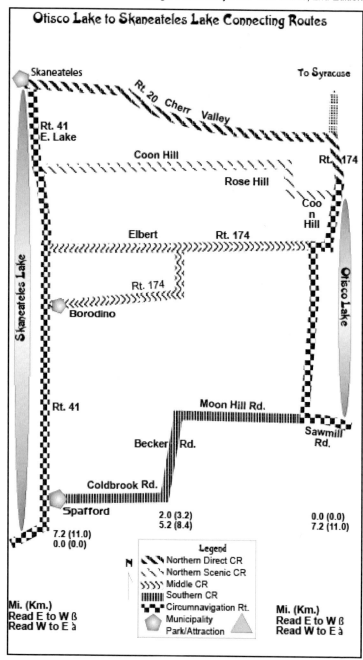

E to W	OTISCO LAKE TO SKANEATELES LAKE	W to E
	NORTHERN DIRECT CONNECTING ROUTE	
Read ↓	MARIETTA TO SKANEATELES	Read up ↑

0.0 (0.0)   NY 174 @ Marietta Village   7.4 (11.9)
Travel North on NY 174
↻ ↻ OTISCO LAKE CIRCUMNAVIGATION
⇔ OTISCO LAKE TO SKANEATELES LAKE: NORTHERN
SCENIC CONNECTING ROUTE.

2.5 (4.0)   NY 20/Cherry Valley Tpk. @ NY 174   4.9 (7.9)
Turn West on to NY 20/Cherry Valley Tpk.

6.7 (10.8)   NY 20/Cherry Valley Tpk.   0.7 (1.1)
Jct. US 20/E. Genesee St.
Continue traveling West on US 20/E. Genesee St.

6.8 (10.9)   US 20/E. Genesee St.   0.6 (1.0)
@ NY 41/E. Lake Rd.
Continue traveling West on US 20/E. Genesee St. to go to
Skaneateles Village.
↻ SKANEATELES CIRCUMNAVIGATION: to travel
clockwise around Skaneateles Lake, turn South on to
NY 41/E Lake Rd.

7.4 (11.9)   NY 321/State St.   0.0 (0.0)
@ US 20/E. Genesee St.
SKANEATELES: See the Skaneateles Circumnavigation
route for information.

E to W	SKANEATELES LAKE TO OTISCO LAKE	W to E
	NORTHERN DIRECT CONNECTING ROUTE	
Read ↓	SKANEATELES TO MARIETTA	Read up ↑

E to W   **OTISCO LAKE TO SKANEATELES LAKE**   W to E
              NORTHERN SCENIC CONNECTING ROUTE
Read ↓   **MARIETTA TO SKANEATELES**   Read up ↑

0.0 (0.0)   NY 174 @ Marietta Village   7.1 (11.4)
Travel North on NY 174.
↻ ↺ OTISCO LAKE CIRCUMNAVIGATION.
↔ OTISCO LAKE TO SKANEATELES LAKE: NORTHERN
DIRECT CONNECTING ROUTE.

0.4 (0.6)   Coon Hill Rd. @ NY 174   6.7 (10.8)
Turn West on to Coon Hill Rd.

1.1 (1.8)   Coon Hill Rd. @ Rose Hill Rd.   6.0 (9.7)
Turn North on to Rose Hill Rd.

1.8 (2.9)   Rose Hill Rd. @ Coon Hill Rd.   5.3 (8.5)
Turn West on to Coon Hill Rd.
Yeah! This discontinuance of Coon Hill Rd. is very strange.

4.5 (7.2)   E. Lake Rd./NY 41 @ Coon Hill Rd.   2.6 (4.2)
↔ SKANEATELES LAKE CIRCUMNAVIGATION ROUTE.
↺ Turn North on to E. Lake Rd./NY 41 to go to
Skaneateles, 2.6 mi. (4.2 km.) North on E. Lake Rd./NY 41.
↻ Turn South on to E. Lake Rd./NY 41 to round
Skaneateles Lake clockwise.

6.5 (10.5)   US 20/E. Genesee St.   0.6 (1.0)
                     @ E. Lake Rd./NY 41
Turn West on to US 20/E. Genesee St.

7.1 (11.4)   NY 321/State St.   0.0 (0.0)
                     @ US 20/E. Genesee St.
SKANEATELES. Refer to the Skaneateles
Circumnavigation Route for information.

E to W   **SKANEATELES LAKE TO OTISCO LAKE**   W to E
              NORTHERN SCENIC CONNECTING ROUTE
Read ↓   **SKANEATELES TO MARIETTA**   Read up ↑

E to W Read ↓	**OTISCO LAKE TO SKANEATELES LAKE MIDDLE CONNECTING ROUTE**	W to E Read up ↑

0.0 (0.0)   NY 174 @ Willowdale Hill Rd.   2.0 (3.2)
Otisco Lake. Turn West on to NY 174.
⇔ ↺ ↻ OTISCO LAKE CIRCUMNAVIGATION
⇔ OTISCO LAKE TO SKANEATELES LAKE: NORTHERN SCENIC CONNECTING ROUTE.

0.7 (1.1)   Elbert Rd. @ NY 174 jct. Rose Hill Rd   1.3 (2.1)
Continue traveling West on Elbert Rd. to go directly to Skaneateles Lake.
⇔ Turn South on NY 174 to intersect with NY 41, which is the main East side of Skaneateles Lake road. At Borodino Hamlet, NY 174 junctions with NY 41. From this intersection you can begin to use the SKANEATELES LAKE CIRCUMNAVIGATION ROUTE.

2.0 (3.2)   E. Lake Rd./NY 41 @ Elbert Rd.   0.0 (0.0)
Skaneateles Lake.
⇔ SKANEATELES LAKE CIRCUMNAVIGATION ROUTE is at this intersection.
↺ Turn South on NY 41 to 'round Skaneateles Lake clockwise from this intersection.
↻ Turn North to 'round Skaneateles Lake counterclockwise from this intersection.

E to W Read ↓	**OTISCO LAKE TO SKANEATELES LAKE MIDDLE CONNECTING ROUTE**	W to E Read up ↑

E to W Read ↓	**OTISCO LAKE TO SKANEATELES LAKE** **SOUTHERN CONNECTING ROUTE**	W to E Read up ↑

0.0 (0.0)   W. Valley Rd./Moon Hill Rd.   **7.2 (11.6)**
@ Sawmill Rd. Otisco Lake
Continue traveling West on to Moon Hill Rd. to go to Skaneateles Lake.

0.6 (1.0)   Moon Hill Rd. @ Becker Rd.   **6.6 (10.6)**
Turn South on to Becker Rd.

2.0 (3.2)   Coldbrook Rd. @ Becker Rd.   **5.2 (8.4)**
Turn West on to Coldbrook Rd.

2.7 (4.3)   NY 41/E. Lake Rd.   **4.5 (7.2)**
@ Coldbrook Rd./Bacon Hill Rd.
↻ SKANEATELES LAKE CIRCUMNAVIGATION ROUTE:
Turn South on to NY 41 to go clockwise.
↺ SKANEATELES LAKE CIRCUMNAVIGATION ROUTE:
counterclockwise, continue traveling Northwest on Bacon Hill Rd. or go North on NY 41.

4.9 (7.9)   Vincent Hill Rd. @ NY 41/E. Lake Rd.   **2.3 (3.7)**
Turn West on to Vincent Hill Rd.

6.3 (10.1)   Glen Haven Rd. @ Vincent Hill Rd.   **0.9 (1.4)**
Turn North on to Glen Haven Rd.

6.5 (10.5)   Glen Haven Rd. Jct. E. Lake Rd.   **0.7 (1.1)**
Bear West on Glen Haven Rd.

7.2 (11.6)   Glen Haven Village   **0.0 (0.0)**
Southern most Village on Skaneateles Lake.
↺↻ Begin to follow the SKANEATELES LAKE CIRCUMNAVIGATION ROUTE from this intersection.

E to W Read ↓	**OTISCO LAKE TO SKANEATELES LAKE** **SOUTHERN CONNECTING ROUTE**	W to E Read up ↑

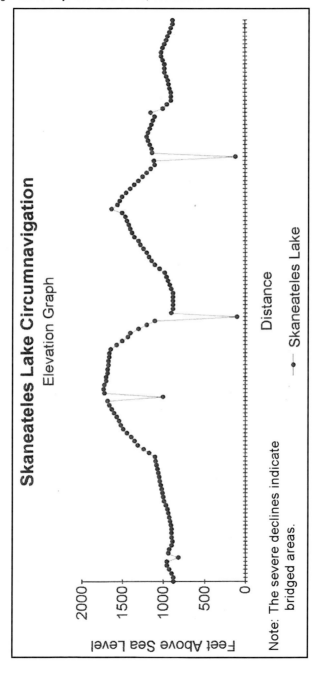

Skaneateles Lake Circumnavigation
Elevation Graph

Feet Above Sea Level

2000 1500 1000 500 0

Distance

Skaneateles Lake

Note: The severe declines indicate
bridged areas.

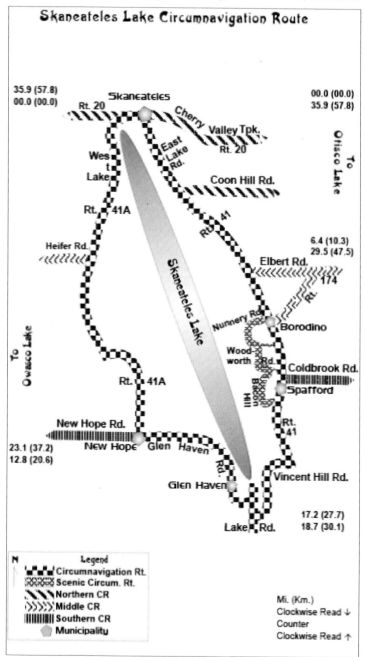

Skaneateles Lake Circumnavigation Route

35.9 (57.8)
00.0 (00.0)

Rt. 20

Skaneateles

Cherry Valley Tpk.
Rt. 20

00.0 (00.0)
35.9 (57.8)

East Lake Rd.

Coon Hill Rd.

West Lake

To Otisco Lake

Rt. 41A

Rt. 41

Heifer Rd.

Elbert Rd.

6.4 (10.3)
29.5 (47.5)

Rt. 174

Skaneateles Lake

Nunnery Rd.

Borodino

To Owasco Lake

Wood-worth Rd.

Coldbrook Rd.

Rt. 41A

Hill Rd.

Spafford

New Hope Rd.

New Hope   Glen Haven

Rt. 41

23.1 (37.2)
12.8 (20.6)

Glen Haven Rd.

Vincent Hill Rd.

Glen Haven

17.2 (27.7)
18.7 (30.1)

Lake Rd.

Legend

N

Circumnavigation Rt.
Scenic Circum. Rt.
Northern CR
Middle CR
Southern CR
Municipality

Mi. (Km.)
Clockwise Read ↓
Counter
Clockwise Read ↑

Ice Covers the Earth

The movie ad read, *Ice Covers the Earth!* Its shock value enhanced by fast moving clips of animals scurrying in front of a glacier barreling down a mountain; a skier frozen in situ; and beautifully colored flowers glistening through the crystal clear ice. An impossible scenario in reality.

At the beginning of the Pleistocene Era, the streams flowing in the Finger Lakes area were carving their courses on the peneplain. At times the streams cut deeply into the softer limestone and sandstone under the flowing water and laid bare the bedrock. Other times these streams were able to widen their channels to form gorges and glens (small gorges) along their paths. Over the course of hundreds of thousands of years some of the stream channels sufficiently widened and deepened at certain points to act as water holding areas which can be considered the forerunners of lakes. Then along came this massive climate change, the ice age. The accumulation and weight of frozen water in what we now call Labrador and Hudson's Bay in Canada pushed the leading edge of the ice flow southward.

Debris, everything from just plain old *dirt* to huge boulders from outcrops of bedrock (granite); from loose sand to chunks of sedimentary rock (shale) to bits of metamorphic rock (gneiss) which the ice had scraped off uplifted or exposed outcroppings, became entrapped and embedded in the flowing ice. Then as if the glacier knew (anthropomorphism and a bit of poetic license) human beings would be inhabiting this part of the earth and establishing political boundaries it the glacier flowing southward almost at what is now the New York - Pennsylvania border. A global warming and then another bout of extensive glaciation and finally a long period of warming with the subsequent retreat of the glacial front back to Labrador.

In the process of flowing southward, the glaciers scraped and dug into the land. The softer rock on the sides of stream beds yielded to the abrading force of harder embedded debris and the ice itself. The force of the ice pushed down and inculcated loose debris from the stream beds exposed soft sedimentary rock layers; which themselves were abraded piece by piece and incorporated into the mass of flowing ice. The force of gravity helped the glacier cut deep into the stream beds' metamorphic and sedimentary layers as some heavy small debris and huge boulders found their way to the bottom of the flowing ice. Hard igneous bed rock, stopped the erosive force of the flowing ice. Leaving behind a gouged landscape of widened streams and preglacial lakes. Then the earth became slightly warmer....

Clockwise	**SKANEATELES LAKE**	Counterclockwise
Read ↓	**CIRCUMNAVIGATION**	Read up ↑

TRAVELER NOTE

Approximately 8 mi. (13 km.) from the starting point in
Skaneateles, the Scenic Diversion Route begins. It
provides an alternative to NY 41 on the East side of
Skaneateles Lake. Both routes, circumnavigating using NY
41 and using the Scenic Diversion, are provided.

0.0 (0.0)   US 20/E. Genesee St.   35.9 (57.8)
                   @ NY 321/State St.
Turn East on to Genesee St.
⇔ OTISCO LAKE TO SKANEATELES LAKE: NORTHERN
CONNECTING ROUTES.
⇔ SKANEATELES LAKE TO OWASCO LAKE:
NORTHERN CONNECTING ROUTE.

SKANEATELES

Information: Skaneateles CofC, PO Box 199, Skaneateles
   13152, 315 685-0552. AC: 315. ZC: 13152.
Services & Facilities: All. Intercity Bus, (rush hour service)
   Centro, Syracuse NY 13205, 315 442-3400.
Accommodations: Motels. B&Bs: Arbor House, 41 Fennell St.,
   685-8966; Aunt Louise's Lake House, 2498 E. Lake Rd.,
   685-5864; Blue Willow Inn, 4423 State Street Rd., 685-
   1101; Frog Pond, 680 Sheldon Rd., 685-0146; Gray
   House, 47 Jordan St., 685-0131; Hobbit Hollow, 3061 W.
   Lake Rd., 685-2791; Hummingbirds Home, 4273 E. Gene-
   see St., 685-5075; Kenlark, 150 E. Genesee St., 685-5414;
   Lady of the Lake, 2 W. Lake St., 685-7997; Sunrise Hill,
   109 Sunrise Hill, 685-6401; Village Inn, 25 Jordan St., 685-
   3405; Westridge, 3143 W. Lake Rd., 685-8054.
Attractions: The Village's architecture has remained in its
   original 19th century splendor. Canal hireboats Midlakes
   Navigation, 11 Jordan St., 545-4318; Charlie Major Nature
   Trail, Old Seneca Tpk & Crow Hill Rd., 685-3473.

0.6 (1.0)   NY 41/E. Lake Rd.   35.3 (56.8)
                   @ NY 20/E. Genesee St.
Turn South on to NY 41/E. Lake Rd.

6.4 (10.3)   Elbert Rd.   29.5 (47.5)
                    @ NY 41/E. Lake Rd.
Continue traveling South on NY 41/E. Lake Rd.
⇔ OTISCO LAKE TO SKANEATELES LAKE: MIDDLE
CONNECTING ROUTE.

8.1 (13.0)   NY 174 & Nunnery Rd.   27.8 (44.7)
                    @ NY 41/E. Lake Rd.

CLOCKWISE TRAVELER NOTE
The primary Skaneateles Lake Circumnavigation Route
continues immediately after the Scenic Diversion Route.
The Scenic Diversion gives you a little change from NY 41.
Your choice! The Scenic Route is about 2 mi. (3.2 km.)
longer.
↻ Clockwise circumnavigators: Continue traveling South
on NY 41. Route directions using NY 41 continue
immediately after the SCENIC DIVERSION or
↻ Turn Southwest on to Nunnery Rd. to use the SCENIC
DIVERSION.
↻ Counterclockwise circumnavigators: Travel North on NY
41.
🔄 OTISCO LAKE CIRCUMNAVIGATION ROUTE. Another
way of going to Otisco Lake is to turn North on to NY 174 at
this intersection. Follow NY 174 to Willowdale Hill Rd. and
you'll be on the Otisco Lake Circumnavigation Route.
BORODINO HAMLET: no services.

CLOCKWISE TRAVELER NOTE
The primary Skaneateles Lake Circumnavigation Route
continues after the Skaneateles Lake Scenic Diversion
Route.

SKANEATELES LAKE CIRCUMNAVIGATION		
Clockwise	**PRIMARY ROUTE**	Counterclockwise
Read ↓	**CONTINUED**	Read up ↑

SKANEATELES LAKE CIRCUMNAVIGATION
Clockwise   **SCENIC DIVERSION**   Counterclockwise
Read ↓   Read up ↑

TRAVELER'S NOTE
Clockwise Travelers: This Scenic Route parallels NY 41.
It is on two lane chip sealed roads.
Counterclockwise Travelers: The primary Skaneateles
Lake Circumnavigation Route continues after the
Skaneateles Lake Scenic Diversion Route.

Toothpicks and building blocks.

00.0 (00.0)   NY 174 & Nunnery Rd.   7.8 (12.6)
                   @ E. Lake Rd./NY 41
        Turn South on to Nunnery Rd.

4.3 (6.9)   Woodworth Rd.   3.5 (5.6)
                   Jct. Nunnery Rd.
        Turn Southeast on to Woodworth Rd.
        If you miss Woodworth you'll end up at NY 41 and then just
        go South on NY 41.

5.6 (9.0)   Bacon Hill Rd. @ Woodworth Rd.   2.2 (3.5)
        Turn South on to Bacon Hill Rd. If you miss the Bacon Hill
        Rd., Woodworth Rd. will take you to NY 41/E. Lake Rd.

7.8 (12.6)   NY 41/E. Lake Rd. @ Bacon Hill Rd.   0.0 (0.0)
  ↻ SKANEATELES LAKE CIRCUMNAVIGATION Route:
Clockwise circumnavigators: Travel South NY 41/E. Lake
Rd. Scenic Diversion bicyclists will join us
The primary Skaneateles Lake Circumnavigation continues
South bound along the East shore from this intersection
with the Scenic Diversion.

SKANEATELES LAKE CIRCUMNAVIGATION
SCENIC DIVERSION

Clockwise   Counterclockwise
Read ↓   Read up ↑

SKANEATELES LAKE CIRCUMNAVIGATION

Clockwise	**PRIMARY ROUTE**	Counterclockwise
Read ↓	**CONTINUED**	Read up ↑

COUNTERCLOCKWISE TRAVELER'S NOTE

The Scenic Diversion gives you a little change from NY 41. Your choice! The Scenic Route is about 2 mi. (3.2 km.) longer.

The primary Skaneateles Lake Circumnavigation Route continues immediately after the SCENIC DIVERSION.

13.6 (21.9)   Bacon Hill Rd. & Coldbrook Rd.   22.3 (35.9)
                   @ NY 41/E. Lake Rd.

↻ Clockwise circumnavigators: Continue traveling South on NY 41/E. Lake Rd.

↻ Counterclockwise circumnavigators: Turn Northwest on to Bacon Hill Rd. to use the SCENIC DIVERSION or

↻ Counterclockwise circumnavigators: Continue to travel North on NY 41.

⇔ OTISCO LAKE TO SKANEATELES LAKE: SOUTHERN CONNECTING ROUTE intersects here.

15.8 (25.4)   Vincent Hill Rd.   20.1 (32.3)
                   @ NY 41/E. Lake Rd.
Turn West on to Vincent Hill Rd.

17.2 (27.7)   Glen Haven Rd.   18.7 (30.1)
                   @ Vincent Hill Rd.
                   Turn North on to Glen Haven Rd.

17.4 (28.0)   Glen Haven Rd.   18.5 (29.8)
                   Jct. E. Lake Rd.
Bear West on to Glen Haven Rd.
This E. Lake Rd. is not NY 41. It leads to Fair Haven and no where else.. Good fishing.

18.4 (29.6)   Glen Haven Village   17.8 (28.6)
                   @ Glen Haven Rd.
Continue North on Glen Haven Rd.
Cayuga County-Onondaga County border.
⇔ OTISCO LAKE TO SKANEATELES LAKE SOUTHERN CONNECTING ROUTE.

23.1 (37.2)   NY 41A/W. Lake Rd.   12.8 (20.6)
                   @ Glen Haven Rd.
↻ Turn North on to NY 41A/W. Lake Rd.
⇔   SKANEATLELES   LAKE   TO   OWASCO   LAKE:
SOUTHERN CONNECTING ROUTE.
NEW HOPE: New Hope Mills, NY 41A, New Hope, 13118;
restaurant, convenience store.

28.4 (45.7)   Heifer Rd. @ NY 41A   7.5 (12.1)
Continue traveling North on NY 41A to circumnavigate
Skaneateles Lake.
⇔ SKANEATELES LAKE TO OWASCO LAKE: MIDDLE
CONNECTING ROUTE.

34.1 (54.9)   West Lake St.   1.8 (2.9)
                   @ NY 41A/W. Lake Rd.
Turn Northwest on to West Lake St.

35.4 (57.0)   US 20/W. Genesee St.   0.5 (0.8)
                   @ West Lake St.
Turn East on to US 20/W. Genesee St.
⇔ SKANEATELES LAKE TO OWASCO LAKE:
NORTHERN CONNECTING ROUTE.
Turn West on to US 20/W. Genesee St. to go to the
northern end of Owasco Lake.

35.9 (57.8)   NY 321/State St.   0.0 (0.0)
                   @ US 20/Genesee St.
SKANEATELES Another Lake and more to enjoy!

| Clockwise | **SKANEATELES LAKE** | Counterclockwise |
| Read ↓ | **CIRCUMNAVIGATION** | Read up ↑ |

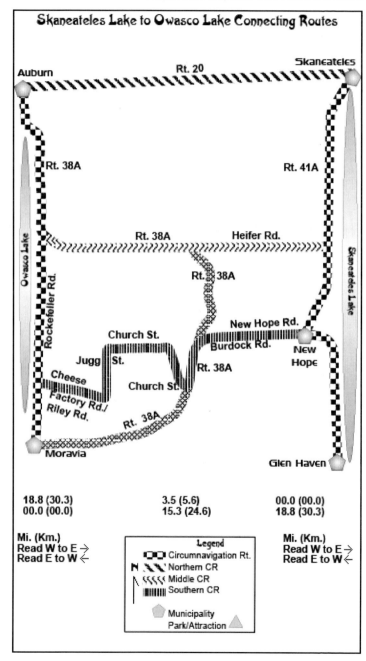

0.0 (0.0)   US 20/Genesee St.   10.6 (17.1)
          @ NY 321/State St. Skaneateles Lake
Travel West on US 20/W. Genesee St.
SKANEATELES

0.5 (0.8)   West Lake Rd.   10.1 (16.3)
          @ US 20/W. Genesee St.
Continue traveling West on US 20.
↺ SKANEATELES LAKE CIRCUMNAVIGATION: counter-
clockwise travelers turn SW on to West Lake Rd.

1.0 (1.6)   NY 41A/W. Lake Rd.   9.6 (15.4)
          @ US 20/W. Genesee St.
Westward Ho! on US 20.
🚲 ↺ NY 41A is the main road on the West side of
Skaneateles Lake. You can turn South here and go around
Skaneateles Lake counterclockwise.

7.3 (11.7)   NY 38A @ US 20   3.3 (5.3)
Continue traveling West on US 20 to go to downtown
Auburn.
🚲 ↺ Turn South on to NY 38A to 'round Owasco Lake
clockwise with the OWASCO LAKE CIRCUMNAVIGATION
route.
Watch out for sewer grates in Auburn! US 20 in Auburn.
does not have a particularly smooth road surface. It is a
wide two lane road with little traffic until you reach the main
business area.
AUBURN: see Owasco Lake Circumnavigation route for
Auburn information.

10.6 (17.1)   St. Boat Ramp @ NY 38A   0.0 (0.0)
          ↺ OWASCO LAKE CIRCUMNAVIGATIONRoute.
Owasco Lake.

E to W Read ↓	**SKANEATELES LAKE TO OWASCO LAKE** **MIDDLE CONNECTING ROUTE**	W to E Read up ↑

0.0 (0.0)   Heifer Rd. W.   5.3 (8.5)
                             @ NY 41A/W. Lake Rd.
Turn West on to Heifer Rd. W. Skaneateles Lake.

1.2 (1.9)   Heifer Rd. Jct. NY 38A   4.1 (6.6)
Continue westward on to NY 38A.

3.2 (5.1)   North Rd./Gahwiler Rd.   2.1 (3.4)
                             @ NY 38A
Continue traveling West on NY 38A. Owasco.

5.3 (8.5)   Rockefeller Rd. @ NY 38A   0.0 (0.0)
Owasco Lake.
⇔ ↻ ↺ OWASCO LAKE CIRCUMNAVIGATION ROUTE
from this intersection.
↺↻ Turn South on to Rockefeller Rd. to go 'round Owasco
Lake clockwise; continue traveling North on NY 38A to
circumnavigate Owasco Lake counterclockwise.

E to W	**SKANEATELES LAKE TO OWASCO LAKE**	W to E
Read ↓	**SOUTHERN CONNECTING ROUTE**	Read up ↑

0.0 (0.0)   Glen Haven Rd. & New Hope Rd.   13.0 (20.9)
                 @ NY 41A/W.Lake Rd.
Travel West on to New Hope Rd.
NEW HOPE: Refer to the Skaneateles Circumnavigation
route for information.

0.9 (1.4)   Old Salt Rd.   12.1 (19.5)
                 @ New Hope Rd. Jct. Burdock Rd.
Continue traveling West on Burdock Rd. The name of the
asphalt simply changes.

1.8 (2.9)   NY 38A/Hollow Rd. @ Burdock Rd.   11.2 (18.0)
Turn South on to NY 38A.
To go directly to Moravia and the southern end of Owasco
Lake, do not follow the directions for the Scenic Way
Route. Simply continue South on NY 38A and you'll be in
Moravia at the Southern end of Owasco Lake. The distance
is about the same as the Scenic Way but NY 38A has a
smoother road surface.
The primary Skaneateles Lake to Owasco Lake: Southern
Connecting Route is continued after the Scenic Way Route.

E to W	**SKANEATELES LAKE TO OWASCO LAKE**	W to E
Read ↓	**SOUTHERN CONNECTING ROUTE CON'T**	Read up ↑

E to W	**SKANEATELES LAKE TO OWASCO LAKE**	W to E
	SCENIC WAY ON THE	
Read ↓	**SOUTHERN CONNECTING ROUTE**	Read up ↑

TRAVELER NOTE
EAST TO WEST - SKANEATELES LAKE TO OWASCO LAKE
Traveling South on NY 38A will bring you directly into Moravia and the southern end of Owasco Lake. It is a 8.9 mi. (14.3 km.) very pleasant ride along NY 38A to Moravia at the southern end of Owasco Lake.
The route description detailed below is a scenic route to Moravia.

3.5 (5.6)   Church St. @ NY 38A   9.5 (15.2)
Turn West on to Church St.

5.4 (8.7)   Jugg St../Corrigan Rd.   7.6 (12.2)
                   @ Church St.
Turn South on to Jugg Rd.
Corrigan Rd. goes North, Jugg St. goes South.

7.0 (11.3)   Jugg St. @ Cheese Factory Rd.   6.0 (9.7)
Turn West on to Cheese Factory Rd.

7.6 (12.2)   Riley Rd. Jct. Cheese Factory Rd.   5.4 (8.7)
Continue traveling West on Riley Rd.

9.4 (15.1)   Rockefeller Rd. @ Riley Rd.   3.6 (5.8)
⇔ ↻ ↺ OWASCO LAKE CIRCUMNAVIGATION ROUTE.
↻ Clockwise 'round Owasco Lake travelers continue traveling South on Rockefeller Rd.
↺ Counterclockwise Owasco Lake travelers turn North on to Rockefeller Rd.

E to W	**SKANEATELES LAKE TO OWASCO LAKE**	W to E
	SCENIC WAY ON THE	
Read ↓	**SOUTHERN CONNECTING ROUTE**	Read up ↑

TRAVELER'S NOTE
WEST TO EAST - OWASCO LAKE TO SKANEATELES LAKE
Traveling North on NY 38A is the most direct way to go to the southern end of Skaneateles Lake from Moravia and the southern end of Owasco Lake. It is a 8.9 mi. (14.3 km.) very pleasant ride along NY 38A Burdock/New Hope Rds. and New Hope where you leave NY 38A.

The SCENIC WAY route description detailed immediately above this Note provides a little diversion from NY 38A. NY 38A is a scenic fine road. You will rejoin the normal connecting route at the Burdock Rd./New Hope Rd. @ NY 38A intersection.

13.0 (20.9)   NY 38A & NY 38   0.0 (0.0)
                 @ Rockefeller Rd./Main St.

⇔ ʊ ʊ OWASCO LAKE CIRCUMNAVIGATION ROUTE.

ʊ Clockwise 'round Owasco turn North on to NY 38.

ʊ Counterclockwise around Owasco Lake travelers turn North on to Rockefeller Rd.

MORAVIA: Refer to the Owasco Lake Circumnavigation route for information.

TRAVELER'S NOTE
There are several ways of going to Cayuga Lake from Moravia. Before you put your pedal down, read them all, each has its own characteristics.

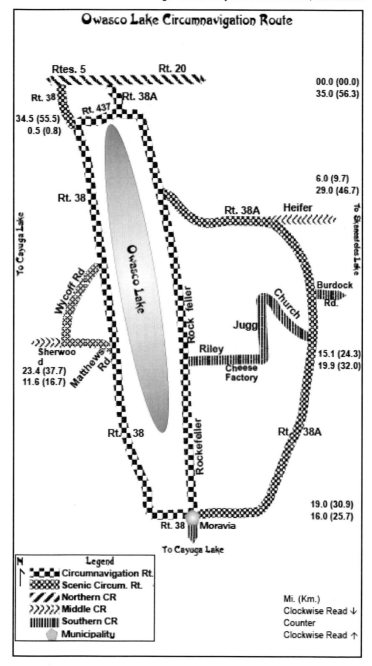

Owasco Lake Circumnavigation Route

Rtes. 5   Rt. 20

Rt. 38   Rt. 38A

Rt. 437

00.0 (00.0)
35.0 (56.3)

34.5 (55.5)
0.5 (0.8)

Rt. 38

6.0 (9.7)
29.0 (46.7)

Rt. 38A   Heifer

To Cayuga Lake

Owasco Lake

To Skaneateles Lake

Wycoff Rd

Rock Teller

Burdock Rd.

Church

Jugg

Riley

Sherwood
23.4 (37.7)
11.6 (16.7)

Matthews Rd.

Cheese
Factory

15.1 (24.3)
19.9 (32.0)

Rt. 38

Rockefeller

Rt. 38A

19.0 (30.9)
16.0 (25.7)

Rt. 38   Moravia

To Cayuga Lake

Legend
N

Circumnavigation Rt.
Scenic Circum. Rt.
Northern CR
Middle CR
Southern CR
Municipality

Mi. (Km.)
Clockwise Read ↓
Counter
Clockwise Read ↑

Debris

Like the debris which confronts you on the road, glacial debris reshaped the topography of the Finger Lakes area. The differences between the two types of debris are of course, how each was created and deposited.

Glaciers receded in starts and stops. When the temperature rose and the ice at the front of the glacier turned into liquid, the sand, stones and boulders precipitated out on to the land. When the temperature fell again the tongue of the glacier extended southward pushing the debris left at the front of the glacier a bit further South. Water flowing from the receding glacier was prodigious and fast moving. Perfect for carrying debris overland or under water to a point where it piled up on top of the debris left at the end of the glacier's tongue. Those ridges between the southern ends of the Fingers are composed of that debris. To a geologist that deposited debris at the end of a glacier is a moraine.

At the southern end of the glacially widened and deepened stream channels the debris, previously suspended in the ice, precipitated out formed a valley head moraine. It is this valley head moraine which blocked the water from the now deepened and chiseled stream valleys. Water from the now formed Finger Lakes was blocked from flowing out. Even more importantly these valley head moraines changed the course of the inlets and outlets for Finger Lake water.

As the glacier receded more and more melt water flowed into the chiseled finger lake valleys. The water rose and pushed through the southern valley head moraine to flow southwards since the southern end of each lake was at a lower elevation than the northern end. The force of the water pushing though the valley head moraine formed steep sided glens and gorges. The lake level dropped and a defined shore line formed.

Over time, water from streams flowing down the land left between each finger lake basin brought silt to the lake's shore. Like almost any river or stream flowing into a water basin, the suspended silt precipitated out to form a delta where the stream and lake meet. In the course of 20,000 years this process was repeated many times. Each time a lower lake level was established. Each time a delta was formed where the stream entered a lake. A step or hanging delta of delta was formed as the lake levels went lower and lower.

In the final phase of glacial recession, glacial erosion so scoured the northern end all the Finger Lakes that the elevation at the northern end became significantly lower than the elevation, above sea level, at the southern end. With a moraine forming a barrier at the southern end of a Lake the water had no where to go but out the northern end and into Lake Ontario (what we now term one part of pre Pleistocene Era Lake Iroquois).

Read ↓   **OWASCO LAKE CIRCUMNAVIGATION**   Read up ↑
Clockwise   Counterclockwise

0.0 (0.0)   NY 38A/Owasco St.   35.0 (56.3)
                         @ US 20/E. Genesee St.
Turn South on to NY 38A/Owasco St.
⇔   SKANEATELES   LAKE   TO   OWASCO   LAKE:
NORTHERN CONNECTING ROUTE.
⇔ OWASCO LAKE TO CAYUGA LAKE: NORTHERN
CONNECTING ROUTES.

AUBURN

Information: Downtown Auburn Bus. Improvement Assn., 131 Genesee St., Auburn NY 13021, 315 252-7874. AC: 315 ZC: 13021.
Bicycling Information: Bike shop. Owasco Velo Club, PO Box 1506, www.owascoveloclub.com; promotes the Owasco Stage Race in June. Bon Ton Roulet a bicycle tour conducted each year by the Auburn & Cortland YMCAs.
Services: All. Hospital. Intercity Bus: Greyhound & Centro commuter bus from Syracuse (with bike hold facility), 315 442-3400.
Accommodations: B&Bs: A Wicher Garden B&B, 5831 Dunning Ave. Rd., 252-1187; Fay's Point Beachhouse, 5008 W. Lake Rd. (NY38S.), 253-9525; Irish Rose, 102 South St., 255-0196; Springside Inn, NY 38 South, 255-0196. Camping: Yaeger Brook Family Cpgd., 252-8969.
Attractions: Merry-Go-Round Playhouse, Emerson Pk., 255-1305; Cayuga Mus. & Case Research Lab., 203 W. Genesee St., 253-8051; Cayuga Co. Agricultural Mus., Emerson Pk., 253-5611; The Seward House, 33 South St., 252-1283; Harriet Tubman Home, 180 S St., 252-2081; Owasco Teyetasta, NY 38A, 253-8051.

3.3 (5.3)   Boat Launch @ NY 38A   31.7 (51.0)
Continue traveling South on NY 38A/East Lake Rd.

6.0 (9.7)   Rockefeller Rd. @ NY 38A   29.0 (46.7)
Turn South on to Rockefeller Rd.; a 2 lane chip sealed road with a somewhat rough surface. It is more scenic and pleasant than riding on NY 38A.
Or continue traveling South on NY 38A. NY 38A goes in land and way far from the Owasco Lake. Using NY 38A, you'll end up in Moravia.

15.1 (24.3)   Riley Rd. @ Rockefeller Rd.   19.9 (32.0)
Continue traveling South on Rockefeller Rd. to continue
your circumnavigation of Owasco Lake.
⇔ SKANEATELES LAKE TO OWASCO LAKE:
SOUTHERN CONNECTING ROUTE: Turn East on to Riley
Rd. to go to Skaneateles Lake.

19.0 (30.6)   NY 38 @ Rockefeller Rd./Main St.   16.0 (25.7)
Turn North on to NY 38.
When you turn North on to NY 38 you will be traveling
clockwise around Owasco Lake. A bit of a round about
way of getting to the West side of Owasco Lake but it is the
only way!

MORAVIA

Services: Groceries, convenience store, hardware store,
gas station, restaurants, & bank.
Lodging: Motels. B&B: Oldest House In Moravia, 52 S.
Main St., 497-0524. Camping: Fillmore Glen St. Pk., Park
Rd., 497-0130; Sevey's Boatyard Cpgrd., Glen Cove Rd.,
496-2092; Empire Haven Nudist Pk., Box 297 Sun Lane,
497-0135.
Attractions: Cayuga-Owasco Lakes Hist. Soc. Mus., 14 W.
Cayuga St., 497-3906; Fillmore Glen St. Pk.; Millard
Fillmore Home at Fillmore Glen St. Pk.; New Hope Mills,
Glen Haven Rd., 497-0783.

Stone stairs constructed by ancient societies?

23.4 (37.7)   Matthews Rd. @ NY38   11.6 (18.7)
Continue North on NY 38 to circumnavigate Owasco Lake.
⇔ ↻ OR use the RURAL RD DIVERSION to spice up your
pedaling.
⇔ OWASCO LAKE TO CAYUGA LAKE: MIDDLE
CONNECTING ROUTE. Turn Northwest on to Matthews
Rd. to go to Cayuga Lake.
Clockwise travelers
The primary Owasco Lake Circumnavigation Route
continues after the Rural Rd. Diversion.

Read ↓	**OWASCO LAKE CIRCUMNAVIGATION**	Read up ↑
Clockwise		Counterclockwise

Read ↓	**OWASCO LAKE CIRCUMNAVIGATION**	Read up ↑
Clockwise	**RURAL RD DIVERSION**	Counterclockwise

0.0 (0.0)   Matthews Rd. @ NY 38   8.4 (13.5)
Turn Northwest on to Matthews Rd.

0.8 (1.4)   Matthews Rd. Jct. Sherwood Rd.   7.6 (12.2)
Continue traveling West on to Sherwood Rd.

2.4 (3.9)   Wycoff Rd. @ Sherwood Rd.   6.0 (9.7)
Turn North on to Wycoff Rd.
⇔ OWASCO LAKE TO CAYUGA LAKE: MIDDLE
CONNECTING ROUTE, continuing West on Sherwood Rd.
will bring you to the middle of Cayuga Lake.

8.4 (13.5)   NY 38 @ Wycoff Rd.   0.0 (0.0)
↻ Turn North on to NY 38 to complete the
circumnavigation of Owasco Lake.

Read ↓	**OWASCO LAKE CIRCUMNAVIGATION**	Read up ↑
Clockwise	**RURAL RD DIVERSION**	Counterclockwise

Read ↓ Clockwise	**OWASCO LAKE CIRCUMNAVIGATION** **PRIMARY ROUTE CONTINUED**	Read up ↑ Counterclockwise

Counterclockwise travelers: The regular Owasco Lake Circumnavigation Route continues after the Rural Rd. Diversion.

29.9 (48.1)   Wycoff Rd. @ NY 38   5.1 (8.2)
↻ **Clockwise travelers:** Continue traveling North on NY 38 to complete the circumnavigation of Owasco Lake.
↺ Counterclockwise **travelers** can turn off on to Wycoff Rd. to use the RURAL RD DIVERSION to spice up their pedal strokes. Using either NY 38 or the Rural Rd Diversion route will bring you to the same point on NY 38. This intersection is the northern end of RURAL RD DIVERSION.

34.5 (55.5)   Sand Pt. Rd./NY 437   0.5 (0.8)
                 @ NY 38/West Lake Rd.
Turn East to Complete the ellipse.
Continue North on NY 38 to go to Auburn.

35.0 (56.3)   Sand Pt. Rd./NY 437   0.0 (0.0)
                 @ NY 38A/East Lake Rd.
Back to where you began!
Turn North on NY 38A/East Lake Rd. to go to Auburn.

Read ↓ Clockwise	**OWASCO LAKE CIRCUMNAVIGATION**	Read up ↑ Counterclockwise

Owasco Lake to Cayuga Lake Connecting Routes

17.4 (28.0)   7.0 (11.3)   00.0 (00.0)
00.0 (00.0)   12.9 (20.8)   17.4 (28.0)

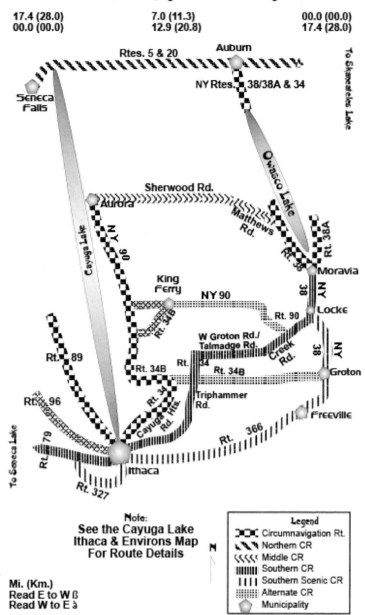

Note:
**See the Cayuga Lake
Ithaca & Environs Map
For Route Details**

N

Mi. (Km.)
Read E to W ß
Read W to E à

Legend
ЭⅭⅭ Circumnavigation Rt.
＼＼＼ Northern CR
‹‹‹‹ Middle CR
||||||| Southern CR
|||| Southern Scenic CR
∷∷∷∷ Alternate CR
⬠ Municipality

E to W Read ↓	**OWASCO LAKE TO CAYUGA LAKE** **NORTHERN CONNECTING ROUTE**	W to E Read up ↑

0.0 (0.0)   US 20/W. Genesee St. @ NY 38A   17.4 (28.0)
Travel West on US 20. **AUBURN:** See the Owasco Lake
Circumnavigation Route for information.
↻ Turn S. on to NY 38A to circumnavigate Owasco Lake.

0.5 (0.8)   Rtes. 34 & 38 @ W. Genesee St.   16.9 (27.2)
Continue traveling West on W. Genesee St. US 20 at this
point becomes a limited access highway and branches off
from W. Genesee St.
↻ Turn South on to NY 38 to go Counterclockwise around
Owasco Lake

4.0 (6.4)   NY 326 @ Genesee St.   13.4 (21.6)
Turn North on to NY 326.

4.9 (7.9)   Rtes. 5&20 @ NY 326   12.5 (20.1)
Turn West on to Rtes. 5&20.

11.8 (19.0)   NY 90 @ Rtes. 5&20   5.6 (9.0)
Continue traveling West to go to Seneca Falls.
↻ CAYUGA LAKE CIRCUMNAVIGATION ROUTE.

12.5 (20.1)   Montezuma Nat'l. Wildlife Refuge   4.9 (7.9)
                    @ Rtes. 5&20
Stop for a look. Bathrooms at Visitors Center.

14.2 (22.9)   Rtes. 318/89 @ Rtes. 5&20   3.2 (5.1)
Continue traveling on Rtes. 5&20 to go to Seneca Falls.
↻ CAYUGA LAKE CIRCUMNAVIGATION ROUTE.

17.4 (28.0)   NY 414 @ Rtes. 5&20   0.0 (0.0)
SENECA FALLS: See the Cayuga Lake Circumnavigation
Route for information.
⇔ CAYUGA LAKE TO SENECA LAKE: NORTHERN
CONNECTING ROUTE

E to W Read ↓	**OWASCO LAKE TO CAYUGA LAKE** **NORTHERN CONNECTING ROUTE**	W to E Read up ↑

E to W	**OWASCO LAKE TO CAYUGA LAKE**	W to E
Read ↓	**MIDDLE CONNECTING ROUTE**	Read up ↑

0.0 (0.0)   NY 38 @ Matthews Rd.   10.2 (16.4)
Turn Northwest on to Matthews Rd.
Owasco Lake, West side.

0.9 (1.4)   Sherwood Rd. Jct. Matthews Rd.   9.3 (15.0)
Continue traveling West on Sherwood Rd. The direction's
the same, only the road name has changed.

10.2 (16.4)   NY 90 @ Sherwood Rd.   0.0 (0.0)
⇔ From this intersection use the CAYUGA LAKE
CIRCUMNAVIGATION ROUTE. Make certain that you
read the Warning at the beginning the Cayuga Lake
Circumnavigation Route.
↻ Turn South on to NY 90 to round Cayuga Lake
clockwise.
↺ Turn North on to NY 90 to go around Cayuga Lake
counterclockwise.
AURORA See entry in the Cayuga Lake Circumnavigation
Route.

TRAVELER NOTE
If you're starting from Aurora and going to Owasco Lake via
the OWASCO LAKE TO CAYUGA LAKE: MIDDLE
CONNECTING ROUTE then you don't really need a note!
If you made it to Aurora from Ithaca via the CAYUGA LAKE
CIRCUMNAVIGATION ROUTE then you deserve an
award.

E to W Read ↓	**OWASCO LAKE TO CAYUGA LAKE** **SOUTHERN CONNECTING ROUTE**	W to E Read up ↑

TRAVELER NOTE

It is impossible to enter Ithaca, at the southern end of Cayuga Lake without descending severely sloped grades. Similarly, it is impossible to go North from Ithaca without ascending severely sloped grades.

0.0 (0.0)   Rockefeller Rd./Main St.   28.0 (45.1)
                   @ Rtes. 38/38A Cayuga St.
Travel South on to NY 38/Main St. to go to Cayuga Lake.
↻ OWASCO LAKE CIRCUMNAVIGATION ROUTE: Clockwise circumnavigators turn North on to NY 38.
↺ OWASCO LAKE CIRCUMNAVIGATION ROUTE: counterclockwise circumnavigators travel North on to Rockefeller Rd. Rockefeller Rd. is simply an extension of Main St., it may be termed something else. Landmark: grocery on your left as you go North on Rockefeller Rd.
⇔ OWASCO LAKE TO CAYUGA LAKE: SOUTHERN DIRECT CONNECTING ROUTE.
MORAVIA: Refer to the Owasco Lake Circumnavigation Route for information.

3.3 (5.3)   NY 90 @ NY 38   24.7 (39.8)
Continue traveling South on NY 38.
⇔ OWASCO LAKE TO CAYUGA LAKE: SOUTHERN DIRECT ROUTE. Turn West on to NY 90.
LOCKE: AC: 607. ZC: 13092. **Service:** convenience store.
Lodging: Bare Bones (Natural) Cpgd., 1090 NY 38, 497-0621. **Attraction:** Earle Estates Meadery, RD 1, Box 246, Tucker Hill Rd., Locke 13092, 607 898-5940.

9.4 (15.1)   NY 222 @ NY 38   18.6 (29.9)
Continue traveling South on NY 38.
NY 222 goes East to Cortland.

GROTON

Services: Grocery, convenience store/gas station, bank, hardware store, and pharmacy.
Public Transit: *Tcat* bus to/from Ithaca, 607 277-4733, Don't forget to ask if there is a bike rack on the bus! Usually these buses only operate on weekdays during the rush hours.
Lodging: B&Bs: Angel Arms, 481 Lafayette Rd., 838-0497;

Austin Manor, 210 Old Peruville Rd., 898-5786; Benn Conger Inn, 206 W Cortland St., 898-5817; Gale House, 114 Williams St., 898-4904; Gleason's, 307 Old Stage Rd., 898-4676; Scandia House, 137 E. Cortland St., 898-3799; Tinkering, 774 Peru Rd., 898-3864; Turtle Dreams, 481 Lafayette Rd., 838-3492.

12.5 (20.1)   NY 34B @ NY 38   15.5 (24.9)
Continue traveling South on NY 38.
🚲 NY 34B will take you directly to the CAYUGA LAKE CIRCUMNAVIGATION ROUTE and the OWASCO LAKE TO CAYUGA LAKE: SOUTHERN DIRECT CONNECTING ROUTE. Simply turn West on to NY 38B and ride for 7.2 mi. (11.7 km.) to the intersection of NY 34 @ NY 34B and read the Circumnavigation Route or the Southern Direct Route from that point.

15.4 (24.8)   NY 366 @ NY 38   12.6 (20.3)
Turn West on to NY 366 to go to Ithaca & Cayuga Lake.
NY 38 goes to Dryden, a larger Village with additional services, facilities and lodging.

FREEVILLE
Services: Local grocery and restaurants.
Public Transit: *Tcat* bus to/from Ithaca, 277-4733, Don't forget to ask if there is a bike rack on the bus!
Lodging: B&Bs: Bountiful Blessings, 147 Lick St., 898-3370; Foxglove, 28 Main St., 844-9602; Yellow Barn, 125A Yellow Barn Rd., 844-4943.

19.1 (30.7)   NY 13 Jct. NY 366   8.9 (14.3)
Turn South on to Rte. 366/13.

20.3 (32.8)   NY 13 @ NY 366   7.7 (12.4)
Continue following NY 366 Southwest to Ithaca.
Do not use NY 13 any further south. It becomes a limited access highway and will only take you to NY 34 which this scenic route is designed to avoid.
You will be descending steep grades from this point into Ithaca. Make certain that your bike, tires, brakes and you are in perfect mechanical condition.

26.5 (42.6)   NY 79 Jct. NY 366   1.5 (2.4)
Continue traveling West on Rtes. 366/79.
Use extreme caution this is a very steep grade on a relatively narrow roadway going South bound.
If you want to go to Cornell University turn North on any of the streets which have signs directing you to Cornell,

Cornell Plantations, or the Veterinary College. If you go into Ithaca you'll only have to climb back up again to go to Cornell.

27.5 (44.4)   Rtes. 366/79/E. State St..   .5 (.8)
                 Jct. Rtes. 366/79/E. Seneca St.
Continue traveling West on Rtes. 79/366 Seneca St.
NY 366 theoretically ends/begins at this intersection.
The major State highways become one way streets in Ithaca. It's not too confusing since the roads/streets are clearly signed.
In front of you is Ithaca Commons, a pedestrian only city mall. Lots of restaurants, stores including a bike shop and camping store. Take a break and have something to drink and eat.

TRAVELER'S NOTE
WEST TO EAST - CAYUGA LAKE TO OWASCO LAKE
Cyclotourists going to Owasco Lake from Cayuga Lake, *i. e.* to Moravia from Ithaca, will actually be traveling East from the Cayuga Lake Inlet along Green St./NY 79 to this intersection. The distances are the same as Green St. and Seneca St. are parallel. If you are traveling from the Inlet, follow the NY 79/Green St. signs to this intersection with NY 366.
Yup! You've got a steep grade upwards to climb as you go to Owasco Lake on NY 366. *Tcat* on the NY 366 route have bike racks. The bus can take you part way up the hill on NY 366. You'll still have lots to climb so there is no sense in wearing yourself out at the beginning of this route.

28.0 (45.1)   Cayuga St.   0.0 (0.0)
                 @ NY 79 West/Seneca St.
                 @ NY 79 East/Green St.
Hey! You're in the center of Ithaca.

| E to W | **OWASCO LAKE TO CAYUGA LAKE** | W to E |
| Read ↓ | **SOUTHERN CONNECTING ROUTE** | Read up ↑ |

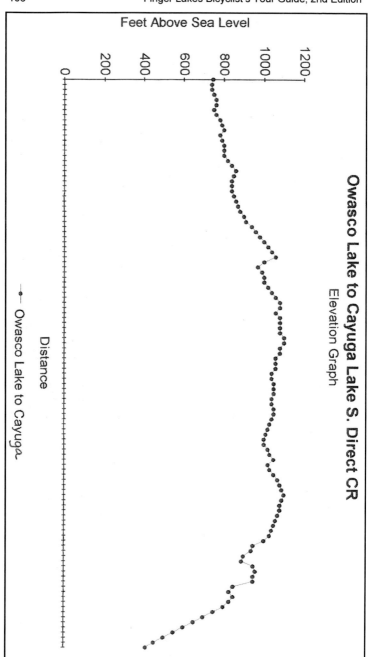

Owasco Lake to Cayuga Lake S. Direct CR

Elevation Graph

	OWASCO LAKE TO CAYUGA LAKE	
E to W	**SOUTHERN DIRECT**	W to E
Read ↓	**CONNECTING ROUTE**	Read up ↑

0.0 (0.0)   Rockefeller Rd./Main St.   21.5 (34.6)
                   @ Rtes. 38/38A Cayuga St.
Travel South on to NY 38/Main St. to go to Cayuga Lake.
↻ OWASCO LAKE CIRCUMNAVIGATION ROUTE, turn
North on to NY 38 to go 'round Owasco Lake clockwise.
↺ OWASCO LAKE CIRCUMNAVIGATION ROUTE, travel
North on to Rockefeller Rd. to go around Owasco Lake
counterclockwise.
MORAVIA: See Owasco Lake Circumnavigation Route for
information.

3.3 (5.3)   NY 90 @ NY 38   18.2 (29.3)
Turn West on to NY 90 to go to Cayuga Lake and Ithaca.
🛏 ↺ Turn West on NY 90 to go to Cayuga Lake, assuming
you don't want to go to Ithaca. You will arrive at Cayuga
Lake about 1/3 the way up from its southern end. Cayuga
Lake is due west, 11.2 mi. (18.1 km.), on NY 90. You will
intersect the CAYUGA LAKE CIRCUMNAVIGATION
ROUTE at King Ferry Village, NY 90 @ NY 34B.
⇔ OWASCO LAKE TO CAYUGA LAKE: SOUTHERN
SCENIC CONNECTING ROUTE, continue traveling South
on NY 38.
LOCKE: AC: 607. ZC: 13092. **Service**: convenience store.
Lodging: Bare Bones (Natural) Cpgd., 1090 NY 38, 497-
0621. **Attraction**: Earle Estates Meadery, RD 1, Box 246,
Tucker Hill Rd., 898-5640.

4.6 (7.4)   West Groton Rd. @ NY 90   16.9 (27.2)
Turn South on to West Groton.
The street names are a bit confusing. The point here is to
turn on to Creek St. Creek St. is very close to the
intersection of Rtes. 90 & W. Groton Rd.

4.8 (7.7)   Creek Rd./Locke Rd.   16.7 (26.9)
                   @ W. Groton Rd. (northern end near NY 90)
Turn South on to Creek Rd./Locke Rd.
At its southern end Creek Rd. is called Locke Rd.
Use care, this is an easy intersection to miss.
Creek Rd. is a well shaded narrow 2 lane chip sealed road
with a gravel shoulder. I really enjoyed riding on this road.
There is negligible traffic on Creek Rd. Since I think

Lockites & Moravians are not used to encountering bicyclists on Creek Rd. make yourself very visible. Make certain that your flashing red light is on.

7.0 (11.3)   W. Groton Rd. (southern end)   14.5 (23.3)
                    @ Locke Rd.
Turn West on to W. Groton Rd.
W. Groton Rd. makes a semi circle around Locke Rd. Connecting NY 34 to NY 90. No map shows this but according to my wheel marks this is the reality.

8.0 (12.9)   NY 34 @ W. Groton Rd.   13.5 (21.7)
Turn South on to NY 34 to go to Ithaca and the southern end of Cayuga Lake. Landmark: "Corner Diner."

12.5 (20.1)   Triphammer Rd. @ NY 34   9.0 (14.5)
                     NY 34B Jct. NY 34
Travel straight South on to Triphammer Rd.
NY 34 makes a broad sweeping turn westward as it junctions with NY 34B. Landmark: restaurant/bar on the curve. At the west edge of the curve it Junctions with NY 34B.
If you pass the Lansing Town Hall then you've gone past this intersection.
⇔ ↺ ↺ LANSING—REMINGTON RD ROUTE: this alternative route South into Ithaca turns off NY 34 just before the dangerous section of NY 34. The Lansing Sunset Route is provided immediately after this Route. The Cayuga Lake Circumnavigation route uses the Lansing Sunset Route to go into Ithaca.
🚲 ↺ ↺ CAYUGA LAKE CIRCUMNAVIGATION Route. Continuing West on NY 34 or NY 34B will bring you to Circumnavigation route.

12.6 (20.3)   Triphammer Rd. @ NY 34B   8.9 (14.3)
Travel South on Triphammer Rd.
There is a 4+ ft. (1.2+ m.) shoulder on Triphammer Rd. from this point to the Community Commons Plaza. In the *Mall* area traffic picks up.
🚲 ⇔ Going East on NY 34B will bring you to NY 38 and the OWASCO LAKE TO CAYUGA LAKE: SOUTHERN SCENIC ROUTE.

16.9 (27.1)   NY 13 @ Triphammer Rd.   4.6 (7.4)
Continue traveling South on Triphammer Rd.
You've passed the *Mall* area. Do not use NY 13. Obey the signs!

17.7 (28.4)   Hanshaw Rd. @ Triphammer Rd.   3.8 (6.1)
This is a complicated intersection. The signage is poor. If
you go straight you'll be on Hanshaw Rd. And you don't
want to be on Hanshaw! Do not follow the "Cornell ←".
You'll be going through Cornell Univ. via Triphammer past
the Johnson Mus.
South bound travelers: turn on to the second street on
your right -Triphammer Rd. going South and down. The
roadway becomes narrower and shoulderless from this
point. A few things in your favor are: more bicyclists and
motorists who are used to bicyclists and a sidewalk. Put on
your flashing light as there are trees over the roadway. Just
keep in your mind that you are descending and going
South.
If you miss Triphammer Rd. you'll be at *Community
Commons* shopping plaza on Upland Rd. Retrace your
steps (tire marks) or just turn on to Upland Rd. It intersects
with Triphammer.
North bound travelers: Triphammer Rd. is the second
street on your left. The roadway surface improves with a
smoother, wider surface and a shoulder from this point
North!

18.9 (30.4)   Wait Rd. @ Triphammer Rd.   2.6 (4.2)
Turn South on Wait Rd. Wait Rd. actually runs Southwest
to East. Don't even ask why! It has to do with land
contours.
South bound riders turn Left. That is keep going down the
hill! Weird but true.
North bound riders turn Right on to Triphammer. That is
keep going up the hill!
I know this sounds strange & you're certainly not going to
be reading this as you descend/ascend the hill! So read &
look at the map before you go down or up!

19.0 (30.6)   Thurston Ave. @ Wait Rd.   2.5 (4.0)
Turn South on to Thurston Ave., *i. e.*, go down the hill!
North bound riders turn North, *i. e.,* keep going up the hill
on Thurston.

19.2 (30.9)   University Dr. @ Thurston Ave.   2.3 (3.7)
Turn West on to University Ave. You've just crossed the
bridge over Fall Creek. Remember you're descending! The
Johnson Mus. is on your way down the hill.
As you ride along the Creek on University Dr. the roadway
narrows & is not particularly smooth. Use the sidewalk if
necessary. Don't forget to take a look at the Creek's bed.

19.8 (31.9)   Lake St. @ University Dr.   1.7 (2.7)
Turn South on to University Dr. It's to hard to explain why
you're now facing Northwest.
South bound travelers: Hang a Left turn.
North bound travelers: Hang a Right turn.

20.4 (32.2)   Linn St. @ University Dr.   1.1 (1.8)
You're flowing South. Keep doin' it!

20.5 (33.0)   Court St. @ Linn St.   1.0 (1.6)
Go West on Court St.

20.7 (33.3)   Cayuga St. @ Court St.   .8 (1.2)
Turn South on Cayuga St.
South of Court St., Cayuga St. is a one way street going
South.
North bound travels are on Tioga St. traveling North.

21.5 (34.6)   Seneca St. @ Cayuga St.   0.0 (0.0)
Hey! You're here. Wanna go up again? Think bus!
Ithaca Commons, ITHACA: Ithaca information is in the
Cayuga Lake Circumnavigation route chapter.
↺ ↻ CAYUGA LAKE CIRCUMNAVIGATION Route
↻ CAYUGA LAKE: RT 89 WEST SIDE ROUTE
↺ ↻ ⇔ LANSING - REMINGTON RD ROUTE
↺ ↻ ⇔ TRIPHAMMER ALTERNATE ROUTE
⇔ OWASCO LAKE TO CAYUGA LAKE: SOUTHERN
SCENIC CONNECTING ROUTE
⇔ CAYUGA LAKE TO SENECA LAKE: SOUTHERN
CONNECTING ROUTE
⇔ ENFIELD LOOP

	OWASCO LAKE TO CAYUGA LAKE	
E to W	**SOUTHERN DIRECT**	W to E
Read ↓	**CONNECTING ROUTE**	Read up ↑

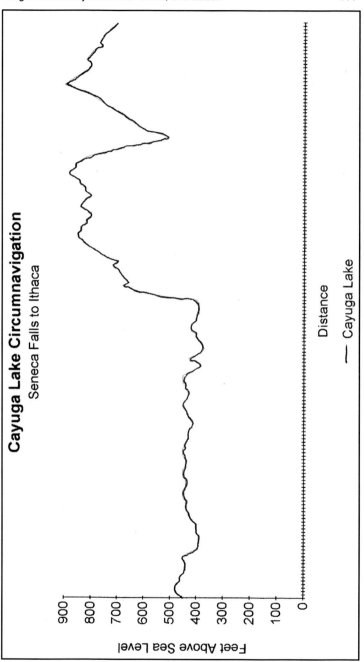

Cayuga Lake Circumnavigation
Seneca Falls to Ithaca

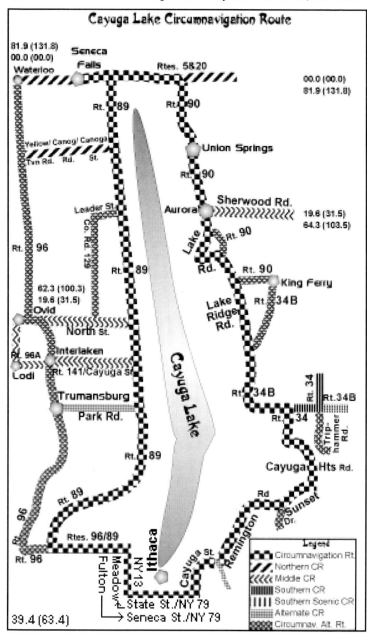

Cayuga Lake Circumnavigation Route

Hills & Routes

Oh what tangled webs we weave in search of the most suitable road to descend or ascend the hill above Ithaca! My original route went straight down steeply sloped NY 34, with its high traffic volume (trucks & RVs), 4 ft. (1.2 m.) guard rail hemmed shoulders. Hey, I did it! Why not the rest of ya'll? True it was scary but no more so than 18 in. (.5 m.) shouldered US 101 in the Russian River area of California.

Ah! There must be a better way, I thought. Out came the maps, highway and topo. Up and down, loaded and unloaded I traversed the hill using one route then another. My legs became super toned without bulk all that spinning does that! I lost a few pounds. I drank prodigious amounts of water. Consumed innumerable chocolate chip cookies from Ithaca's bakeries and groceries. The 11 tooth chain ring + 34 tooth cog served me well! And yet each route had its own peculiarity which said, just go via NY 34 and hope for the best.

So I wrote long winded caveats and warnings about NY 34. I reworked NY 89 into the NY 89 West Side Route from Seneca Falls to Ithaca (as well as providing the normal circumnavigation route reading clockwise from Ithaca to Seneca Falls). I added the NY 96 Trajectory Route to account for NY 89's strange small shoulders on its most steeply sloped southern end.

And then a brilliant thought, I'm in the latter part of the 20th Century! Use the power of the 'puter! On to the e-mail and web sites I went. Looking for info. Finding none. Finding some. To sort out the confusion of which route to take came a rescuer in the form of a bicycling advocate from Ithaca. He suggested that, climbing up and down the hill along all those routes in 1 or 2 days caused elevated oxygen levels in my brain, the cause of my confusion. More importantly, he sorted out the pluses and minuses of each route and provided information on alternatives.

The result of all this research were three more trips to Ithaca, to ascend and descend; loaded and unloaded; and most importantly, eat chocolate chip cookies. I removed most of the caveats and warnings after configuring new routes of delight and wonder. The hill is still steep but the ride is nicer and less congested with motor vehicles. Besides, you'll meet some bicyclists along the way!

TRAVELER'S NOTE

The clockwise route around Cayuga Lake is fraught with an extreme
southward and downward slope on all roads leading into Ithaca
on the East side of Cayuga Lake. The roads, Rtes. 89 and 96,
leading into Ithaca on the West side are not as severely sloped.
Thanks glaciers!

The CAYUGA LAKE RT 89 WEST SIDE ROUTE is provided after
the CAYUGA LAKE CIRCUMNAVIGATION ROUTE so that you
do not have to transpose directions and mileage traveling South
along the West shore of Cayuga Lake from Seneca Falls to
Ithaca. Should you choose to go counterclockwise along
Cayuga Lake.

Your bicycle and you must be in superb mechanical order with
excellent brakes, tires and rims to conquer the inclines/declines
on the East side of Cayuga Lake without problems.

Another alternative is to take a bus which has bike racks. Tompkins
Consolidated Area Transit (*Tcat*) buses operate on a regular
schedule from the Cornell University area to Ithaca on the East
side of the Lake; and on a limited schedule to various points
higher on the *hill* above Ithaca as well as to Trumansburg on
the West side of Cayuga Lake. Refer to the Ithaca, Lansing and
Trumansburg Public Transit Information paragraphs.

There are several options on the Cayuga Lake Circumnavigation
routes besides the NY 89 West Side Route. Most are short

sections using rural roads instead of the major State highways. The major optional routes are the NY 96 Trajectory and the NY 96 Projectile Routes which provide directions along NY 96 rather than NY 89 to/from Ithaca to the Cayuga Lake to Seneca Lake: Interlaken - Lodi Middle Connecting Route. NY 96 has the gentlest slope from Ithaca to Trumansburg, ~10 mi. (~16 km.).

0.0 (0.0)   Rtes. 5&20 @ NY 414   83.9 (135.0)
Travel East on Rtes. 5&20.
⇔ OWASCO LAKE TO CAYUGA LAKE: NORTHERN CONNECTING ROUTE.
⇔ CAYUGA LAKE TO SENECA LAKE: NORTHERN CONNECTING ROUTE.

Although Seneca Falls is on the West side of Cayuga Lake, we'll begin here to go clockwise around the Lake. Seneca Falls is the City at the northern end of Cayuga Lake.

SENECA FALLS
Information: Seneca Falls Heritage Area Visitor Ctr., 115 Fall St., Seneca Falls NY 13148, 315 568-2703. AC: 315. ZC: 13148.
Bicycling Information: The Visitors Ctr. has a walking/bicycling route around the Village. Nearest bike shop is in Geneva, ~9 mi. (14 km.) west. Seneca-Cayuga Canal multi-use trail is being developed to link Seneca Falls, Geneva and the Erie Canal.
Services: All. Intercity bus stop from both Rochester and Syracuse. Canal locks.
Lodging: Motels. B&Bs: B&Bs: Barrister's, 56 Cayuga St., 568-0145; Hubbell House, 42 Cayuga St., 568-9690; John Morris Manor, 2138 NY 89, 568-9057; VanCleef Homestead, 86 Cayuga St., 568-2275. Guion House, 32 Cayuga St., 568-8129; Ileen's, 69 Cayuga St., 568-6092. Camping: Cayuga Lake St. Pk., 2678 Lower Lake Rd., 568-5163/800 456-2267; Cayuga Lake Campgrounds, 2546 NY 89, 568-0919; Oak Orchard Cpgd., PO Box 148 Rte. 89 N., 365-3000. Eagle View, 12850 Armitage Rd., Savannah 13146, 315 365-2249.
Attractions: Women's Rights Nat'l. Historic Pk., 136 Fall St., 568-2991; Elizabeth Cady Stanton House, 31 Washington St., 568-2991; National Women's Hall of Fame, 76 Fall St., 568-8060; Seneca Falls Hist. Soc., 55 Cayuga St., 568-8412; Becker 1880 House Mus., 55 Cayuga St., 568-8412; Seneca-Cayuga Canal; Erie Canal Cruise Lines, Erie Canal Cruise Lines, 5 Water St., 962-1771; Montezuma Nat'l. Wildlife Refuge, 3395 Rtes. 5&20 East, 568-5987; Cayuga-Seneca Canal, NYS Canal Corp., 800 422-6257; Montezuma Winery, 2981 Auburn Rd., 568-8190;

3.2 (5.1)   Rtes. 318/89 @ Rtes. 5&20   80.8 (130.0)

Continue traveling West on Rtes. 5&20 to go clockwise around Cayuga Lake.

↻ ⇔ SENECA LAKE RT 89 WEST SIDE ROUTE. The directions in this Route read from North to South along NY 89 on the West side of Cayuga Lake from Seneca Falls to Ithaca. Turn South on NY 89 to go around the Lake, counterclockwise.

4.9 (7.9)   Montezuma Wildlife Refuge   79.0 (127.1)
                   NY 90 @ Rtes. 5&20
Stop for a look! Sorry, no bicycling on the Wildlife Drive. If you arrive at sunrise/sunset you're in for a birders delight.

5.6 (9.0)   NY 90 @ Rtes. NY 5& US 20   78.3 (126.0)
Turn South on to NY 90 to circumnavigate Cayuga Lake clockwise.
⇔ OWASCO LAKE TO CAYUGA LAKE NORTHERN DIRECT ROUTE, continue traveling East on Rtes. 5&20 to go to Auburn and Owasco Lake.
Many of the Villages along the shore have a public beach. At times the slope to the Lake can be severe.
Information: NYS NY 90 Assoc., PO Box 587, Union Springs, NY 13160, 800 889-5836.

6.7 (10.8)   Lock Rd. @ NY 90   77.2 (124.2)
Continue traveling South on NY 90.
Turn West (towards the Lake) to see Lock 1, the Mud Lock, of the Seneca/Cayuga Canal. Nice place to picnic. Portable toilet. The Lock is about ¾ mi. (1.2 km.) from NY 90.

8.4 (13.5)   Genesee St. @ NY 90   75.5 (121.5)
Continue traveling South on NY 90.
CAYUGA: ZC:13034. AC: 315. **Lodging:** Eagle Rock B&B, Cayuga 13034, 889-5925; Twin Oaks Cpgd., RD #1, Lake Rd., 889-5189.

12.5 (20.1)   NY 326 @ NY 90   69.4 (111.6)
Continue traveling South on NY 90.

UNION SPRINGS

Info.: Union Springs Village, PO Box 99, Union Springs NY 13160, 315 889-7341. AC: 315. ZC: 13160.
Services: convenience & other stores.
Lodging: B&B: Dill's Run, 8632 NY 90, 889-5007.
Attractions: Frontenac Mus., NY 90, 889-5836.

19.6 (31.5)   Sherwood Rd. @ NY 90   64.3 (103.5)
⇔ OWASCO LAKE TO CAYUGA LAKE: MIDDLE CONNECTING ROUTE, turn East on to Sherwood Rd. to

go to Owasco Lake.

AURORA

Info.: Aurora Arts & Merchants Assn., c/o Cayuga Lake-Nat'l Bank, Main St., Aurora NY 13026. AC: 315. ZC: 13026.

Services: bakery, restaurants, hardware, book & other specialty stores.

Lodging: B&Bs: The Aurora Inn, Main St., 364-8888; Dills Run, 8639 NY 90, 889-5007; Camping: Long Pt. St. Pk., 2063 Lake Rd., 497-0130.

Attractions: Morgan Opera House (theater), Main St., 364-5437; Howland Stone Mus., NY 90, 364-5514; Long Pt. St. Pk., Lake Rd. at NY 90, 497-0130. MacKensie-Childs Ltd., (home furnishings), Main St., 364-7123; Long Point Winery, 1485 Lake Rd., 364-6990; Wells College.

20.9 (33.6)   Lake Rd. (northern entrance)   63.0 (101.1)
                 @ NY 90
Bear Southwest on to Lake Rd. Landmark: Sign "To Long Pt. St. Pk." A bit hilly, particularly at the southern end of *this* Lake Rd. A shady very nice diversion from NY 90. OR continue South on NY 90 which is actually hillier than Lake Rd.

22.6 (36.4)   Lake Rd. (southern entrance)   61.3 (98.7)
                 @ NY 90
Turn South on to NY 90.
Lake Rd. is discontinuous so it is back to NY 90.

Counterclockwise circumnavigators: Turn West on to Lake Rd. It's a fine diversion from NY 90. Landmark on NY 90: Sign: "To Long Pt. Bait Shop."

25.8 (41.5)   Clearview Dr. Jct. Lake Ridge Rd.   58.1 (93.5)
                     @ NY 90
Travel straight South on to Lake Ridge Rd. Landmark: Triangle Family Diner and sign "King Ferry/Trevelan Winery ↑. Lake Ridge Rd. is gently hilly at its beginning and end but level in between. It is shady and has views of the Lake.
OR Continue traveling on NY 90 into King Ferry. The distance is about the same to the next intersection. Rtes. 90 & 34B will be a smoother ride than Lake Ridge Rd. Lake Ridge Rd. is a two lane no shoulder chip sealed road with very little traffic.
RT 90 TRAVELER'S DIRECTIONS
These directions will guide you to NY 34B @ Lake Ridge Rd. from this intersection, just in case you decided to continue on NY 90 rather than riding on Lake Rd. Of course you can go into King Ferry and then return to this intersection, it's only a 1 mi. (1.6 km.) to King Ferry.

25.8 (41.5)   Clearview Dr. Jct. Lake Rd.   58.1 (93.5)
                     @ NY 90
Continue traveling on NY 90 around the right angle curve.

26.8 (43.1)   NY 34B @ NY 90   54.7 (88.0)
Turn South on to NY 34B. You're in King Ferry. Now you can read the next entry on the route.
🚲 OWASCO LAKE TO CAYUGA LAKE: SOUTHERN CONNECTING ROUTES: Traveling due East on NY 90 from this intersection in King Ferry will take you directly to NY 34 and then westward to NY 38, at Locke

KING FERRY
Info.: Genoa Mus. & Visitor Ctr., NY 34B, King Ferry, NY 13081, 315 364-8202. AC: 315. ZC: 13081.
Services: Convenience store/gas station.
Lodging: Motel. Camping: Blackrock Campsites, Ledyard Rd., 364-8962.
Attractions: Genoa Rural Life Mus., NY 34B, 364-8202. King Ferry Winery, Lake Rd., 364-5100.

29.2 (47.0)   NY 34B @ Lake Ridge Rd.   54.7 (88.0)
Turn South on to NY 34B. NY 34B/Ridge Rd.
Counterclockwise: travelers: this intersection comes into NY 34B at an acute angle just north of NYSGE power plant.

36.4 (58.6)   NY 34 Jct. NY 34B   47.5 (76.4)

Clockwise travelers: Turn South on to NY 34. Before turning on to NY 34, turn on your front light and your back red flashing light. Make yourself highly visible. Ride to Cayuga Heights Rd. where you will exit NY 34.

卐 ⇔ ↻ ↺ TRIPHAMMER ALTERNATE ROUTE. Ride West on NY 34B South for .7 mi. (1.1 km.) to Triphammer Rd. Use the Triphammer Rd. Alternate Route from that intersection. The Triphammer Alternate Route has the gentlest slopes leading into Ithaca on the East side of Cayuga Lake. Gentlest is a relative term!

Counterclockwise travelers: Continue North on NY 34B to go counterclockwise around Cayuga Lake. If you made it up to this point from Ithaca then you deserve a medal!

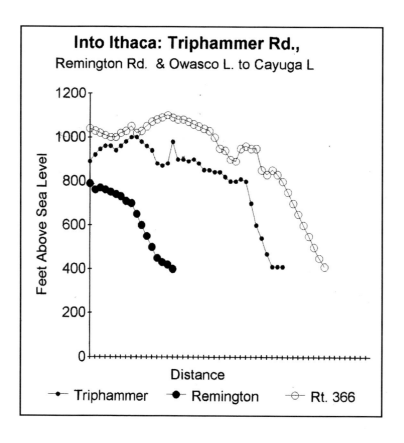

Into Ithaca: Triphammer Rd.,
Remington Rd. & Owasco L. to Cayuga L

LANSING

Info.: Town Supervisor, Town Hall, 29 Auburn Rd., Lansing NY 14882. AC: 607. ZC: 14882.

Cycling info.: given the steep slope on all roads leading into Ithaca here's some bus information from Lansing. Call the bus co. (607 277-7433) to make certain that the Lansing bus has a bike rack. At this intersection, southbound buses are at 7 & 8AM; 2:30 PM; Flag driver for the 5:20 PM bus.

The Village and Town of Lansing is in the process of upgrading all of its roads to make them bicycle friendly. Included in the plans and current construction projects are bike lanes, share the road signs, wider roadways and shoulders where possible. You'll notice the enhancements when you cross the Town border into neighboring Towns. 3 cheers!

Services: Convenience stores and gas stations.

Lodging: B&Bs: Federal House, 175 Ludlowville Rd., 533-7362; Rogue's Harbor, 2079 E Shore Dr., 533-3535; Salmon Creek, 212 Ludlowville Rd., 533-4623; The Old Townsend Place, 1616 Ridge Rd. Rte. 34B, 533-8955; A Lakefront Inn, 533-4804; Blue Cayuga on the Water, 280-7435. Camping: Myers Point/Lansing Town Park, Marine Rd. off Rt. 34B, 533-7388.

39.6 (63.7)   Cayuga Hts. Rd. @ NY 34   44.3 (71.3)
DO NOT GO ANY FURTHER SOUTH ON RT 34. It is dangerous to go any further South on NY 34. As you have noticed, NY 34 is heavily trafficked with RVs, trucks and autos; the downward and southward slope is very steep (~70°+); and the <4 ft. (<1.2 m.) shoulder is hemmed by guard rails. Certainly not pleasurable bicycling.

TURN Southwest on to Cayuga Hts. Rd. You can't miss this intersection. There is a big sign and a left turn lane. Use extreme care making this turn. Traffic is heavy. Dismount your bike if it is safer to make the turn dismounted.

41.2 (66.3)   NY 13 @ Cayuga Hts. Rd.   <42.7 (<68.7)
Continue traveling South on Cayuga Hts. Rd. Sorry but bicycles are banned on NY 13.

<41.3 (<66.4)   Sunset Dr. @ Cayuga Hts. Rd.   42.6 (68.6)
Turn Southwest on to Sunset Dr. This is a somewhat obscure intersection since the street sign is blocked by trees. And that should tell you something about Sunset Dr. Although there is very little auto traffic on Sunset Dr. make

yourself visible to motorists. It is a narrow shady street with a number of curves.

If you miss Sunset Dr. ride South and turn West on to the next street, Remington Rd.

41.7 (67.1)   Remington Rd. @ Sunset Dr.   43.2 (69.5)
Turn Southwest on to Remington Rd.

Although there is very little auto traffic on Remington Rd. make yourself highly visible to potential motorists. It is a narrow shady street with a number of curves and a steep decline at its southern end. A delightful ride.

Be careful on the final very steep .1 mi. (.2 km.). Remington Rd. exits almost directly on to busy East Shore Dr.

42.5 (68.3)   East Shore Dr. @ Remington Rd.   41.4 (66.6)
                   Cayuga St. @ Remington Rd.

Go straight West on to Cayuga St. Use extreme care crossing East Shore Dr., it is a busy street.

If you go North on East Shore Dr. under the Rte. 13 overpass you'll find the Tompkins County Information office. Stop in and tell them you're a bicycle tourist. Make certain they record it in some manner. It is the best way to improve cycling conditions.

                    Counterclockwise/North bound travelers
Do not travel North on NY 34. It is dangerous for bicyclists to use NY 34 going North from this intersection. Use Remington Rd. or use the Triphammer Alternate Route. You can not ride on NY 13.

43.6 (70.2)   Seneca St./NY 79 @ Cayuga St.   40.3 (64.9)
Turn West on to W. Seneca St./NY 79.

Hey! You're in the center of Ithaca. In front of your bike is Ithaca Commons, a pedestrian only city mall. It has a camping supply stores, a bike shop (there is another bike shop on Seneca St. as you travel West to the Inlet bridge), restaurants, and other stores. Stop and have something to eat and drink, you deserve it!

CLOCKWISE TRAVELER'S INFORMATION

Clockwise circumnavigators and West bound travelers (to Watkins Glen at Seneca Lake's southern end) have to make a few decisions. NY Rtes. 79, 89 and 96 each have their own roadway and bridge over the Cayuga Lake Inlet. All routes leading North from Ithaca involve climbing steeply graded roads. However the State highways on the West Side of Cayuga Lake do have wider shoulders and roadways than those roads (NY Rtes. 34 & 366) on the East side of Cayuga Lake leading North from Ithaca.

Here are your choices:

1. CAYUGA LAKE CIRCUMNAVIGATION ROUTE: Turn North on Meadow Dr. and then West on Buffalo Rd./NY 89 (Right lane) to go North close to the Lake shore on NY 89 to Seneca Falls. NY 89 has a narrow shoulder for about 4 mi. (6.4 km.) but it has low traffic volumes during the day.

2. RT 96 PROJECTILE ROUTE: Turn North on Meadow Dr. and then go West on Buffalo Rd./NY 96 (Middle & Left lanes) to go North a bit inland from the Lake. NY 96's shoulder is narrow only for the first .5 mi. (.8 km.). But it has more traffic than NY 89. NY 96's slope is also less than NY 89's.

3. CAYUGA LAKE TO SENECA LAKE: SOUTHERN CONNECTING ROUTE: Continue traveling West on NY79/ Seneca St. to go to Watkins Glen/Seneca Lake. NY 79's initial slope up from Ithaca is a continual rise and is has steep rise in elevation rather than an up and down type of rise to the top of the ridge. NY 79 has some traffic since it is the main road between Ithaca and Watkins Glen. There is a connection between NY 96 and NY 79 as well as the Enfield Loop with this route.

4. ENFIELD LOOP takes you to NY 79 and the Cayuga Lake to Seneca Lake: Southern Connecting Route. NY 327 is a little used road with a wide shoulder. However it is an up and down type of road. You can also use this route to go north to Trumansburg on NY 96.

Decisions! Decisions! Decisions! Since you'll probably be in Ithaca for at least one night put off deciding what to do and enjoy yourself. That's really what cyclotouring is all about.

ITHACA

Information: Tompkins County CVB, 904 E. Shore Dr., Ithaca, NY 14850, 800 284-8422/607 272-1313. ZC: 14850. AC: 607.

Bicycling Information: Bicycle shops: there are at least 4 bike shops in Ithaca. Finger Lakes Cycling Club, www.flcycling.org, full schedule of rides, visitors are welcome to ride with Club members (helmets necessary). Check the web site.

Services: All. Hospital.

Public Transit: Intercity bus service: Greyhound, Adirondack Trailways and Shortline. The bus station is on NY 13 between Seneca St. and State St.

Local bus: Tompkins Consolidated Area Transit (*Tcat*), 737 Willow Ave., Ithaca NY 14850, 607 277-7433, www.tcatbus.com. All *Tcat* buses have bicycle racks. Two bicycles can be accommodated on each bus. Most of the city buses to the Cornell Campus and Mall area on Triphammer Rd. operate on a ½ hour schedule from Green St. near the Ithaca Commons.

The suburban buses to Cayuga Heights, Lansing, Trumansburg, Groton & Freeville operate on a ~2-3 hour schedule from 6 AM to 6PM. Suburban buses operate on a limited weekend schedule. To leave Ithaca you must climb, use the bus if necessary.

Lodging: For clarity all are in Ithaca, area code 607. Motels. B&Bs: A Touch of Country, 119 Enfield Main Rd., 272-9435; Amazing Grace, 136 Hunt Hill Rd., 277-8888; Annie's Garden, 220 Pearl St., 273-0888; Applegate House, 272 N. Applegate Rd., 272-6519; Besemer Station Inn, 2024 Slaterville Rd., 539-6319; Buttermilk Falls, 110 E. Buttermilk Falls Rd., 272-6767; Coddington Guest House, 130 Coddington Rd., 275-0021; Cottage Garden Inn, 107 Crescent Pl., 277-7561; Edgewood, 514 Edgewood Pl., 592-1817; Ezra's, 48 Wedgewood Dr., 257-1155; Frog Haven Women's B&B, 578 W. King Rd., 272-3238; Frogs Way, 211 Rachel Carson Way, 275-0249; Godwin House, 1184 Ellis Hollow Rd., 277-0747; Hound & Hare, 1031 Hanshaw Rd., 257-2821; Inn @ City Lights, 1319 Mecklenberg Rd., 227-3003; Inn on Columbia, 228 Columbia St., 272-0204; Macintire's Cottage, 217 Eastern Heights Dr., 273-8888; Mi Peru, 153 Reach Run, 272-7287; Station Restaurant & Sleeping Cars, 806 W. Buffalo St., 272-2609; Stone Quarry House, 26 Quarry Rd., 272-0556; Suzan's Guest House, 208 1/2 Utica St., 272-5173; Sweet Dreams, 228 Wood St., 272-7727; Thomas Farm, 136 Thomas Rd., 539-7477; Veralma-The 1850 House, 211 Hudson St., 275-9519; William Henry Miller Inn, 303 N. Aurora St., 256-4553.

Camping: Robert H. Treman St. Pk., NY 327 @ NY 13S, RD #10, 273-3440/800 456-2267; Buttermilk Falls St. Pk., NY 13S, 271-5761; Spruce Row Cpgd., 2271 Kraft Rd., 387-9225; Taughannock Falls St., Pk., Taughannock Pk. Rd. (NY 89), 387-6739; Willowood Cpgd., 272-6087.

Attractions: The Hanger Theater, NY 89 at Cass Pk., 273-4497; Cornell Plantations, One Plantation Rd., 255-3020; DeWitt Hist. Soc. of Tompkins Co., 401 E. State St., 273-8284; Herbert F. Johnson Mus. of ANY, University Ave., Cornell Campus, 255-6464; Sapsucker Woods Bird Sanctuary, 159 Sapsucker Woods Rd., 254-2473; Sciencenter, 601 First St., 272-0600; Cayuga Nature Ctr., 1420 Taughannock Blvd., 273-6260; Circle Greenway, 108 E. Green St., 274-6570; Allan H. Treman St. Marine Pk., NY 89, (No camping); Alcyone Charters, City Dock, 272-7963; Cayuga Breeze, 704 W. Buffalo St., 272-4868; Cornell University. Ithaca College. NYS Agricultural College & NYS Veterinary College.

COUNTERCLOCKWISE & OWASCO LAKE BOUND TRAVELER'S INFORMATION

The hill on the East side of Cayuga Lake going either North around Cayuga Lake or Northwest to Owasco Lake has a very steep slope. Much steeper than the roads on the West side of the Lake. You have several options going North from Ithaca.

🚲 ⇔ ↺ ↻ TRIPHAMMER ALTERNATE ROUTE. This route has the gentlest (a relative term) slope up the hill but there some traffic. It goes through the Cornell Univ. campus.

↺ ↻ CAYUGA LAKE CIRCUMNAVIGATION Route using Remington Rd. and Cayuga Hts. Rd. This route is steep but it has views of the Lake and negligible motor traffic.

⇔ OWASCO LAKE TO CAYUGA LAKE: SOUTHERN CONNECTING ROUTES. The Direct Southern Connecting Route uses Triphammer Rd.; the Scenic Southern Connecting Route uses NY 366.

🚲 Using a bus to by pass the most severe incline. Purists, don't laugh! Make your life a bit easier. Use the *Tcat* bus to take you up the hill to the Cornell University Campus or higher. There are more hills to climb along all routes going North and West once you rise above Ithaca. Refer to the Ithaca public transit information paragraphs.

44.1 (71.0)	NY 13/Meadow Dr. @ W. Seneca St./NY 79	39.8 (64.1)

Turn North on to Meadow Dr.

⇔ CAYUGA LAKE TO SENECA LAKE: SOUTHERN CONNECTING ROUTE.

🚲 ENFIELD LOOP.

CLOCKWISE TRAVELER'S NOTE

The primary Cayuga Lake Circumnavigation Route using NY 89, continues immediately after the Triphammer Alternate Route, Lansing - Remington Rd. Route and the NY 96 Projectile Route.

Read ↓ Clockwise	**CAYUGA LAKE CIRCUMNAVIGATION** **PRIMARY ROUTE CONTINUED**	Read up ↑ Counterclockwise

Read ↓   **CAYUGA LAKE CIRCUMNAVIGATION**   Read up ↑
Clockwise   **TRIPHAMMER ALTERNATE ROUTE**   Counterclockwise

TRAVELER'S NOTE

This Tour Guide uses three routes to ascend the hill above Ithaca on the East side of the Lake:

Cayuga Lake Circumnavigation Route which uses the Lansing-Sunset Alternate Route;

Owasco Lake to Cayuga Lake: Southern Scenic Connecting Route which uses NY 366;

Owasco Lake to Cayuga Lake: Southern Direct Connecting Route which uses this Triphammer Alternate Route.

I've separated out two of the routes between Lansing at the northern high point on the *hill* and Ithaca at the southern valley end of the *hill* because some travelers might want to use a different path than the one provided in the Route they are following.

The Triphammer Alternate Route has the gentlest (relative term) rise in elevation from the valley floor to the top of the *hill*. There is always the option of using a bus with bike racks to take you at least part way up the *hill*.

0.0 (0.0)   NY 34B @ NY 34   9.5 (15.3)
Travel East on Rtes. 34/34B.
↻ ↺ CAYUGA LAKE CIRCUMNAVIGATION Route.
⇔ ↻ ↺ LANSING-REMINGTON RD ROUTE: goes South into Ithaca from this intersection. The CAYUGA LAKE CIRCUMNAVIGATION ROUTE uses this Route.

.5 (.8)   NY 34B Jct. NY 34   9.0 (14.5)
Travel straight East on to NY 34B.
NY 34 makes a broad sweeping turn northward as it junctions with NY 34B.

.6 (.9)   NY 34B @ Triphammer Rd.   8.9 (14.3)
                  NY 34 @ Triphammer Rd.
Turn South on to Triphammer Rd.
Landmark: Gas station/convenience store & hardware store on NY 34B.
Landmark: Crossroads restaurant/bar on the NY 34 curve.
⇔ OWASCO LAKE TO CAYUGA LAKE: SOUTHERN DIRECT CONNECTING ROUTE.
🚍 Traveling East on NY 34B will bring you to NY 38 and the Owasco Lake to Cayuga Lake: Southern Scenic Connecting Route.
🚍 ↻ ↺ LANSING-REMINGTION ROUTE: traveling West

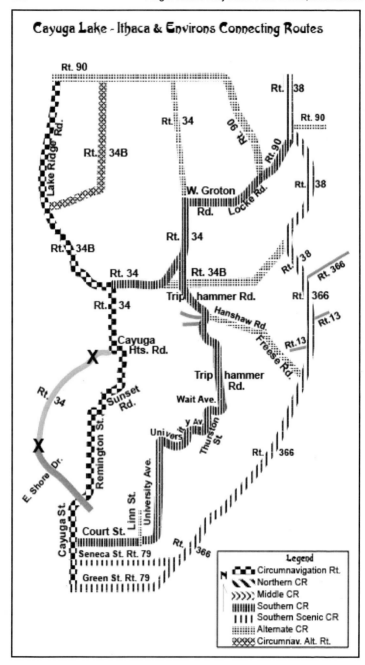

Cayuga Lake - Ithaca & Environs Connecting Routes

Legend

Circumnavigation Rt.
Northern CR
Middle CR
Southern CR
Southern Scenic CR
Alternate CR
Circumnav. Alt. Rt.

from this intersection will bring you to one of the other Routes going South into Ithaca. The CAYUGA CIRCUMNAVIGATION ROUTE uses the Lansing-Remington Rd. route to go into Ithaca.

4.9 (7.9)   NY 13 @ Triphammer Rd.   4.6 (7.4)
Continue traveling South on Triphammer Rd.
You've passed the *Mall* area. Do not use NY 13. Obey the signs!

5.7 (9.2)   Hanshaw Rd. @ Triphammer Rd.   3.8 (6.1)
This is a complicated intersection. The signage is strange. If you go straight you'll be on Hanshaw Rd. And you don't want to be on Hanshaw! Do not follow the "Cornell ←".
South bound travelers turn on to the second street on your Right--Triphammer Rd. going South and down. The roadway becomes narrow and shoulderless from this point. A few things in your favor are more bicyclists and motorists who are used to bicyclists; and a sidewalk. Put on your flashing light as there are trees over the roadway. Just keep in your mind that you are descending and going South.
If you miss Triphammer Rd. you'll be at *Community Commons* shopping plaza on Upland Rd. Retrace your steps or just turn on to Upland Rd. It intersects with Triphammer.
North bound travelers, Triphammer Rd. is the second street on your Left. The road surface improves by being smoother, wider and with a shoulder from this point North!
⇔ OWASCO LAKE TO CAYUGA LAKE: SOUTHERN SCENIC CONNECTING ROUTE. Traveling East on Hanshaw Rd. for 1.7 mi. (2.7 km.) to the Y intersection of Freese Rd and Lower Creek Rd. Use Freese Rd. to go to NY 366. Or use Upper Creek Rd. to go to NY 366. Upper Creek Rd. has more hills. From the intersection of NY 366 use the Connecting Route's directions.

6.9 (11.1)   Wait Rd. @ Triphammer Rd.   2.6 (4.2)
Turn South on Wait Rd.
South bound riders turn Left. That is, keep going down the hill! Weird but true. Wait Rd. actually runs Southwest to East. Don't even ask! But it has to do with land contours.
North bound riders turn Right on to Triphammer. That is keep going up the hill!
I know this sounds strange & you're certainly not going to be reading this as you descend the hill! So read & look at the map before you go down or up!

7.0 (11.3)   Thurston Ave. @ Wait Rd.   2.5 (4.0)
Turn South on to Thurston Ave., *i. e.*, go down the hill!
North bound riders, keep going up the hill on Thurston.

7.2 (11.6)   University Dr. @ Thurston Ave.   2.3 (3.7)
Turn West on to University Ave. You've just crossed the
bridge over Fall Creek. Remember you're descending! The
Johnson Mus. is on your way down the hill.
As you go along the Creek on University Dr. the roadway
narrows and is not particularly smooth. Use the sidewalk if
necessary. Don't forget look down into the Creek's bed.

7.8 (12.6)   Lake St. @ University Dr.   1.7 (2.7)
Turn South on to University Dr. It's to hard to explain why
you're now facing Northwest.
South bound travelers: Hang a Left turn.
North bound travelers: Hang a Right turn.

8.4 (13.5)   Linn St. @ University Dr.   1.1 (1.8)
You're flowing South. Keep doin' it!

8.5 (13.7)   Court St. @ Linn St.   1.0 (1.6)
Go West on Court St.

8.7 (14.0)   Cayuga St. @ Court St.   .8 (1.3)
Turn South on Cayuga St.
South of Court St., Cayuga St. is a one way street going
    South.
North bound travelers are probably on Tioga St. traveling
    North.

9.5 (15.3)   Seneca St. @ Cayuga St.   0.0 (0.0)
You're here. Wanna go up again? Thinking of the bus?
Ithaca Commons.
ITHACA: See the Cayuga Lake Circumnavigation route.

CAYUGA LAKE CIRCUMNAVIGATION
Read ↓   **TRIPHAMMER ALTERNATE ROUTE**   Read up ↑
Clockwise   Counterclockwise

Is the Sailor Bicycling?

CAYUGA LAKE CIRCUMNAVIGATION

Clockwise   Counterclockwise
Read ↓   **LANSING - REMINGTON RD ROUTE**   Read up ↑

TRAVELER'S NOTE

This Tour Guide uses three routes to ascend the hill above Ithaca on the East side of the Lake: Cayuga Lake Circumnavigation Route which uses the Lansing-Sunset Alternate Route; Owasco Lake to Cayuga Lake: Southern Scenic Connecting Route which uses NY 366; and the Owasco Lake to Cayuga Lake: Southern Direct Connecting Route which uses this Triphammer Alternate Route.

I've separated out two of the routes between Lansing at the northern high point on the *hill* and Ithaca at the southern valley end of the *hill* because some travelers might want to use a different path than the one provided in the Route they are following.

Of the three Routes, Triphammer Rd. has the gentlest (relative term) climb. There is always the option of using a bus with bike racks to take you at least part way up the *hill*.

0.0 (0.0)   NY 34 Jct. NY 34B   7.2 (11.6)
Clockwise travelers: Turn South on to NY 34. Before turning on to NY 34, turn on your front light and your back red flashing light. Make yourself highly visible. Ride to Cayuga Heights Rd. where you will exit NY 34.
⇆ ⇔ ↺ ↻ TRIPHAMMER ALTERNATE ROUTE. Ride

West on NY 34B South for .7 mi. (1.1 km.) to Triphammer Rd. Use the Triphammer Rd. Alternate Route from that intersection. The Triphammer Alternate Route has the gentlest slopes leading into Ithaca on the East side of Cayuga Lake. Gentlest is a relative term!
Counterclockwise travelers: Continue North on NY 34B to go counterclockwise around Cayuga Lake. If you made it up to this point from Ithaca then you deserve a medal!
LANSING: Refer to the text in the main Cayuga Lake Circumnavigation Route.

3.2 (5.1)   Cayuga Hts. Rd. @ NY 34   4.0 (6.4)
DO NOT GO ANY FURTHER SOUTH ON RT 34
It is dangerous to go any further South on NY 34. As you have noticed, NY 34 is heavily trafficked with RVs, trucks and autos; the downward and southward slope is very steep (~70º+); and the <4 ft. (<1.2 m.) shoulder is hemmed by guard rails. Certainly not pleasurable bicycling.
TURN Southwest on to Cayuga Hts. Rd. You can't miss this intersection. There is a big sign and a left turn lane. Use extreme care making this turn. Traffic is heavy. Dismount your bike if it is safer to make the turn dismounted.

4.8 (7.7)   NY 13 @ Cayuga Hts. Rd.   <2.4 (3.9)
Continue traveling South on Cayuga Hts. Rd. Sorry but bicycles are banned from NY 13.

<4.9 (<7.9)   Sunset Dr. @ Cayuga Hts. Rd.   2.3 (3.7)
Turn Southwest on to Sunset Dr. This is a somewhat obscure intersection since the street sign is blocked by trees. And that should tell you something about Sunset Dr. Although there is very little auto traffic on Sunset Dr. make yourself visible to motorists. It is a narrow shady street with a number of curves.
If you miss Sunset Dr. ride South and turn West on to the next street, Remington Rd.

5.3 (8.5)   Remington Rd. @ Sunset Dr.   1.9 (3.1)
Turn Southwest on to Remington Rd.
Although there is very little auto traffic on Remington Rd. make yourself highly visible to potential motorists. It is a narrow shady street with a number of curves and a steep decline at its southern end. A delightful ride.

6.1 (9.8)   East Shore Dr. @ Remington Rd.   1.1 (1.8)
                   Cayuga St. @ Remington Rd.
Be careful on the final very steep .1 mi. (.2 km.). Remington

Rd. exits almost directly on to busy East Shore Dr.
Go straight West on to Cayuga St. Use extreme care
crossing Lake Shore Dr. It is a busy street.
If you go North on East Shore Dr. under the Rte. 13
overpass you'll find the Tompkins County Information
office. Stop in and tell them you're a bicycle tourist. Make
certain they record it in some manner. It's the best way to
improve cycling conditions.
Counterclockwise/North bound travelers: **Do not travel
North on NY 34**. It is dangerous for bicyclists to use NY 34
going North from this intersection. Use Remington Rd. or
use the Triphammer Alternate Route. You can not ride on
NY 13.

7.2 (11.6)   Seneca St./NY 79 @ Cayuga St.   0.0 (0.0)
Turn West on to W. Seneca St./NY 79.
Hey! You're in the center of Ithaca. In front of your bike is
Ithaca Commons, a pedestrian only city mall. It has a
camping supply stores, a bike shop (there is another bike
shop on Seneca St. as you travel West to the Inlet bridge),
restaurants, and other stores. Stop and have something to
eat and drink, you deserve it!
ITHACA: Refer to Ithaca information in the Cayuga Lake
Circumnavigation Route for information.
↻ ↺ CAYUGA LAKE CIRCUMNAVIGATION Route
↻ ↺ CAYUGA LAKE: RT 89 WEST SIDE ROUTE
↻ ↺ ↔ TRIPHAMMER ALTERNATE ROUTE
↔ OWASCO LAKE TO CAYUGA LAKE: SOUTHERN
SCENIC CONNECTING ROUTE
↔ CAYUGA LAKE TO SENECA LAKE: SOUTHERN
CONNECTING ROUTE
↔ ENFIELD LOOP

CAYUGA LAKE CIRCUMNAVIGATION
Clockwise   Counterclockwise
Read ↓   **LANSING - REMINGTON RD ROUTE**   Read up ↑

Read ↓	**CAYUGA LAKE CIRCUMNAVIGATION**	Read up ↑
Clockwise	**RT 96 PROJECTILE ROUTE**	Counterclockwise

0.0 (0.0)   Seneca St./NY 79 @ Cayuga St.   17.2 (27.7)
Turn West on to W. Seneca St./NY 79.
You're in the center of Ithaca. In front of your bike is Ithaca Commons, a pedestrian only city mall. It has camping supply stores, a bike shop, restaurants, and other stores. Stop and have something to eat and drink, you deserve it!

.5 (.8)   NY 13/Meadow Dr. @ Seneca St.   16.7 (26.9)
Turn North on Meadow Dr./NY 13.

.6 (.9)   Buffalo St./NY 89 & NY 96   16.6 (26.7)
               @ Meadow Dr./NY 13
Turn West on to Buffalo St.
Hope you made up your mind which route to take. Once you are on the Inlet Bridge there is no turning back! Except for U turns on the other side!

.7 (1.1)   NY 13/Fulton Ave.   16.5 (26.6)
               @ Buffalo St./NY 89 & NY 96
Travel West on to the Inlet Bridge.
⇔ Fulton Ave./NY 13 allows you to go back to NY 79/ Seneca St. if you suddenly change you mind about going around Cayuga Lake and want to go to Watkins Glen and Seneca Lake using the CAYUGA LAKE TO SENECA LAKE: SOUTHERN CONNECTING ROUTE.
🚲 ⇔ Traveling South on NY 13 for ~2 mi. (~3.2 km.) will bring you to Buttermilk Falls St. Pk.; Robert Treman St. Pk., and the ENFIELD LOOP ROUTE which connects with the CAYUGA LAKE TO SENECA LAKE: SOUTHERN CONNECTING ROUTE. The Enfield Loop also has a connection with the NY 96 Projectile & NY 96 Trajectory Routes at Trumansburg.

3.2 (5.1)   Hayts Rd. @ NY 96   14.0 (22.5)
Continue traveling North on NY 96.
🚲 For those of you who are a bit tired of NY 96 and a bit adventurous, turn West on to Hayts Rd. Travel 4.2 mi. (6.8 km.) to Haleysville Rd. Turn North on to Haleysville Rd. and ride for 4.1 mi. (6.6 km.) to NY 96.
🚲 If you turn South on to Haleysville Rd., you'll be at NY 79, the Cayuga Lake to Seneca Lake: Southern Connecting Route after pedaling for .5 mi. (.8 km.). There you can

catch the Enfield Loop or go to Watkins Glen or back to Ithaca.

9.4 (15.1)   Halseyville Rd. @ NY 96   7.8 (12.6)
Continue traveling North on NY 96.

ᛋ ⇔ Use Halseyville Rd. by traveling South to go to NY 79 and the Cayuga Lake to Seneca Lake: Southern Connecting Route. If you cross NY 79 to NY 327 then you'll be on the Enfield Loop. This is a basically level (as level as any roads can be between two lakes) route.

9.6 (15.4)   Park Rd. @ NY 96   7.6 (12.2)
Continue traveling North on NY 96.

ᛋ ↻ ↺ If you'd like to see the Taughannock Falls or go to NY 89, turn East on to Park Rd. You are at a significantly higher elevation than either the Falls or NY 89 at this point on NY 96. Thus you'll be descending. If you do go to the Falls, save yourself a climb and start using NY 89 from Park Rd. @ NY 89 on the CAYUGA LAKE CIRCUMNAVIGATION ROUTE.

11.1 (17.9)   Cayuga St. @ NY 96   6.1 (9.8)
                     Frontenac Rd. @ NY 89
Continue North on NY 96.
Cayuga St. goes to NY 89 via Frontenac Rd. (name of Cayuga St. on NY 89).

TRUMANSBURG

Info.: Trumansburg Village, 56 E. Main St., Trumansburg, NY 14886, 607 387-9254. AC: 607. ZC: 14886.

Services: grocery, bank gas station, convenience store, restaurants, hardware store, and art galleries.

Lodging: B&Bs: Copper Beacons, 3883 CR 143, 387-5240; Gothic Eyes, 112 E. Main St., 387-6033; Halsey House, 2057 Trumansburg Rd., 387-5428; McLallen House, 30 McLallen St., 387-3892; Mom's Place, 5040 Perry City Rd., 387-5597; Morning Glory B&B, 89 Cayuga St., 387-5305; Reunion House, 7550 Willow Creek Rd., 387-6553; Sunburst Hill, 9818 Watermark Rd., 387-3165; Taughannock Farms Inn, 2030 Gorge Rd., 387-7711; Westwind, 1662 Taughannock Blvd., 387-3377; White Gazebo Inn, 151 E. Main St., 387-4952.

Camping: Taughannock Falls St. Pk., NY 89 Taughannock Pk. Rd., 387-6739; Spruce Row Campsites (on ridge above the Lake & St. Pk., off 96), 2271 Kraft Rd., 387-9225; Kingtown Beach Campsite, 9305 Kingtown Beach Rd., 387-5688.

Attractions: Cayuga Lakeside Stables, 9186 Booth Rd., 387-9050; Bellwether Hard Cider, 9070 NY 89, 387-9464; Frontenac Point

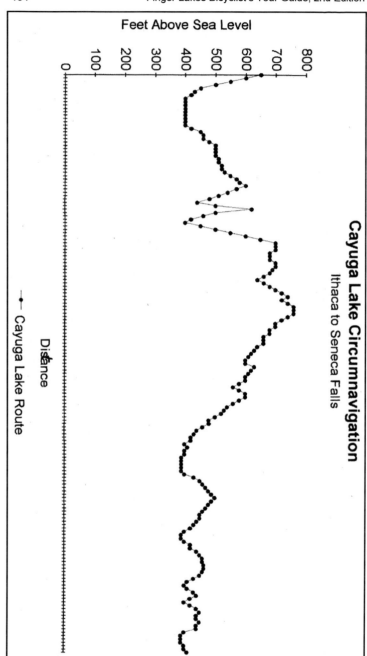

Vineyard, 9501 NY 89, 387-9619; Glenhaven Farm (fruit wines), 6121 Sirrine Rd., 387-9031; Taughannock Falls; Grassroots Music Festival (August), book lodging at least a month in advance if you're going to be in the area during the festival.

17.1 (27.5)   NY 96A @ NY 96   .1 (.2)
⇔ CAYUGA LAKE TO SENECA LAKE: INTERLAKEN - LODI MIDDLE CONNECTING ROUTE: Turn West on to NY 96A and to go to Seneca Lake.

17.2 (27.7)   Cayuga St./Co. Rd. 141 @ NY 96   0.0 (0.0)
⇔↺↻ CAYUGA LAKE TO SENECA LAKE: INTERLAKEN - LODI MIDDLE CONNECTING ROUTE: Turn East on to Cayuga St./Co. Rd. 141 and go to NY 89.

INTERLAKEN
Info.: Trumansburg Area CofC, PO Box 478, Trumansburg, NY 14886, 607 387-9254.
Services: convenience store/gas station, bank, restaurant.
Lodging: Glass Magnolia B&B, 8347 N. Main St., 532-8356;
Attractions: Lively Run Goat Dairy, 8978 CR 142, 532-4647. Americana Vineyards Winery, 4367 E. Covert Rd., 387-6801; Lucas Vineyards, 3862 CR 150, 532-4825.
Deere Haven Mus., PO Box 14 CR 141, 532-4288; Interlaken Hist. Soc. & Farmers Mus., Main St. NY 96, 532-9227.

Read ↓	**CAYUGA LAKE CIRCUMNAVIGATION**	Read up ↑
Clockwise	**RT 96 PROJECTILE ROUTE**	Counterclockwise

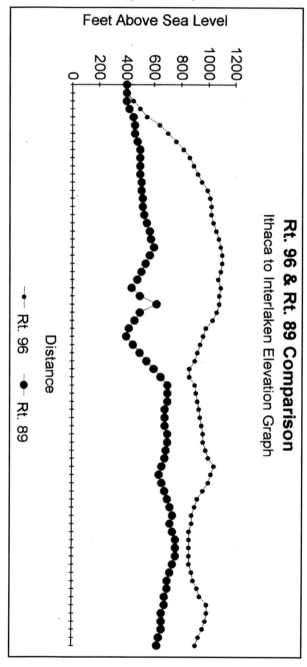

Rt. 96 & Rt. 89 Comparison
Ithaca to Interlaken Elevation Graph

| Read ↓ | **CAYUGA LAKE CIRCUMNAVIGATION** | Read up ↑ |
| Clockwise | **PRIMARY ROUTE CONTINUED** | Counterclockwise |

You've made your decision! Ya' on your way North on the West side of Cayuga Lake, that is traveling clockwise around the Lake.

COUNTERCLOCKWISE TRAVELER'S NOTE
The primary Cayuga Lake Circumnavigation Route using NY 89, continues immediately after the NY 96 Projectile Route, the Lansing-Remington Rd. Route and the Triphammer Alternate Route.

44.3 (71.3)   Buffalo St./NY 89 & NY 96   39.6 (63.7)
                   @ Meadow Dr.
Turn West on to Buffalo St.
Hope you made up your mind which route to take. Once you are on the Inlet bridge there is no turning back! Except for U turns on the other side!

44.4 (71.5)   NY 13/Fulton Ave.   39.5 (63.6)
                   @ Buffalo St./NY 89 & NY 96
⇔ You will pass NY 13/Fulton Ave. as you go to the Inlet bridge. It is a one way southbound street. Fulton Ave./NY 13, will allow you to go back to NY 79/Seneca St. if you suddenly change you mind about going around Cayuga Lake and want to go to Watkins Glen and Seneca Lake using the CAYUGA LAKE TO SENECA LAKE: SOUTHERN CONNECTING ROUTE.
⇔ Traveling South on NY 13 for ~2 mi. (~3.2 km.) will bring you to Buttermilk Falls St. Pk.; Robert Treman St. Pk., and the ENFIELD LOOP ROUTE which connects with the CAYUGA LAKE TO SENECA LAKE: SOUTHERN CONNECTING ROUTE.

45.1 (72.6)   NY 89/Taughannock Blvd.   38.8 (62.4)
                   @ Cass Park & Allan H. Treman St. Pk.
Continue traveling North on to NY 89/Taughannock Blvd.
Bike Path: there are a few entrances to the bike path which parallels NY 89 for about 1 mi. (1.6 km.). Or you can just cross the grass to the Path.

52.9 (85.1)   Park Rd. @ NY 89   31.0 (49.9)
Continue North on NY 89, to completely 'round the Lake.
⇔ Turn West on Park Rd. to go through Taughannock Falls St. Pk. to Trumansburg via Jacksonville and Falls Rds. (turn North on Jacksonville Rd.). See the RT 96

TRAJECTORY ROUTE for more details. A very hilly and steep~2 mi. (~3.2 km.) from NY 89 to NY 96.
TRUMANSBURG: Trumansburg is actually on NY 96. Refer to the RT 96 TRAJECTORY Route for information. You can reach the Village by going through the Park; or by turning West on Frontenac Rd.

54.5 (87.7)   Frontenac Rd. @ NY 89   29.4 (47.3)
Continue traveling North on NY 89.
⇔ Turn West on to Frontenac Rd. to go to Trumansburg. It is a hilly 1 mi. (1.6 km.) to the Village. From Seneca Rd. @ NY 96 you'll be able to use the RT 96 TRAJECTORY ROUTE.

61.6 (99.1)   Cayuga St./Co. Rd. 141 @ NY 89   22.3 (35.9)
Continue traveling North on NY 89 to go to Seneca Falls.
⇔ CAYUGA LAKE TO SENECA LAKE: INTERLAKEN - LODI MIDDLE CONNECTING ROUTE turn West on to Cayuga St./Co. Rd. 141 to go to Seneca Lake.
↻ ⇔ **Counterclockwise** travelers should turn West on to Cayuga St./Co. Rd. 141 to go to NY 96 and use the RT 96 TRAJECTORY ROUTE to grandly enter Ithaca.

65.6 (105.6)   North St./Ovid Rd. @ NY 89   18.3 (29.5)
Continue traveling North on NY 89.
⇔ CAYUGA LAKE TO SENECA LAKE: MIDDLE CONNECTING ROUTE

75.5 (121.5)   Canoga St. @ NY 89   8.4 (13.5)
Continue North on NY 89.
⇔ CAYUGA LAKE TO SENECA LAKE: NORTHERN SCENIC CONNECTING ROUTE, turn West on to Canoga St. to go to Seneca Lake.

78.3 (126.0)   Garden St. @ NY 89   5.6 (9.0)
Turn West on to Garden St. to return to Seneca Falls. Seneca Falls is 2.5 mi. (4 km.) West of this point. Garden St. takes you directly into Seneca Falls.
Cayuga Lake St. Pk. (camping & cabins), refer to the Cayuga Lake Circumnavigation Route for information.

81.5 (131.2)   Rtes. 5&20 @ NY 89   2.4 (3.9)
Turn West on Rtes. 5&20 to go to Seneca Falls.
Turn East on to Rtes. 5&20 to go to NY 90 and the East side of Cayuga Lake.
⇔ CAYUGA LAKE TO SENECA LAKE NORTHERN CONNECTING ROUTE, turn West on to Rtes. 5&20 to go to Seneca Falls, Geneva and Seneca Lake.

⇔ OWASCO LAKE TO CAYUGA LAKE NORTHERN DIRECT CONNECTING ROUTE, turn East on Rtes. 5&20 to go to Auburn and Owasco Lake.

83.2 (133.9)   Montezuma Wildlife Refuge.   0.7 (1.1)
                  @ Rtes. 5&20
Turn West on to Rtes. 5&20 to go to Seneca Falls.

83.9 (135.0)   NY 90 @ Rtes. 5&20   0.0 (0.0)
Hey! You've rounded Cayuga Lake! Take a well deserved rest. Eat out and imbibe some of the wine you bought along the way!

Read ↓	**CAYUGA LAKE CIRCUMNAVIGATION**	Read up ↑
Clockwise	**PRIMARY ROUTE**	Counterclockwise

Counterclockwise	**CAYUGA LAKE**	Clockwise
N to S	**RT 89 WEST SIDE**	S to N
Read down ↓	**SENECA FALLS TO ITHACA**	Read up ↑

TRAVELER'S NOTE

This CAYUGA LAKE RT 89 WEST SIDE ROUTE is provided so that you do not have to transpose directions and mileage traveling South along the West shore of Cayuga Lake. It leads into Ithaca on NY 96 rather than on NY 89. A small change on a better road for climbing out of Ithaca.

All roads at the southern end of Cayuga Lake slope steeply downward as you progress southward into Ithaca.

0.0 (0.0)   Rtes. 5&20 @ NY 414   43.8 (70.5)
Travel East on Rtes. 5&20.
SENECA FALLS: info. In Cayuga Lake Circumnavigation Route.
Wanna cut off 5 mi. (8 km.) from the trek to Ithaca from Seneca Falls? Simply do the following:

  0.0 (0.0)   Rtes. 5&20 @ NY 414   2.9 (4.7)
  Turn South on NY 414. Go over the Canal.
  Signs will direct you to Cayuga St. Pk.

  .5 (.8)   Garden St. @ NY 414   2.4 (3.9)
  Turn East on to Garden St.

  2.9 (4.7)   NY 89 @ Garden St.   0.0 (0.0)
  Turn South on to NY 89.
  The entrance to Cayuga St. Pk. is almost at your front wheel!
  ⇔ Follow the CAYUGA LAKE WEST SIDE ROUTE from this intersection.

↻ CAYUGA LAKE CIRCUMNAVIGATION ROUTE: Travel East on Rtes. 5&20.
⇔ OWASCO LAKE TO CAYUGA LAKE: NORTHERN CONNECTING ROUTE, Travel East on to Rtes. 5&20.
⇔ CAYUGA LAKE TO SENECA LAKE: NORTHERN DIRECT CONNECTING ROUTE: Travel West on to Rtes. 5&20.

2.4 (3.9)   Rtes. 5&20 @ NY 89   41.4 (66.6)
Turn South on to NY 89.

5.9 (9.4)   Garden St. @ NY 89   37.9 (61.0)
Continue traveling South on NY 89.

Folks bicycling directly from Seneca Falls join us here. See the entry directly above. Cayuga Lake St. Pk.
There are many wineries along NY 89. Most are less than 1 mi. (1.6 km.) inland from NY 89.

9.2 (14.9)   Canoga St. @ NY 89   34.6 (55.7)
Continue traveling South on NY 89
⇔ CAYUGA LAKE TO SENECA LAKE: NORTHERN SCENIC CONNECTING ROUTE.

16.9 (27.2)   S. Townline Rd. @ NY 89   26.9 (43.3)
Continue traveling South on NY 89.

ROMULUS & POPLAR BEACH

Info.: Town of Romulus 1435 Prospect Ave., PO Box 177, Willard NY 14588. Romulus' AC: 315 or 607; ZC: 14541.The Town of Romulus extends from Cayuga Lake to Seneca Lake. Unfortunately, the former Seneca Army Depot prevents you from going from Lake to Lake at this point.

Bicycling Information: Use the Cayuga Lake to Seneca Lake: Middle Connecting Route to go to between the Lakes.

Services: Romulus Village: ~2.4 mi. (3.9 km.) West on S. Townline Rd. Grocery, bank, gas station, convenience store. Poplar Beach Village: ~2 mi. (3.2 km.) South on NY 89. Convenience store/gas station. Also Ovid Village has a grocery etc.
Seneca Transit Service, 5537 Rt. 96A, (toll free) 866 736-3220., no bike racks but allows bikes to be transported inside the bus if the wheelchair area is not being used.

Lodging: B&Bs: B&Bs: 1843 House, 5976 Rte. 89, 607 869-5304; Yale Manor, 563 Yale Farm Rd., 315 585-2208. Camping both on Seneca Lake): Kendaia Cpgd., 5919 NY 96A (1 km. n of Sampson St. Pk.), 315 585-2244; Sampson St. Pk., NY 96A, 315 585-6392.

Attractions: Dean's Cove St. Marine Boat Launch Pk., NY 89; Buttonwood Grove Winery, 607 869-9760; Cobblestone Winery, 5102 NY 89, 315 569-5966; Goose Watch Winery, 5480 NY 89, 315 549-2599; Knapp Vineyard, 2770 CR 128 (Emsberger Rd.), 607 869-9271; Lakeshore Winery, 5132 NY 89, 549-7075; Swedish Hill Vineyard (Seneca Lake), 4565 NY 414, 315 549-8326; Naval & Air Force Mus at Sampson St. Pk. (Seneca Lake), 315 585-6392; Sampson St. Pk., NY 96A

22.0 (35.4)   North St./Ovid Rd. @ NY 89   21.8 (35.1)
Continue traveling South on NY 89.
⇔ CAYUGA LAKE TO SENECA LAKE: MIDDLE CONNECTING ROUTE.

25.8 (41.5)   Cayuga St./Co. Rd. 141 @ NY 89   18.0 (29.0)
Continue traveling South on NY 89 to use 89 to go into
Ithaca.   Directions continue after the NY 96 Trajectory
Route. But I suggest that you use the NY 96 Trajectory to
go to Ithaca.
⇔ ↻ NY 96 TRAJECTORY ROUTE. Turn West on to Co.
Rd. 141/Cayuga St. to use NY 96 to go into Ithaca.
⇔ CAYUGA LAKE TO SENECA LAKE: INTERLAKEN -
LODI MIDDLE CONNECTING ROUTE, turn West on to Co.
Rd. 141/Cayuga St. to go to Lodi Village and Seneca Lake.
↻ CUYUGA LAKE RT 89 WEST SIDE Route is continued
immediately following the NY 96 Trajectory Route.
A few bits and pieces to help you make a decision.
   1. Both roads, NY 89 & NY 96, arrive in Ithaca at the
   same intersection.
   2. Both the NY 89 and the NY 96 trajectory into Ithaca
   are described in this text.
   3. The distance from this point to Ithaca is almost the
   same using either road.
   4. NY 89's shoulder narrows South of Taughannock Falls
   St. Pk., ~7 mi. (11.3 km.) South of this intersection on NY
   89 and becomes very narrow, <1.5 ft. (<.4 m.), on the
   steepest portions ~3 mi. (~5 km.) before Ithaca.
   5. NY 96 has a wider shoulder except for the last .5 mi.
   (.8 km.) before Ithaca.
   6. Going any further South and then crossing over to NY
   96 will involve climbing higher on the ridge between the
   two Lakes.
   7. NY 96 follows an inland route about 5-10 mi. (8-16
   km.) from the Cayuga Lake shore.

Counterclockwise	**CAYUGA LAKE**	Clockwise
N to S	**RT 89 WEST SIDE ROUTE CON'T**	S to N
Read down ↓	**ITHACA TO SENECA FALLS**	Read up ↑

Counterclockwise	**CAYUGA LAKE**	Clockwise
N to S	**RT 96 TRAJECTORY**	S to N
Read down ↓	**INTERLAKEN TO ITHACA**	Read up ↑

25.8 (41.5)   Cayuga St./Co. Rd. 141 @ NY 89   18.0 (29.0)
Turn West on to Cayuga St./Co. Rd. 141.
⇔ ↻ ↺ CAYUGA LAKE CIRCUMNAVIGATION ROUTE
⇔ ↻ ↺ RT 89 WEST SIDE ROUTE
⇔ ↻ ↺ RT 96 PROJECTILE ROUTE
⇔ CAYUGA LAKE TO SENECA LAKE: INTERLAKEN - LODI MIDDLE CONNECTING ROUTE

26.5 (42.6)   NY 96 @ Cayuga St./Co. Rd. 141   17.3 (27.8)
Turn South on to NY 96.
🏠 If you turn North on to NY 96 you'll to Ovid and eventually to the North end of Seneca Lake at Geneva.

INTERLAKEN
Information: Trumansburg Area CofC, PO Box 478, Trumansburg, NY 14886, 607 387-9254. AC: 607 ZC:14847.
Services: convenience store, restaurant, etc.
Lodging: 1488Glass Magnolia B&B, 8347 N. Main St., 532-8356.
Attractions: Deere Haven Mus., PO Box 14 CR 141, 532-4288; Interlaken Hist. Soc. & Farmers Mus., Main St. Rte. 96, 532-4213/532-9227; Lively Run Goat Dairy, 8978 CR 142, 532-4647; Americana Winery, 4367 E. Covert Rd., 387-6801; Lucas Vineyards, 3862 CR 150, 532-4825.

26.7 (43.0)   NY 96A @ NY 96   17.1 (27.5)
Continue traveling South on NY 96 to go to Ithaca and the southern end of Cayuga Lake.
🏠 ⇔ ↻ ↺ SENECA LAKE CIRCUMNAVIGATION ROUTE. Turning North on NY 96A will take you to Lodi Village, NY 414 and Upper Lake Rd. A straight line route to Seneca Lake!

32.7 (52.3)   NY 227 @ NY 96   11.1 (17.9)
             Main St. @ Hector St.
Continue traveling South on NY 96 to go to Ithaca.
🏠 Thinking of going to Seneca Lake or Watkins Glen? Since you are partially up the ridge between Seneca & Cayuga Lakes you might as well know that there is this connecting road from here. Turn Southwest on to NY 227/ Hector St. to go to Watkins Glen and the southern end of Seneca Lake. NY 227 junctions with NY 79, the Cayuga

Lake to Seneca Lake: Southern Connecting Route, ~10 mi.
(16 km.) south of this intersection. Be aware that there are
no services, only beautiful scenery between Trumansburg
(Cayuga Lake) & Burdett (Seneca Lake).
TRUMANSBURG: Info. in the NY 96 Projectile Route.

33.9 (54.6)　　　　Falls St. @ NY 96　　　　　　　　9.9 (15.9)
Continue traveling South on NY 96.
Turn East on to Falls St./Jacksonville Rd. to go into
Taughannock Falls St. Pk. (camping/cabins). Luckily you
are above the Falls so its a downward road! Falls St./
Jacksonville Rd. intersects with Park Rd. which will take
you eastward into the Park and to NY 89.

36.4 (58.6)　　　　Jacksonville @ NY 96　　　　　　　7.4 (11.9)
To Ithaca, continue South on NY 96.
Just a cross roads but it does have a B&B & campground:
Spruce Row Cpgd., 2271 Kraft Rd., 387-9225.

43.2 (69.5)　　　　NY 96/Buffalo St..　　　　　　　　　.6 (.9)
　　　　　　　　　Jct. NY 13/Fulton Ave.
Continue traveling East on Buffalo St.
NY 96 turns South on to Fulton Ave.
ᛋ CAYUGA LAKE TO SENECA LAKE: SOUTHERN
CONNECTING Route.　you are planning to go to Watkins
Glen and Seneca Lake turn South on to Fulton Ave. go 1
block to NY 79/W. Seneca St. @ Fulton Ave. and begin
climbing!

43.3 (69.7)　　　　Meadow Dr./NY 89 @ Buffalo St.　　　.5 (.8)
Turn North on to Meadow Dr. to use NY 89 and return from
whence you came, the northern end of Cayuga Lake/
Seneca Falls or wherever (Seneca Lake via the Middle
Connecting Route).

43.8 (70.5)　　　　Cayuga St. @ Buffalo St.　　　　　0.0 (0.0)
ITHACA. Yeah! I know you've been in Ithaca for at least ½
a mi./.8 km. but it is from Cayuga St. and Seneca Ave. (one
block South at the Ithaca Commons) from which all
directions in Ithaca emanate in this book.

Counterclockwise	**CAYUGA LAKE**	Clockwise
N to S	**RT 96 TRAJECTORY**	S to N
Read down ↓	**ITHACA TO INTERLAKEN**	Read up ↑

Clockwise	**CAYUGA LAKE**	Counterclockwise
N to S	**RT 89 WEST SIDE ROUTE CON'T**	S to N
Read down ↓	**SENECA FALLS TO ITHACA**	Read up ↑

COUNTERCLOCKWISE - SOUTH TO NORTH
TRAVELER'S NOTE

Hopefully you're using the Cayuga Lake Circumnavigation Route. This West Side NY 89 Route is simply a duplication of the Cayuga Lake Circumnavigation Route which allows folks to not have to transpose directions and distances when traveling South on the West side of Cayuga Lake from Seneca Falls to Ithaca.

The Seneca Lake West Side Route using NY 89 is continued after the NY 96 Trajectory Route as you read from the bottom of the page upwards.

There is a slight discontinuity of distance indicators due to the use of NY 96 as the for the West Side Route as the major road on which to base distances.

25.8 (41.5)   Cayuga St./Co. Rd. 141   16.5 (26.6)
                 @ NY 89
Continue traveling South on NY 89
⇔ ↺ RT 96 PROJECTILE ROUTE
⇔ CAYUGA LAKE TO SENECA LAKE: INTERLAKEN - LODI CONNECTING ROUTE

33.2 (53.4)   Park Rd. @ NY 89   9.1 (14.6)
Continue traveling South on NY 89. The shoulder begins to get progressively narrower from this point southward. The slope downwards also becomes steeper as you go southward.
Taughannock Falls St. Pk. (camping), 607 387-6739.
TRUMANSBURG: info. In the Rt. 96 Trajectory Route

41.0 (66.0)   NY 89/Taughannock Blvd.   1.3 (2.1)
                 @ Allan H. Treman St. Pk. & Cass Pk.
Continue traveling South on to NY 89/Taughannock Blvd. Bike Path. The entrance to the bike path which parallels NY 89 for about 1 mi. (1.6 km.) is at the Hanger Theater/ Treman St. Pk. entrance. Use care when crossing NY 89.

41.7 (67.1)   NY 13/Fulton Ave.   .6 (1.0)
                 @ Buffalo St./NY 89 & NY 96
Travel East on Buffalo St.
NY 89 essentially ends at this point. You are now in Ithaca. NY 96 junctions with NY 89 in the middle of the Inlet bridge!

⇔ CAYUGA LAKE TO SENECA LAKE: SOUTHERN CONNECTING ROUTE. You will pass Rtes. 13/96/Fulton Ave. as you exit from the Inlet bridge. It is a one way southbound street. NY 96 turns South at Fulton Ave./NY 13. Fulton Ave./NY 13, will allow you to go to NY 79/ Seneca St. if you suddenly change you mind about going into Ithaca and immediately want to go to Watkins Glen and Seneca Lake. Ha! Ha! Its a steep climb up NY 79.
⅏ ENFIELD LOOP.

41.8 (67.3)   @ Meadow Dr./NY 13 Buffalo St.   .5 (.8)
Continue traveling East on Buffalo St.
Meadow Dr./NY 13, is another one way street and it allows you to go up the west side of the Lake. Essentially a U turn.

42.3 (68.1)   Cayuga St. @ Buffalo St.   0.0 (0.0)
Ithaca. Yeah! I know you've been in Ithaca for at least ½ a mi./.8 km. but it is from Cayuga St. and Seneca Ave. (one block South at the Ithaca Commons) from which all directions in Ithaca emanate in this book.

Clockwise	**CAYUGA LAKE**	Counterclockwise
N to S	**RT 89 WEST SIDE ROUTE**	S to N
Read down ↓	**ITHACA TO SENECA FALLS**	Read up ↑

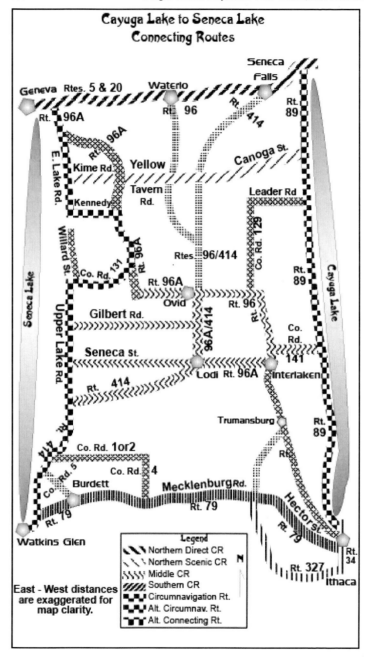

Cayuga Lake to Seneca Lake Connecting Routes

| Read ↓ | **CAYUGA LAKE TO SENECA LAKE** | Read up ↑ |
| E to W | **NORTHERN DIRECT CONNECTING ROUTE** | W to E |

CLOCKWISE TRAVELER'S NOTE

There are two Northern Connecting routes between Cayuga and Seneca Lakes--Direct and Scenic. You choose!

0.0 (0.0)   NY 414 @ Rtes. 5&20   9.6 (15.4)
Turn West on to Rtes. 5&20 (NY 5/US 20)
⇔ ↻ ↺ CAYUGA LAKE CIRCUMNAVIGATION Route
⇔ ↺ CAYUGA LAKE: RT 89 WEST SIDE ROUTE
⌂ ⇔ CAYUGA LAKE TO SENECA LAKE: NORTHERN SCENIC CONNECTING ROUTE begins about 9.2 mi. (14.9 km.) at Canoga St. @ NY 89 on the Circumnavigation and NY 89 West Side Routes. It is also accessible from Rtes. 414 and 96 by traveling South on those roads for 9 mi. (14.5 km.) to Yellow Tavern Rd.
SENECA FALLS: see beginning Cayuga Lake chapter.

3.2 (5.1)   NY 96 @ Rtes. 5&20   6.4 (10.3)
Continue traveling West on Rtes. 5&20.
Lock 4, Seneca/Cayuga Canal.
NY 96 travels South almost half way between Cayuga Lake and Seneca Lake.
Traveling North on NY 96 will eventually take you into Rochester.

WATERLOO

Info.: Village of Waterloo, Main St., 315 539-9131, Waterloo NY 13165. AC: 315. ZC: 13165.
Services: All.
Lodging: Motels. B&Bs: Gridley Inn, 36 W. Main St., 539-5192; Through the Grapevine, 108 Virginia St., 539-8620. Camping: Hidden Harbor, 1076 Rtes. 5&20, 539-8034; Waterloo Harbor, PO Box 27, 539-8848; Canalside Destinations, Rtes. 5&20, 781-6682
Attractions: McClintock House, 16 Williams St., 568-2991; Peter Whitmer House, Aunkst Rd., 539-2552; Waterloo Library/Terwilliger Mus., 31 E. Williams St., 539-0533, Waterloo Memorial Day Mus., 35 E Main St.; Lock 4, Seneca-Cayuga Canal.

7.3 (11.7)   NY 96A @ Rtes. 5&20   2.3 (3.7)
Connectors, continue to travel West on Rtes. 5&20.
⇔ ↻ SENECA LAKE CIRCUMNAVIGATION Route. Turn
South on to NY 96A to circumnavigate Seneca Lake
clockwise.

7.5 (12.1)   Waterfront Pk. & Path @ Rtes. 5&20   2.1 (3.4)
Enter Waterfront Pk., follow the sidewalk/trail along the
shore. The path is much nicer and safer than Rtes. 5&20.
Don't forget to look for the Seneca Lake whale!
GENEVA: info. In Seneca Lake Circumnavigation Rte.

9.6 (15.4)   NY 14 @ Rtes. 5&20   0.0 (0.0)
The Waterfront Pk. trail follows the Lake shore. At Castle
St. you exit and go on to the Rtes. 5&20 roadway. Cross
Rtes. 5&20 only at a traffic light! Then go up the ramp on
Rtes. 5&20 to NY 14.
⇔ ↻ SENECA LAKE CIRCUMNAVIGATION ROUTE.
Turn South on to NY 14 to go counterclockwise around
Seneca Lake.
⇔ CAYUGA LAKE TO SENECA LAKE: NORTHERN
SCENIC CONNECTING ROUTE.

Read ↓   **CAYUGA LAKE TO SENECA LAKE**   Read up ↑
E to W   **NORTHERN DIRECT CONNECTING ROUTE**   W to E

0.0 (0.0)   Canoga St. @ NY 89   8.1 (13.0)
Turn West on to Canoga St.
Canoga Hamlet, Cayuga Lake: No services.
⇔ ↻ ↺ CAYUGA LAKE CIRCUMNAVIGATION Route
⇔ ↺ CAYUGA LAKE: RT 89 WEST SIDE ROUTE

0.7 (1.1)   Seybolt Rd. @ Canoga St.   7.4 (11.9)
Turn South on to Seybolt Rd.

0.9 (1.4)   Yellow Tavern Rd. @ Seybolt Rd.   7.2 (11.6)
Turn West on to Yellow Tavern Rd.

2.5 (4.0)   NY 414 @ Yellow Tavern Rd.   5.6 (9.0)
Continue traveling West on Yellow Tavern Rd.
Turn North on to NY 414 to go to Seneca Falls.

4.5 (7.2)   NY 96 @ Yellow Tavern Rd.   3.6 (5.8)
Continue traveling West on Yellow Tavern Rd. to go to
Seneca Lake.
Turn North on to NY 96 to go to Waterloo.

7.0 (11.3)   NY 96A   1.1 (1.8)
          @ Yellow Tavern Rd./Kime Rd.
Continue West on Kime Rd. Follow the asphalt westward!
Yup, the road's the same, the name's different.
⇔ ↻ ↺ SENECA LAKE CIRCUMNAVIGATION.

8.1 (13.0)   East Lake Rd. @ Kime Rd.   0.0 (0.0)
⇔ ↻ SENECA LAKE CIRCUMNAVIGATION ROUTE.
Turn South on to E. Lake Rd. to go clockwise.
⇔ ↺ SENECA LAKE CIRCUMNAVIGATION ROUTE.
Turn North on E. Lake Rd. to go counterclockwise.

WEST TO EAST TRAVELER'S NOTE
There are two Northern Connecting routes between
Cayuga and Seneca Lakes--Direct and Scenic. You
choose!

Read ↓ E to W	**CAYUGA LAKE TO SENECA LAKE MIDDLE CONNECTING ROUTE**	Read up ↑ W to E

0.0 (0.0)   North St./Ovid Rd. @ NY 89   6.3 (10.0)
Turn West on to North St.

1.6 (2.6)   NY 96 @ North St.   4.7 (7.6)
Continue traveling North actually West on NY 96. to go to Seneca Lake.
⇥ Going North on NY 96 takes you to Waterloo and the Northern Connecting Route between Cayuga & Seneca Lakes
⇥ ↻ ↺ Going South on NY 96 takes you to Trumansburg & from there to Ithaca via the NY 96 Trajectory and Projectile Routes.

4.0 (6.4)   Rtes. 96A/414   2.3 (3.7)
                   @ NY 96/North St.
↺ SENECA LAKE CIRCUMNAVIGATION ROUTE (counterclockwise). Travel on to NY 96A **North** to encounter Seneca Lake at Willard. Use the directions from Willard Rd. @ NY 96A.
↻ SENECA LAKE CIRCUMNAVIGATION RT (clockwise). NY 414 & NY 96A junction and go South at this intersection. If you are planning to travel South to Watkins Glen from this intersection you can turn South on to Rtes. 96A/414 or use the primary Upper Lake Rd. route, see the direction entry after Ovid information.
⇥ NY 96 junctions with NY 414 and goes due North to Waterloo from this intersection.
⇥ ↻ NY 96 goes South to Interlaken from this intersection. From Interlaken you can use the Cayuga Lake Circumnavigation Route, the NY 89 Cayuga Lake West Side Route, and the NY 96 Trajectory and NY 96 Projectile Routes.

OVID
Services: Grocery, convenience store/gas station, hardware store, bank, other local shops.
Lodging: Motels. B&Bs: Driftwood, 7401 Wyers Pt. Rd., 532-4324; Silver Strand, 7398 Wyers Pt. Rd., Tillinghast Manor, 7246 S. Main St., 869-3584; Camping: Ridgewood Cpgd., 6590 Cayuga Lake Rd. (NY 89), 869-9787.
Attractions: Bonavista St. Golf Course, 7194 CR 132, 869-5482; Ovid Historical Soc. Mus., 7203 S. Main St., 869-

5222; Three Bears Hist. Site, South Main St. Rte. 414, 869-3818; Bonavista St. Golf Course, 7194 CR 132, 869-5482; Willard Wildlife Mgt. Area, CR 132, 526-6596. Cayuga Ridge Estate Winery, 6800 NY 89 at Elm Beach Rd., 869-5158; Hosmer Winery, 6999 Rte. 89, 869-3393; Sheldrake Point Vineyards, 7448 CR 153, 532-9401; Thirsty Owl Wine Co., 6799 Elm Beach Rd., 869-5805.

4.8 (7.7)   Gilbert Rd. @ Rtes. 96A/414 South   1.5 (2.4)
Turn West on Gilbert Rd. to go to Seneca Lake.
Traveling South on Rtes. 96A/414 will take you to the southern ends of Cayuga Lake or Seneca Lake depending on which road you use after Lodi.

6.3 (10.0)   Upper Lake Rd.   0.0 (0.0)
                    @ Gilbert Rd.
↺ SENECA LAKE CIRCUMNAVIGATION Route.   Turn South on to Upper Lake Rd. to 'round Seneca Lake clockwise.
↻ SENECA LAKE CIRCUMNAVIGATION Route.   Turn North on to Upper Lake Rd. to go around Seneca Lake counterclockwise. Yup! You're at Seneca Lake.

Read ↓	**CAYUGA LAKE TO SENECA LAKE**	Read up ↑
E to W	**MIDDLE CONNECTING ROUTE**	W to E

Read ↓	**CAYUGA LAKE TO SENECA LAKE**	Read up ↑
	INTERLAKEN - TO LODI	
E to W	**MIDDLE CONNECTING ROUTE**	W to E

0.0 (0.0)   Cayuga St./Co. Rd. 141   7.8 (12.6)
@ NY 89 - Cayuga Lake
Turn West on to Cayuga St./CR 141 to go to Seneca Lake.
↻ ↺ CAYUGA LAKE CIRCUMNAVIGATION Route.
↺ CAYUGA LAKE: RT 89 WEST SIDE ROUTE.

1.3 (2.0)   NY 96 @ Cayuga St./Co. Rd. 141   6.5 (10.5)
Turn South on to NY 96.

1.5 (2.4)   NY 96A @ NY 96   6.3 (10.1)
Turn West on to NY 96A North. Confused? Don/t be! NY
96A actually ends here! Even more confused? NY 96A is
follows a North-South alignment at this point.
↻ ↺ CAYUGA LAKE CIRCUMNAVIGATION.
↺ CAYUGA LAKE RT 89 WEST SIDE ROUTE: RT 96
TRAJECTORY ROUTE will take you to Ithaca and the
southern end of Cayuga Lake. NY 96 has the best
shoulders leading into Ithaca.

6.4 (10.3)   NY 414 @ NY 96A   1.4 (2.3)
Co. Rd. 136/W. Seneca St. @ NY 96A
Continue to travel West on to Seneca St.

SENECA LAKE CIRCUMNAVIGATION
Route options
🚲 ↺ ⇔ Clockwise: You can also turn South on to NY414
to go to Watkins Glen and the southern end of Seneca
Lake.
🚲 ↺ ⇔ Counterclockwise: Going North on Rtes. 96A/414
will take you counterclockwise around Seneca Lake via the
SENECA LAKE CIRCUMNAVIGATION ROUTE and you
will encounter riders on that Route at Willard. This is the
best option for Seneca Lake counterclockwise travelers, as
you will only be riding on Upper Lake Rd. for a very short
distance if you choose that option.
A note is necessary here. The Seneca Lake
Circumnavigation Route uses two State highways NY 96A
& NY 414; and various rural roads, Lake Rd., Upper Lake
Rd. and Schuyler Co. Rd. 4, as a way to go around the
Lake. From this intersection, NY 96A is the north bound
road used for going around the Lake. NY 414 is the south

bound road used to go around the Lake. W. Seneca St./Co. Rd. 136 connects Rtes. 414/96A with Upper Lake Rd., the road described in the Seneca Lake Circumnavigation route.

LODI

Info.: As with so many other places in rural America, Lodi has seen better days. With the closing of the Seneca Army Depot, a few of its residents and businesses have gone elsewhere. But the ice cream store is still there! As are lots of friendly folks.

Lodging: B&Bs: Fox and the Grapes, 9496 NY 414, 582-7528; Maxsom's, 9404 NY 414, 582-6248; Seneca Lakeside, 9048 Barbara Rd., 582-6487; At Vineyards Edge, 1533 Caywood Rd., 582-7223. Camping: Sunset on Seneca, 8453 Lower Lake Rd., 582-6030.

Attractions: Lodi Hist. Soc., S. Main St. NY 414, 582-6511; Lamoreaux Landing Wine Cellars, 9224 NY 414, 582-6011; Shalestone Vineyard, 9681 NY 414, 582-6600; Silver Thread Vineyard, 1401 Caywood Rd. 582-6116; Wagner Vineyards, 9322 NY 414, 582-6450.

7.8 (12.6)   Upper Lake Rd   0.0 (0.0)
                    @ W. Seneca St./Co Rd. 136

↺ ↻ SENECA LAKE CIRCUMNAVIGATION Route. Turn North or South. Be careful at this intersection. Make certain that you turn South on to Upper Lake and not on to Lower Lake Rd. Lower Lake Rd. is very narrow and descends steeply to the Lake. Make a NY ∠ turn on to Upper Lake Rd at the cemetery.

If you go North, you'll pass the road leading down to Lodi Pt. St. Marine Pk. (day use only, beach It is a fairly steep 1.2 mi. (1.9 km.) descent to the Park. Come up the same way you went down.

Read ↓	**CAYUGA LAKE TO SENECA LAKE**	Read up ↑
	LODI TO INTERLAKEN	
E to W	**MIDDLE CONNECTING ROUTE**	W to E

| Read ↓ | **CAYUGA LAKE TO SENECA LAKE** | Read up ↑ |
| E to W | **SOUTHERN CONNECTING ROUTE** | W to E |

TRAVELER'S NOTE
EAST TO WEST - ITHACA TO WATKINS GLEN

Do not expect this route between Cayuga Lake and Seneca Lake to take you 2 or 3 hours to ride. Besides the initial climb up from Ithaca, there are several rises in elevation as you progress West towards Watkins Glen. Although this Route appears short in distance, it may rapidly exhaust you physically. Make certain that you have sufficient snacks and water as there are few replenishment points along the way. Make certain that your bicycle is in excellent condition.

0.0 (0.0)   Cayuga St. Seneca St./NY 79   25.2 (40.6)
Travel West on Seneca St./NY 79.
Ithaca Commons.
↺ ↻ CAYUGA LAKE CIRCUMNAVIGATION Route.
⇔ OWASCO LAKE TO CAYUGA LAKE SOUTHERN CONNECTING ROUTES
↻ CAYUGA LAKE RT 89 WEST SIDE ROUTE
↻ CAYUGA LAKE RT 96 TRAJECTORY ROUTE

0.4 (0.2)   Meadow Dr./NY 13   24.8 (39.9)
     @ Seneca St./NY 79
Continue traveling West on Seneca St. Cross Cayuga Lake Inlet Channel.
⇔ Meadow Dr. is a one way North bound street which allows you to turn on to NY Rtes. 96/89. Use it to go North along the West side of Cayuga Lake via NY 89 or NY 96. Use either the CAYUGA LAKE CIRCUMNAVIGATION ROUTE; the CAYUGA LAKE WEST SIDE ROUTE/RT 96 TRAJECTORY ROUTE.

0.5 (0.8)   Fulton Ave./Rtes. 13/34/96 S   24.3 (39.1)
     @ W. Seneca St./NY 79
Fulton Ave./Rtes. 13/96 is a one way street going South
⇔ ENFIELD LOOP: Turn on to NY 96 South. The Enfield Loop is another way to reach the ridge along which NY 79 flows! The ENFIELD LOOP directions are at the end of this Route.

0.7 (1.3)   Floral Ave./NY 13A   24.5 (39.4)
                   @ NY 79/Hector St./Mecklenberg Rd.
Continue West on NY 79. You will be climbing a steep
slope as you go West.

3.5 (5.7)   Hector St./NY 79   21.7 (34.9)
                   Jct. Mecklenberg Rd./NY 79
Continue to follow NY 79 westward. The street name
changes but the route number doesn't!

8.6 (13.8)   NY 327/Enfield Rd.   16.6 (26.7)
                   @ NY 79/Mecklenberg Rd.
Continue traveling West on NY 79/Mecklenberg Rd.
⇔ ENFIELD LOOP directions are provided at the end of
this Southern Connecting Route. Go to Ithaca via the
Enfield Loop! Don't think this is a flat ride!

12.6 (20.3)   NY 228 @ NY 79   12.6 (20.3)
Continue traveling West on NY 79 to go to Seneca Lake.
NY 228 goes North to Perry. There it meets NY 227 which
will take you to Trumansburg & NY 96, North of Ithaca, and
intersects with the RT 96 TRAJECTORY ROUTE.
MECKLENBERG

16.2 (26.1)   NY 227 @ NY 79   9.0 (14.5)
Continue traveling on NY 79.
⑅ NY 227 goes North to Perry and Trumansburg. At
Trumansburg it intersects with NY 96 and the RT 96
TRAJECTORY ROUTE. Hey I had to tell you this, if not
you'll go to Ithaca and only have to come up to the ridge
again.

20.6 (33.1)   Co. Rd. 4 @ NY 79   4.6 (7.4)
Continue traveling on NY 79.
⇔ ↻ SENECA LAKE CIRCUMNAVIGATION ROUTE:
NAT'L FOREST NY You're way up thar'! If you want to go
to Finger Lakes Nat'l. Forest along the ridge (well almost
along the ridge). CR 4 is a very pleasant road. Although it
does have more severe ups and downs than NY 414 (the
main Seneca Lake road) which it parallels.

21.6 (34.8)   Co. Rd. 5 @ NY 79   3.6 (5.8)
Continue traveling West to go to Watkins Glen.
⑅ ↻ Turn North on to CR 5 to go around Seneca Lake
counterclockwise. A mile (1.6 km.) North, CR 5 junctions
with NY 414, the major road nearest the shore, used in the
SENECA LAKE CIRCUMNAVIGATION ROUTE.

BURDETT

Bicycling Information: Going West on NY 79 is a steep decline into Watkins Glen. Going East on NY 79 to Ithaca, you've got a lot more to climb.

Services: Restaurant, local convenience store.

Lodging: B&Bs: Sunset on Seneca, 3221 NY 414, 535-6973; Red House Country Inn, FLNF Picnic Area Rd., 546-8566; Country Gardens, 5116 NY 414, 546-2272. Chalet Leon at Hector Falls Motel, 3835 NY 414, 546-7171.

Attractions: Catharine Valley Winery, 4201 NY 414, 546-5300; Skyland Farm Art Gallery, 4966 Rt. 414, 546-5050.

23.3 (37.5)   NY 414   1.9 (3.1)
                   Jct. NY 79 & NY 227/228

Turn South on to NY 414 to go to Watkins Glen.
Continuing Southwest on to Rte. 414/79 will bring you into Watkins Glen and the southern end of Seneca Lake. Theoretically NY 79 begins/ends at this intersection.
↺ SENECA LAKE CIRCUMNAVIGATION ROUTE. Turning North on NY 414 will allow you to go North along the East side of Seneca Lake.

TRAVELER'S NOTES

NY 414 declines very steeply going into Watkins Glen. The roadway was being enlarged in 1998. Hopefully the State will put at least a 12 ft. (3.7 m.) shoulder on each side of the road. On *race* weekends this road has a considerable amount of traffic. Make certain that you and your bicycle are in perfect mechanical condition. Check your brakes, tires, rims and gear before you begin the descent.

WEST TO EAST - WATKINS GLEN TO ITHACA

You've just conquered the cliff! The small sign states: *NY 227/228 to NY 79* ⇨. Landmark: opposite this intersection, across NY 414 is DeWitt Concrete. You have a lot more to climb! Turn West, actually Rtes. 227/228/79 meet NY 414 at an angle, on to these roads. It is easy to miss this intersection!

25.2 (40.6)   NY 14/Franklin St.   0.0 (0.0)
                   Jct. NY 414/Fourth St.
                   @ NY 409/Upper Glen Rd.

WATKINS GLEN: see Seneca Lake Circumnavigation Route for information.

You've just past Watkins Glen Village's Chute Pk. (beach; campsites; lots of RVs & pick ups with housing on them) but you don't have to climb any hills!

Here's the story about this intersection.
NY 414 & NY 14 junction and go South on Franklin St. .5
mi. (.8 km.) South on Franklin St. is Watkins Glen St. Pk.,
lower entrance for camping.

⇔ SENECA LAKE TO KEUKA LAKE: SOUTHERN
CONNECTING ROUTE. NY 409/Upper Glen Rd. and the
is opposite your tire.

↺ SENECA LAKE CIRCUMNAVIGATION ROUTE. Going
North on NY 14 will set you on the clockwise course 'round
Seneca Lake.

↻ SENECA LAKE CIRCUMNAVIGATION ROUTE. Of
course the opposite is true at this intersection, going East
on Rtes. 414/228/79 will set you on the xounterclockwise
course around Seneca Lake.

TRAVELER'S NOTE
WEST TO EAST - WATKINS GLEN TO ITHACA
& COUNTERCLOCKWISE
SENECA LAKE CIRCUMNAVIGATORS

Do not expect this route between Seneca Lake and
Cayuga Lake to take you 2 or 3 hours to ride. Besides the
initial cliff going North/West from Watkins Glen, there is
almost a continual rise in elevation as you progress East
towards Ithaca. Although this Route appears short in
distance, it may rapidly exhaust you physically. Make
certain that you have sufficient snacks and water. Make
certain that you and your bicycle are in excellent condition.

Read ↓	SENECA LAKE TO CAYUGA LAKE	Read up ↑
E to W	SOUTHERN CONNECTING ROUTE	W to E

0.0 (0.0)   Fulton Ave./Rtes. 13/34/96 S   19.0 (30.6)
                   @ Seneca St./NY 79
         Turn South on to Rtes. 13/96

4.2 (6.8)   NY 327/Enfield Falls Rd.   14.8 (23.8)
                   @ Rtes. 13/34/96/Danby Rd.
         Turn West on to NY 327.

10.7 (17.2)   NY 79/Mecklenberg Rd.   8.3 (13.4)
                   @ NY 327/Enfield Falls Rd.
         Turn East on to NY 79/Mecklenberg Rd. to return to Ithaca.
         This is a loop after all!
         ⇔ CAYUGA LAKE TO SENECA LAKE: SOUTHERN
         CONNECTING ROUTE. Turn West on to NY 79/
         Mecklenberg Rd. to go to Watkins Glen and Seneca Lake.
         ⇥ ⇔ Continue traveling due North on Haleysville Rd. for
         3.5 mi. (5.6 km.) to intersect with NY 96 north of Ithaca,
         Trumansburg, the RT 96 TRAJECTORY ROUTE and the
         RT 96 PROJECTILE ROUTE.

15.8 (25.4)   Hector St./NY 79   3.2 (5.1)
                   Jct. Mecklenberg Rd./NY 79
         Continue to follow NY 79 eastward.

18.6 (30.0)   Floral Ave./NY 13A   0.4 (0.6)
                   @ NY 79/Hector St./Mecklenberg Rd.
         Continue East on NY 79.

19.0 (30.6)   Fulton Ave./Rtes. 13/34/96 S   0.0 (0.0)
                   @ NY 79/State St.
         Back where you started the Enfield Loop.
         Continue traveling East on NY 79 to go to Ithaca commons.
         Both Fulton Ave./Rtes 13/34/96 and State St./NY 79 are
         one way streets.

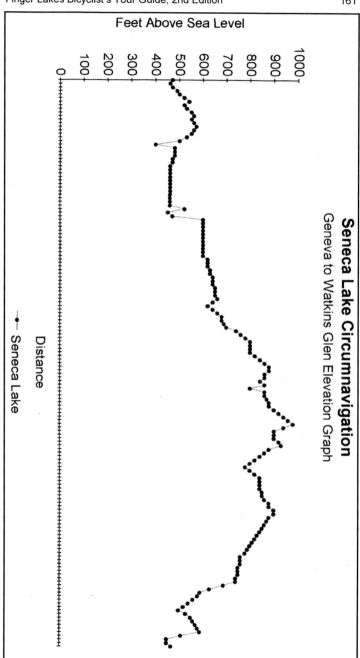

Seneca Lake Circumnavigation

Geneva to Watkins Glen Elevation Graph

Feet Above Sea Level

Distance

Seneca Lake

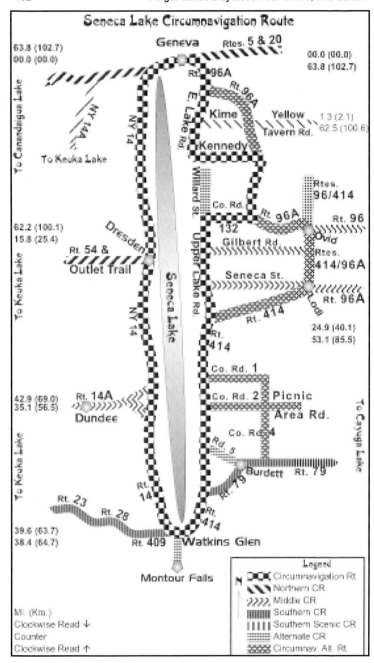

Seneca Lake Circumnavigation Route

Size and Depth

During World War II the United States Navy established a training facility on Seneca Lake. Sailors were given the requisite basic training on land at the Sampson facility. The recruits marched to the dock on Seneca Lake to board ships to gain the sea legs necessary for life on board. Not small sail boats or motor yachts but real working Navy vessels including submarines.

One important part of the Sampson facility was the training of Navy aviators. Pontoon equipped training and larger planes swooped low over the water, perhaps looking for the submarine!

Today, the Navy is gone. The Army which assumed responsibility for the base is also gone. In its place is a large State Park with a World War II Museum and land awaiting a proper use.

Here's the data on the Finger Lakes

Lake	Length mi. (km.)	Width mi. (km.)	Depth ft. (m.)	Elev. ft. (m.)
Otisco	5.7 (9)	0.75 (1.2)	66 (20)	784 (239)
Skaneateles	15 (24)	1.5 (2.4)	350 (106)	300 (91)
Owasco	11 (33)	1.2 (1.9)	177 (53)	770 (235)
Cayuga	40 (64)	3.5 (5.6)	435 (132)	381 (116)
Seneca	35 (56)	3.0 (4.8)	618 (188)	444 (135)
Waneta	3.0 (5)	0.5 (.8)	29 (9)	1098 (335)
Keuka	20 (32)	2.0 (3.2)	186 (57)	709 (216
Canandaigua	16 (26)	1.5 (2.4)	274 (84)	686 (209)
Honeoye	4.5 (7)	0.75 (1.2)	30 (9)	803 (245)
Canadice	3.0 (5)	0.3 (.48)	84 (25)	1096 (334)
Hemlock	7.5 (12)	0.5 (0.8)	90 (27)	896 (273)
Conesus	7.7 (12)	0.75 (1.2)	66 (20)	818 (249)

Read ↓   **SENECA LAKE CIRCUMNAVIGATION**   Read up ↑
Clockwise   Counterclockwise

TRAVELER NOTE

The roads leading into Watkins Glen, on both sides of the Lake, are steeply sloped downward and southward. Make certain that you and your bicycle are well prepared for the descent or ascent.

0.0 (0.0)   Rtes. 5&20 @ NY 96A   78.0 (125.5)
Turn South on to NY 96A.

⇔ CAYUGA LAKE TO SENECA LAKE: NORTHERN DIRECT CONNECTING ROUTE, travel East on Rtes. 5&20 to go to Seneca Falls and Cayuga Lake.

⇔ SENECA LAKE TO KEUKA LAKE: NORTHERN CONNECTING ROUTE, travel West on Rtes. 5&20 to go to Penn Yan and Keuka Lake.

GENEVA

Info.: Geneva Area CofC, 35 Lakefront Dr., Geneva NY 14456, 315 789-1776, www.genevany.com. AC: 315 ZC: 14456.

Bike Info.: Geneva Bicycle Center, 489 Exchange St., 789-5922, rentals.

Services: All. Hospital. Intercity bus: Trailways & Greyhound. Seneca Transit

Lodging: Motels. B&Bs: Belhurst, PO Box 609 NY 14, 781-0201; Farr Inn, 164 Washington St., 789-7730; Geneva On The Lake, 1001 Lochland Rd., 789-7190; Gentle Giants, 1826 CR 4, 781-2723; LaFayette, 107 LaFayette Ave., 781-0068; Paradise on the Lake, 4136 High Banks Rd., 585-9901. Camping: Both in Romulus, ~8-9 mi. S. of Geneva, Kendaia Cpgd., 5919 NY 96A (9 mi./14 km. S), 585-2244; Sampson St. Pk., NY 96A (10 mi./16 km. S), 585-6392; Cheerful Valley (Phelps NY), NY 14, (8 mi./13 km. N), 781-1222; Junius Ponds (Phelps NY), 1475 W. Townline Rd. (9 mi./14 km. N.), 781-5120.

Attractions: Mike Weaver Drain Tile Mus. and Rose Hill Mansion, Rt.96A, 789-3848; Geneva Historical/Prouty-Chew Mus./ Balmanno Cottage, 543 S. Main St., 789-5151. Smith Opera House, 82 Seneca St., 781-5483. Seneca Lake Whale Watch Festival, 35 Lakefront Dr., 781-0820. Seneca Lake St. Pk. (day use), Rtes. 5&20 at the Lake, 789-2331. Wineries: Billsboro Winery, 4760 W. Lake Rd. (5 mi. S on 14), 789-9538; Nagy's New Land Vineyards & Winery, 623 Lerch Rd.(5 mi. S on E. Lake Rd.), 585-4432; White Springs Farm Estate Winery, 65 White Springs Ln., 719-0341; Belhurst Winery, 4069 Rt. 14,

781-0201. Geneva Cubs Baseball, McDonough Pk., 789-2827; NYS Agricultural Experiment Station (grapes, fruit and wine specialties), 787-2211. Fishing: charters, City Dock. Hobart & William Smith Colleges, 337 Pulteney St., 781-3000.

1.6 (2.6)   E. Lake Rd. @ NY 96A   76.4 (123.0)
Turn South on to E. Lake Rd.
Those of us who use the E. Lake Rd. to Kennedy Rd. to NY 96A scenic route will join riders who continued South on 96A, ~8 mi. (~13 km.), down the pike.
Ontario County - Seneca County border.

2.2 (3.4)   Kime Rd./Yellow Tavern Rd.   75.8 (122.0)
                   @ E. Lake Rd.
Continue traveling South on E. Lake Rd. or NY 96A.
⇔ CAYUGA LAKE TO SENECA LAKE: NORTHERN SCENIC CONNECTING ROUTE, turn East on to Kime Rd./ Yellow Tavern Rd. to go to Cayuga Lake.

9.0 (14.5)   Kennedy Rd. @ E. Lake Rd.   69.0 (111.0)
The sign states, "Federal Property. No Thru Road." Do not go through the fence. Obey the sign (otherwise you might be confronted with a few MPs) and turn East on to Kennedy Rd. Eventually this will be a through road to Sampson St. Pk. If the sign is missing, yell yippee! and go through to the Park!

10.2 (16.4)   NY 96A @ Kennedy Rd.   67.5 (108.6)
Turn South on to NY 96A.
Camping: Kendaia Cpgd., 5919 NY 96A (9 mi./14 km. S), 585-2244.
Counterclockwise Travelers: You can continue North on NY 96A rather than turning West on to Kennedy Rd. The distance to Geneva at the North end of the Lake is about the same whether you use 96A or E. Lake Rd. Those of us who use the Kennedy Rd. to E. Lake Rd. to NY 96A scenic

route will join riders who continued North on 96A, ~8 mi. (~13 km.), up the pike.

11.8 (19.0)   Sampson St. Pk. @ NY 96A   66.2 (106.5)
Continue traveling South on NY 96A
Camping: Sampson St. Pk., 6096 NY 96A, Romulus 14541, 315 585-6392/camping reservations: 800 456-2267; bike rentals at the park, the rental folks have a limited supply of repair items but will call the Geneva Bicycle Shop for almost instantaneous parts delivery.
↻ **TRAIL ROUTE:** A 4.9 mi. (7.9 km.) from Sampson St. Pk. to Willard along the Lake shore. The Willard end of the Trail is 1.7 mi. (2.7 km.) from the Seneca Lake Circumnavigation Route intersection: Willard Rd. @ NY 96A. The stone dust/pea gravel surface is very easy to ride on except for except for bikes with slicks. If you are continuing to go 'round the Lake clockwise or are out for a short jaunt you will have to ascend from the Lake shore to NY 96A @ Upper Lake Rd./Willard Rd. Worth the effort but it is steep in parts for loaded cyclotourists.
Attractions: Sampson WW-2 Naval Mus., Sampson St. Pk., NY 96A, Romulus 14541, 800 357-1814/315 585-6203.
Note: Travelers should read the next entry, Willard Rd. @ NY 96A before they push down their pedal on the Trail!

15.7 (25.3)   Willard Rd. @ NY 96A   62.3 (100.3)
You'll recognize this intersection by the wide sweeping curve which is fine for motorists but makes my life a bit harder since its a triangle type of intersection where $a^2+b^2 \neq c^2$!
You can continue traveling South on NY 96A, meeting the Upper Lake Rd. riders about 10 mi. (16 km.) South of this intersection.
We're going to get off NY 96A and go on to shadier Upper Lake Rd. to travel South.
The key to this intersection and taking either Upper Lake Rd. southward or the Sampson St. Pk. Trail northward is knowing the location of Bonavista Golf Course, sign on NY 96A in either direction states: "Bonavista Golf Course ⇧."
↻ **Clockwise travelers** will exit NY 96 directly on to Co. Rd. 132A/Upper Lake Rd. (assuming you are following the signs to the Golf Course). Simply follow the signs to the Golf Course, its much easier than reading these directions and you'll be on Upper Lake Rd./CR 132/131.
If you do not plan to use Upper Lake Rd. as the primary road South then continue traveling South on NY 96A and disregard every bit of the directions in the rest of this entry.

But you'll be missing a very nice ride southward.

↺ Counterclockwise **travelers**: If you have been traveling North on Upper Lake Rd. & have arrived at this intersection. Turn West on to Willard Rd. At the end of Willard Rd.. past the prison, bar and pizzeria; down the slope and around a curve you'll find a stone dust/ path going North to Sampson St. Pk. Go North on the Trail!

If you have been traveling North on NY 96A. Follow the "Willard ⇧" sign. Travel straight West on to Willard Rd. Go past the prison and bar/pizzeria; down the slope and around a curve to find the Trail to Sampson St. Pk.

If you do not plan to use the Trail, then continue traveling straight from the intersection of Upper Lake Rd./Co. Rd. 132 @ Willard Rd. on to CR 132A. At NY 96A, cross to the other side of the 96A, the northbound side.

If you are traveling North on NY 96A and don't want to use the Trail, disregard the entire discussion of this intersection and let centrifugal force take you around the curve. Simply, continue traveling North on NY 96A to Geneva.

WILLARD: Restaurant/bar, pizzeria & prison.

16.3 (26.2)   Upper Lake Rd./Co. Rd. 132   61.7 (99.3)
                     (northern entrance)
                     @ Willard Rd.

Follow the signs to Bonavista Golf Course. I must warn you that there are a few significant short but steep hills from this intersection to the Golf Course entrance. After that Upper Lake Rd. (also termed Co. Rds. 132, 131, and Co. Rd. 136) has flat rolling hills. A much better and more interesting ride than NY 96A.

17.4 (28.0)   Gilbert Rd. @ Upper Lake Rd.   60.6 (97.5)
Continue traveling South on Upper Lake Rd.
⇔ CAYUGA LAKE TO SENECA LAKE: MIDDLE CONNECTING ROUTE Turn East on to Gilbert Rd. to go to Ovid and Cayuga Lake.

21.5 (34.6)   Co. Rd. 136 @ Upper Lake Rd.   56.5 (90.9)
Continue South on Upper Lake Rd.
Upper Lake Rd. has a very steep but very short up & down hill just after the cemetery going South.
Be careful not to turn on to Lower Lake Rd. Lower Lake Rd. is a one lane steeply sloped road to the Lake and Lodi Pt. St. Marine Pk. (day use, beach).
⇔ CAYUGA LAKE TO SENECA LAKE: INTERLAKEN TO LODI MIDDLE CONNECTING ROUTE. Turn East on to CR 136/Seneca St. to go to Lodi and Cayuga Lake as well as

the NY 96 Trajectory and Projectile Routes.

24.4 (39.3)   NY 414/96A   53.6 (86.3)
                  @ Upper Lake Rd. (Southern end)
      Turn South on to NY 414.

25.7 (41.7)   CR 1/Beckhorn Rd. @ NY 414   52.3 (84.2)
      The sign points to Co. Rd. 1 & Finger Lakes Nat'l. Forest.
      ↻ ⇔ NATIONAL FOREST PARALLEL ROUTE. If you'd
      like a change from NY 414 use this parallel Route.
      If you go to the Forest using Co. Rd. 1 and expect to find a
      campground you're in for a big surprise! You will have to
      travel South on Co. Rd. 4 & then East on Co. Rd. 2 (part of
      the Nat'l. Forest Parallel Route) to go to the Nat'l. Forest
      campground.
      Seneca County - Schuyler County Border

CLOCKWISE TRAVELER'S NOTE
The   SENECA   LAKE   CIRCUMNAVIGATION   Route
continues immediately after the National Forest Parallel
Route.

Read ↓   **SENECA LAKE CIRCUMNAVIGATION**   Read up ↑
Clockwise   **PRIMARY ROUTE CONTINUED**   Counterclockwise

TRAVELER'S NOTE
This is a more scenic ride than NY 414. The NYS Dep't. of Transportation flattens out the hills on NY 414 by building culverts and bridges over streams and rivers. That's one thing that makes a State road a State road. Schuyler Co. hasn't done much flattening to Co. Rds. 1, 2 & 4! Thus using this Parallel Route will be more demanding.

0.0 (0.0)   CR 1/Beckhorn Rd. @ NY 414   11.6 (18.7)
Turn East on to Co. Rd. 1/Beckhorn Rd.
↺ **Counterclockwise travelers:** Turn North on to NY 414. Hope you enjoyed NY 4 as much as I did!
VALOIS: No services. Poplar Ridge Winery, 9872 NY 414, 582-6421.

1.5 (2.4)   CR 4 @ CR 1   10.1 (16.3)
Turn South on to Co. Rd. 4.
The Nat'l. Forest is 1.7mi (2.7km) further East on Co. Rd. 1.

4.4 (7.1)   CR 2/Hector St./Picnic Area Rd.   7.2 (11.6)

@ CR 4
Continue traveling South on Co. Rd. 4.
Some of the hills on the next section of Co. Rd. 4 are short
& steep.
To go to the Nat'l. Forest Cpgd. turn East on to Co. Rd. 2/
Picnic Area Rd. The Cpgd. is 2 mi. (3.2 km.) East of this
intersection. The last .5 mi. (.8 km.) is a dirt road. Water,
access point to the Finger Lakes Trail, hiking ONLY on the
Trail. Very beautiful! B&B: Red House Country Inn, Picnic
Area Rd., 607 546-8566 (see Burdett information).
To return to NY 414 turn West on to Co. Rd. 2/Hector St.
LOGAN: Just a crossroads but there are a few businesses
along Co. Rd. 4 going southward.

9.1 (14.6)   NY 79 @ Co. Rd. 4   2.5 (4.0)
↻ Turn West on to NY 79 to go to NY 414, Watkins Glen
and southern end of Seneca Lake.
↺ Turn North on to CR 4 to go to Geneva and the northern
end of Seneca Lake.
⇔ CAYUGA LAKE TO SENECA LAKE: SOUTHERN
CONNECTING ROUTE continue to travel East on to NY 79
to go to Ithaca and the southern end of Cayuga Lake.

9.9 (15.9)   Co. Rd. 5 @ NY 79   1.7 (2.7)
Continue traveling South on NY 79 to go to Watkins Glen
and the southern end of Seneca Lake.
CR 5 is a connecting road between Burdett & NY 414.

11.6 (18.7)   NY 414 Jct. NY 79   0.0 (0.0)
Wasn't that fun & enjoyable!
↻ You're back on the main Seneca Lake Circumnavigation
Route. Read the directions from this intersection.
↺ Counterclockwise **travelers:** Turn East on to NY 79 to
use this PARALLEL NAT'L FOREST ROUTE.
⇔ CAYUGA LAKE TO SENECA LAKE: SOUTHERN
CONNECTING ROUTE. Turn East on to NY 79 to go to
Ithaca and the southern end of Cayuga Lake.

Read ↓   **SENECA LAKE CIRCUMNAVIGATION**   Read up ↑
                NAT'L FOREST PARALLEL ROUTE
Clockwise   Counterclockwise

"Behind the cascading water, deep in the hillside the explorers found a cave. Not even their native guides knew of its existence."

Read ↓   **SENECA LAKE CIRCUMNAVIGATION**   Read up ↑
Clockwise   **PRIMARY ROUTE CONTINUED**   Counterclockwise

COUNTERCLOCKWISE TRAVELER'S NOTE
The primary SENECA LAKE CIRCUMNAVIGATION ROUTE continues immediately after the National Forest Parallel Route.

28.0 (45.1)   Co. Rd. 2/Hector St. @ NY 414   50.0 (80.5)
Continue traveling South on NY 414.
⇔ NAT'L FOREST PARALLEL ROUTE: Turn East on to Co. Rd. 2/Hector St. Co. Rd. 2 intersects with Co. Rd. 4, the Nat'l. Forest Parallel Route, 2.3 mi. (3.7 km.) East of this intersection.
To go to Finger Lakes National Forest, Blueberry Cpgd. turn East on to Co. Rd. 2/Hector St. It is 3.7 mi. (6.0 km.) to the Cpgd. The last .5 mi. (.8 km.) on a dirt road.

HECTOR:
Info.: Finger Lakes Natl. Forest, 5218 Rt. 414, 546-4470. Finger Lakes Trail Conference, 6111 Visitor Center Rd., Mt. Morris NY 14510, 585 658-9320. AC: 607 ZC: 14841.
Services: convenience store/gas station.
Lodging: B&Bs: Magnolia Place, 5240 NY 414, 546-5338; Norbud Farm, 5245 Norbud Rd., 546-8388; Shandon Inn, PO Box 71, 546-4245; Windswept Farms, 3934 Tichenor Rd., 546-2864. Camping: Finger Lakes Natl. Forest, 546-4470.
Attractions: Wineries: Atwater Estate Vineyards, 5055 Rt. 414, 546-8463; Bloomer Creek Vineyard, 5315 NY 414, 546-5027; Chateau Lafayette Reneau, NY 414, 546-2062; Finger Lakes Champagne House, 6075 NY 414, 546-5115; Hazlitt 1852 Vineyards, 5712 Rt. 414, 546-9463; Leidenfrost Vineyards, 5677 NY 414, 546-2800; Logan Ridge Wine Cellars, 3800 Ball Diamond Rd., 546-6600; Rasta Ranch Vineyards, 5882 NY 414, 546-2974; Red Newt Cellars, 3675 Tichenor Rd., 546-4100; Standing Stone Vineyards, 9934 NY 414, 582-6051; Tickle Hill Winery, 3839 Ball Diamond Rd., 546-7740.

35.0 (56.3)   Co. Rd. 5/Lake Rd. @ NY 414   43.0 (69.2)
Continue traveling South on NY 414.
Turn Southeast to go to Burdett.

↳ ⇔ CAYUGA LAKE TO SENECA LAKE: SOUTHERN
CONNECTING ROUTE. Co. Rd. 5 intersects with NY 79,
the connecting road at Burdett. If you're going directly to
Ithaca, you'll save yourself a steep hill by turning here.
BURDETT: Refer to the Cayuga Lake to Seneca Lake:
Southern Connecting Route for information.

37.8 (60.8)   Rtes. 79/227 @ NY 414   40.2 (64.7)
Continue traveling South on Rtes. 414/79 to go to Watkins
Glen and the South end of Seneca Lake.
We are pedaling down a steep southward grade going into
Watkins Glen. Make certain that your bicycle is in perfect
mechanical order.
⇔ ↺ NAT'L FOREST PARALLEL ROUTE. Turn East on to
Rtes. 79/227.
⇔ CAYUGA LAKE TO SENECA LAKE: SOUTHERN
CONNECTING ROUTE. Turn   East on to Rtes. 79/227 to
go to Ithaca.

39.6 (63.7)   NY 14/Franklin St.   38.4 (64.7)
                     Jct. NY 414/Fourth St.
                     @ NY 409/Upper Glen Rd.
Here's the story about this intersection since you can go a few ways
from this point. However, I expect that you'll probably spend a
day in Watkins Glen.
⇔ ↺ SENECA LAKE CIRCUMNAVIGATION: turning North on NY
14 will set you on the continuing clockwise course 'round
Seneca Lake.
⇔ SENECA LAKE TO KEUKA LAKE: SOUTHERN CONNECTING
ROUTE, travel due West on to NY 409/Upper Glen Rd. Your tire
is pointing to NY 409.
↺ Of course the opposite is true at this intersection, going East on
Rtes. 414/228/79 will set you on the counterclockwise course
around   Seneca   Lake   via   the   SENECA   LAKE
CIRCUMNAVIGATION Route;
⇔ and on the CAYUGA LAKE TO SENECA LAKE: SOUTHERN
CONNECTING ROUTE.
NY 414 junctions with NY 14/Franklin St. and goes South. That's
pretty clear since the signs say so!
You've just past Watkins Glen Village's Chute Pk. (beach;
campsites; lots RVs & pick ups w/caps). .5 mi. (.8 km.) South on
Franklin St./NY 14/414 is the Watkins Glen St. Pk., lower
entrance for camping. Yup! You guessed it! The upper entrance
to Watkins Glen (not a camping area) is way high on NY 409.

TRAVELER'S NOTE COUNTERCLOCKWISE & WEST TO EAST - WATKINS GLEN TO ITHACA

Do not expect the route between Seneca Lake and Cayuga Lake to take you 2 or 3 hours. Besides the initial cliff going North/East from Watkins Glen, there is almost a continual rise in elevation as you progress East towards Ithaca. Although this Route appears short in distance, it may rapidly exhaust you physically. Make certain that you have sufficient snacks and water. Make certain that your bicycle is in excellent condition.

WATKINS GLEN

Information: Schuyler County CofC, 100 N. Franklin St., Watkins Glen 14891, 800 607-4552/607 535-4300. AC: 607. ZC: 14891.

Bike info.: Bike shop.

Services: All; hospital; camping supply store.

Lodging: Motels. B&Bs: 1871 Benjamin Hunt Inn, 305 6th St., 535-6659; Avant Garden, 209 Sixth St., 368-9066; Clarke House, 102 Durland Pl., 535-7965; Glen Manor House, 134 E. 4th St., 535-9737; Longhouse Manor, 3625 NY 14 at Adams Rd., 535-2565; Seneca Clipper Inn, 436 S. Franklin St., 535-2441; Seneca Lake Watch, 104 Seneca St., 535-4490; The Gables, 400 E. 4th St., 535-9604; Lamplighter Inn, 200 E. 4th St., 535-0031; Madison Guest House, 413-415 S. Madison Ave., 535-9096; Professors' Inn, 3651 NY 14N, 535-8000; Tudor Rose, 102 Durland Pl., 535-6768; Camping: Clute Mem. Pk. Cpgd., 155 S. Clute Park Dr., 535-4438; KOA Kampgrounds, NY 414S, 535-7404; Watkins Glen St. Pk., Franklin St., 535-4511/800 456-2267.

Attractions: Watkins Glen St. Pk., Franklin St., 535-4511. Watkins Glen International, 2790 CR 16, 535-2486, www.theglen.com. When there is an event at the raceway it might be difficult to obtain loding in Watkins Glen. Check the schedule. International Motor Racing Mus., 610 S. Decatur St., 535-9044; Farm Sanctuary, 3100 Aikens Rd., Tyrone, 583-2225. Wineries: Cascata Winery at The Professors' Inn, 3651 NY 14N, 535-8000; Castel Grisch Estate Winery, 3380 CR 28, 535-9614; Chateau D'Esperance, 29 N. Franklin St., 535-2944; Lakewood Vineyards, 4024 NY 14, 535-9252.

MONTOUR FALLS

Information: Montour Falls is the Village 1.5 mi. (2.4 km.) South of Watkins Glen on NY 14. Montour Falls is the southern most village on the New York State Barge Canal System. From the Marina it is possible to go to Duluth MN/Thunder Bay ON on Lake Superior; New York NY and Halifax NS on the Atlantic; and New Orleans LA on the Gulf Coast by boat. AC: 607.

Services & Facilities: hospital, grocery.
Accommodations: Motels. B&Bs: At The Falls, 101 Genesee St., 535-2445; Wisteria Way, 400 College Ave., 535-0158. Camping: Montour Marina, Seneca Lake, 535-9397; Havana Glen Cpgd., Havana Glen Rd., 535-9476.
Attraction: Montour (Sha-qua-na) Falls.

42.9 (69.0)   NY 14A Jct. NY 14   35.1 (56.5)
Continue traveling North on NY 14.
To go diagonally to Keuka Lake and Penn Yan turn North on to NY 14A. It is 21.2 mi. (31.1 km.) to Penn Yan using NY 14A all the way! At Dundee, the SENECA LAKE TO KEUKA LAKE: MIDDLE CONNECTING ROUTE meets NY 14A. Using NY 14A instead of NY 14 will bring you inland and on a shorter route rather than riding along the Seneca Lake Shore. But there will be other places to cut off & go to Keuka Lake as you go up the shore.

48.8 (78.5)   Co. Rd. 44 @ NY 14   29.2 (47.0)
Continue traveling North on NY 14. CR 44 goes to Dundee/

50.4 (81.1)   Co. Rd. 42 @ NY 14   27.6 (44.4)
Continue traveling North on NY 14 to complete your trek around Seneca Lake.
⇔ CAYUGA LAKE TO SENECA LAKE: MIDDLE CONNECTING ROUTE. Turn West on to NY 42 to go to Dundee & NY 14A. NY 14A will take you to Keuka Lake and Penn Yan.

55.6 (89.5)   Co. Rd. 36/Plum Pt. Rd. @ NY 14   22.4 (36.0)
Continue traveling North on NY 14 to circumnavigate Seneca Lake.
Turn West on Co. Rd. 36/Plum Pt. Rd. to go to Himrod.

62.2 (100.1)   NY 54 @ NY 14   15.8 (25.4)
Continue traveling North on NY 14.
⇔ SENECA LAKE TO KEUKA LAKE: OUTLET TRAIL CONNECTING ROUTE. The Outlet Route is the most direct & shortest way to go Penn Yan and Keuka Lake. Turn West on to NY 54.
The *Keuka Outlet Trail* is almost below your pedals. Backpedal a few bike lengths to the bridge on NY 14. Look down! The last time I used the Trail a huge tortoise followed me as I was riding. I think it was faster than me! At the minimum, hybrid tires are necessary. But it is an efficient way to go to Penn Yan and Keuka Lake. Turn on to Seneca St. to go down to the Trail. Seneca St. is on the East side of NY 14 at your wheel.

Turn East on to NY 54 to go to Dresden and the Seneca Lake shore.

DRESDEN: refer to the Seneca Lake to Keuka Lake: Outlet Trail Route for Dresden information.

75.6 (121.7)   Rtes. 5&20 @ NY 14   2.4 (3.9)
Turn East on to Rtes. 5&20 to return to the starting point.
⇔ Turn West on to Rtes. 5&20 to go to Keuka Lake or Canandaigua Lake.

78.0 (125.5)   NY 96A @ Rtes. 5&20   0.0 (0.0)
A long ride but well worth it. **GENEVA**
↺ ↻ SENECA LAKE CIRCUMNAVIGATION Route: turn South on to NY 96A to go to Watkins Glen and the southern end of Seneca Lake.
⇔ CAYUGA LAKE TO SENECA LAKE: CONNECTING ROUTES
⇔ CAYUGA LAKE TO KEUKA LAKE: CONNECTING ROUTES.

Read ↓   **SENECA LAKE CIRCUMNAVIGATION**   Read up ↑
Clockwise   Counterclockwise

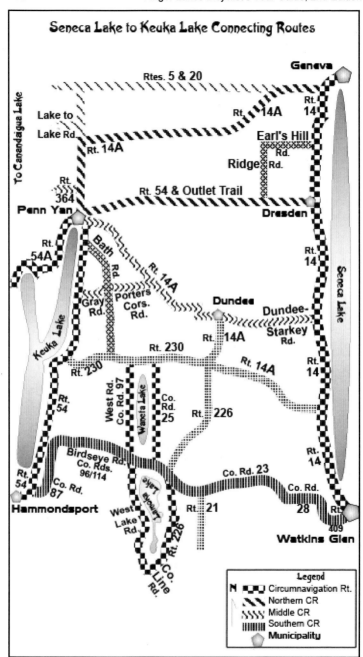

Read ↓	**SENECA LAKE TO KEUKA LAKE**	Read up ↑
E to W	**NORTHERN CONNECTING ROUTE**	W to E

0.0 (0.0)   NY 96A @ Rtes. 5&20   20.6 (33.2)
Travel West on Rtes. 5&20 to go to Penn Yan and Keuka
Lake.
↻ ⇔ SENECA LAKE CIRCUMNAVIGATION Route: turn
South on to NY 96A to go to Watkins Glen and the
southern end of Seneca Lake.
⇔ CAYUGA LAKE TO SENECA LAKE: NORTHERN
DIRECT CONNECTING ROUTE: travel East on Rtes. 5&20
to go to Seneca Falls and Cayuga Lake.

2.1 (3.4)   E. Castle St. @ Rtes. 5&20   18.5 (29.8)
Continue traveling on Rtes. 5&20 or on the bike path at the
shore. If you are on the bike path, cross Rtes. 5&20 at a
traffic light. Rtes. 5&20 is too dangerous to *run across*!
A bit of a grammar lesson here is in order. All of us locals
term Routes NY 5 and US 20 as one entity, *5&20* usually
said very rapidly.
GENEVA: Turn North on to E. Castle St. to go to the
Geneva business area (bike shop). Refer to the Seneca
Lake Circumnavigation Route for Geneva information.

2.7 (4.3)   NY 14 @ Rtes. 5&20   17.9 (28.8)
Continue traveling West on Rtes. 5&20.
↻ SENECA LAKE CIRCUMNAVIGATION Route: turn
South on to NY 14 to 'round Seneca Lake counterclock-
wise. You've just climbed a ramp on Rtes. 5&20. When you
are traveling West on Rtes. 5&20, a ramp leads you NY 14.
You can not make a left hand turn across 5&20 to go on to
NY 14. The ramp is the first street going right after leaving
the Lake shore. The signs leading you to NY 14 are very
obscure.

4.6 (7.4)   Rtes. 14A/245 @ Rtes. 5&20   16.0 (25.7)
Turn South on to Rtes. 14A/245 to go to Penn Yan and
Keuka Lake.
⇔ Travel West on Rtes. 5&20 to go to Canandaigua Lake.

7.8 (12.6)   NY 245 Jct. NY 14A   12.8 (20.6)
Continue traveling South on NY 14A to go to Keuka Lake.
⇔ Keuka Lake Middle Connecting Route. Going West on
to NY 245 will take you to Naples and the southern end of
Canandaigua Lake.

8.3 (13.4)   Lake to Lake Rd. @ NY 14A   12.3 (19.8)
⇔ KEUKA LAKE TO CANANDAIGUA LAKE: ROLLIN'
HILLS CONNECTING ROUTE turn West on to Lake to
Lake Rd. .7 mi. (1.1 km.) West on Lake to Lake Rd. at Post
Rd. the official Connecting Route intersects with Lake to
Lake Rd.

9.0 (14.5)   Post Rd. @ NY 14A   11.6 (18.7)
⇔ KEUKA LAKE TO CANANDAIGUA LAKE: ROLLIN'
HILLS CONNECTING ROUTE: turn North on to Post Rd.
and begin to follow the Rollin' Hills Connecting Route from
this intersection.

19.7 (31.7)   NY 364 @ NY 14A   0.9 (1.4)
Continue riding South on NY 14A into Penn Yan to
circumnavigate Keuka Lake.
⇔ KEUKA LAKE TO CANANDAIGUA LAKE: MIDDLE
CONNECTING ROUTE, turn West on to NY 364.

20.4 (32.8)   NY 54A & NY 54 North @ NY 14A   0.2 (0.3)
Continue traveling South on NY 14A to 'round Keuka Lake,
clockwise.
⇔ ↻ Turn West/South on to NY 54A to go to the West
Branch of Keuka Lake and around Lake Keuka Lake
counterclockwise.
⇔ SENECA LAKE TO KEUKA LAKE: OUTLET TRAIL
CONNECTING ROUTE, turn East, well really North, on to
NY 54 North to go to Dresden and Seneca Lake. The well
maintained dirt Outlet Trail parallels NY 54.

20.6 (33.2)   NY 54 South Jct. NY 14A   0.0 (0.0)
↻ KEUKA LAKE CIRCUMNAVIGATION Route: turn South
on to NY 54 to 'round Keuka Lake, clockwise.
⇔ Use NY 14A to go diagonally to Seneca Lake via
Dundee.
PENN YAN: The KEUKA LAKE CIRCUMNAVIGATION
Route has the Penn Yan information.

Read ↓   **SENECA LAKE TO KEUKA LAKE**   Read up ↑
E to W   **NORTHERN CONNECTING ROUTE**   W to E

TRAVELER'S NOTE

The Keuka Lake Outlet Trail essentially parallels NY 54. This is a "Rails to Trails" trail in the process of being improved. Currently it is a wide 10 ft. (3 m.) cleared and maintained dirt trail. It is very beautiful and wooded. I saw large tortoises, beautiful birds, magnificent butterflies, as well as the usual mammals scurrying about on the path.

DRESDEN

BiKE Info.: The (Keuka Lake) Outlet Trail: Dresden to Penn Yan, 2375 NY 14A, Penn Yan 14527, 315 536-3791. Crossroads Bike Rentals, 88 Main St.(NY 54 @ NY 14), Dresden 14441, 315 531-5311.
Services: Convenience store/gas station.
Attractions: Robert Ingersoll Mus., 61 Main St., Dresden 14441, 315 536-1074; Outlet Trail.
Lodging: Dresden Manor B&B, 58 Cornelia St., 536-2552.

0.0 (0.0)   Seneca St./ NY 54 @ NY 14   5.0 (8.0)
Turn West on to NY 54.
↻ ↺ SENECA LAKE CIRCUMNAVIGATION Route.
⇔ Outlet Trail: A well maintained dirt trail connecting Penn Yan to Dresden. The entrance to the Outlet Trail is below your wheel! Go to the bridge on NY 14. Look down! Thar' it is! Just ride down Seneca St. and you'll find your wheel at the Trail access point.

5.0 (8.0)   NY 14A @ NY 54   0.0 (0.0)
↻ KEUKA LAKE CIRCUMNAVIGATION Route, turn South on to NY 54 to 'round Keuka Lake, clockwise.
⇔ The Penn Yan entrance to the Outlet Trail is at the Birkett Mills building on NY 54 North.
PENN YAN: Refer to the Keuka Lake Circumnavigation Route for Penn Yan information.

| Read ↓ | **SENECA LAKE TO KEUKA LAKE** | Read up ↑ |
| E to W | **MIDDLE CONNECTING ROUTE** | W to E |

TRAVELER'S NOTE

This route connects the middle of Seneca Lake to the middle of the East Branch of Keuka Lake.

0.0 (0.0)   Co. Rd. 42 @ NY 14   11.0 (17.7)
Turn West on to either CR 42 or CR 40 to go to the middle of Keuka Lake (East Branch/East side).
🚲 ↺ Seneca Lake clockwise travelers use CR 42/ Dundee/ Lakemont Rd. to go to Dundee.
🚲 ↺ Seneca Lake Counterclockwise travelers use CR 40/ Dundee/Starkey Rd. to go to Dundee.
The distance is about the same using either CR 40 or CR 42. CR 40 is just North of CR 42 and Pythagogoras helps you cut off a few miles!

2.0 (3.2)   Co. Rd. 40 Jct. Co. Rd. 42   9.0 (14.5)
                   @ Jessup Rd.
Continue traveling West on CR 40.

3.2 (5.1)   NY 14A @ Co. Rd. 40/Seneca St.   7.8 (12.6)
Turn North on to NY 14A/Main St. CR 40/Dundee/Starkey Rd. is renamed Seneca St. in Dundee.

DUNDEE

Info.: Dundee CofC, PO Box 12, Dundee 14837.
     AC: 607. ZC: 14837.
Services: Restaurants, grocery, bank, hardware and other stores.
Lodging: B&Bs: 1819 Red Brick Inn, 2081 Route 230, 243-8844; Keuka Overlook Inn, 5777 Old Bath Rd., 292-6877; Nautical Nights, 4280 Locust Rd., 243-7703; Scottish Glen, 107 Maclean Ln., 243-5678; South Glenora Tree Farm, 546 South Glenora Rd., 243-7414; Sunrise Landing, 4986 Apple Rd., 243-7548; Tobehanna Creek, 4229 Perry Hill Rd., 243-7616.
Attractions: Dundee Hist. Soc., 26 Seneca St., 243-7047. Wineries: Fulkerson Winery, 5576 NY 14, 243-7883; Glenora Wine Cellars, 5435 NY 14, 243-9500; Hermann J. Wiemer Vineyard, PO Box 38 NY 14, 243-7971; Hickory Hollow, 5289 NY 14, 243-9114; Keuka Overlook Wine Cellars, 5777 Old Bath-Gardner Rd., 292-6877; McGregor Vineyard, 5503 Dutch St., 292-3999; Villa Bellangelo, 150 Poplar Pt., 243-8602; Woodbury Vineyards, 4141 NY 14, 243-8925.

3.4 (5.5)   NY 14A/Main St.   7.6 (12.2)
                   Jct. NY 14A/Millard Rd.
Follow the NY 14A North signs. This is simply a right angle
turn but if the sign is missing....

4.9 (7.9)   NY 230 @ NY 14A   6.1 (9.8)
Continue traveling North on NY 14A.
NY 230 does lead South and intersects with the Keuka
Lake Circumnavigation Route in 7.7 mi. (12.4 km.).

6.4 (10.3)   Porters Corners Rd. @ NY 14A   4.6 (7.4)
Turn West on to Porters Corners. Rd. to go to the Middle of
Keuka Lake's East Branch.
🚲 ↻ The most direct route to Penn Yan and the northern
end of the East Branch of Keuka Lake is to travel
Northwest on NY 14A. Penn Yan is 8 mi. (12.8 km.) from
this intersection.

8.4 (13.5)   Co. Rd. 17/Bath Rd.   2.4 (4.2)
                   @ Porters Cors. Rd.
Turn North on to CR 17/Bath Rd.

8.6 (14.2)   Gray Rd. @ Co. NY 17/Bath Rd.   2.2 (3.5)
Turn West on to Gray Rd.

11.0 (17.7)   NY 54 @ Gray Rd.   0.0 (0.0)
↻ KEUKA LAKE CIRCUMNAVIGATION Route: Turn South
on to NY 54 to go to Hammondsport & the southern end of
Keuka Lake.
↺ KEUKA LAKE CIRCUMNAVIGATION Route: Turn North
on to NY 54 to go to Penn Yan & the northern end of the
East Branch of Keuka Lake.
Penn Yan is 8.5 mi. (13.6 km.) North from this point on NY
54. Hammondsport is 4.8 mi. (7.8 km.) South from this
point on NY 54.

| Read ↓ | **SENECA LAKE TO KEUKA LAKE** | Read up ↑ |
| E to W | **MIDDLE CONNECTING ROUTE** | W to E |

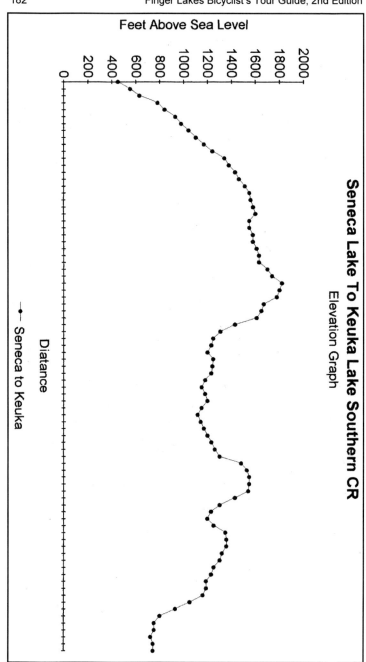

Seneca Lake To Keuka Lake Southern CR

Elevation Graph

Feet Above Sea Level

Distance

Seneca to Keuka

Hey! These Aren't Finger Lakes

These two lakes, Waneta Lake and Lamoka Lake, smack in the middle of the Finger Lakes Region are geologically not Finger Lakes! Both Lakes were formed by geologic processes other than glacial action on the peneplain. There is so little geologic information available on these two Lakes that a dissertation can be written on them.

A delightful ride around these two Lakes can be accomplished in one day. The two Lakes are beautifully situated in a valley between Seneca Lake and Keuka Lake. Once you reach the Lakes it is a basically level route. But getting there involves a bit of ascending and descending!

Although each Lake has its own circumnavigation route, their proximity makes it ideal to do a figure 8 ride around the two Lakes.

TRAVELER'S NOTE

There are no services past the intersection of Tyrone Hamlet or NY 226 @ Co. Rd. 23. Be prepared.

Clockwise	**WANETA - LAMOKA FIGURE 8**	Counterclockwise
Read ↓	**WANETA LAKE CIRCUMNAVIGATION**	Read up ↑

0.0 (0.0}   NY 54 @ NY 230   10.7 (17.2)
Turn East on to NY 230.
⇔ ↻ ↺ KEUKA LAKE CIRCUMNAVIGATION Route.
Lodging: Wright's Cottages on Waneta Lake, 9472 Lakeshore Dr., 292-6786; Heart's Delight Campsites (Waneta Lake), 9533 Lakeshore Dr., 607 292-6955

1.9 (3.1)   Co. Rd. 97/West Lake Rd.   8.8 (14.2)
                   @ NY 230
Continue traveling East on NY 230.
↺ ☞ Turn South on to go counterclockwise around Waneta Lake or to begin a figure 8 around both Lakes. Or to begin a true figure 8 (☞ symbol) around both Lakes. Steuben County - Schuyler County border.

2.3 (3.7)   Co. Rd. 25 @ NY 230   8.4 (13.5)
↺ Turn South on CR 25.
☞ ↺ Figure 8 and counterclockwise Waneta Lake bicyclists turn West on to NY 230 to complete their routes.

5.8 (9.3)   Co. Rd. 23 @ Co. Rd. 25   4.9 (7.9)

↺ Turn West on to CR 23 to complete the circumnavigation of Waneta Lake.

↷ Turn East on CR 23 to do the figure 8. CR 23 will take you to the Lamoka Lake Circumnavigation Route, going clockwise 'round that Lake.

⇔ SENECA LAKE TO KEUKA LAKE: SOUTHERN CONNECTING ROUTE.

6.5 (10.5)   West Lake Rd./Co. Rd. 24/97   4.2 (6.8)
                   @ Co. Rd. 23

↺ Turn North on to West Rd./CR 24/97 to complete the circumnavigation of Waneta Lake.

It is easy to miss this intersection. West Lake Rd. has a very small street sign on the South side of CR 23. It does not have a numerical marking - Schuyler CR 24. As it crosses the Schuyler Co. - Steuben Co. border it is renumbered as CR 97/West Lake Rd. Politics!

↷ Figure 8 travelers, turn East on to CR 23.

↺ Lamoka Lake counterclockwise circumnavigators turn South on to West Lake Rd.

10.0 (16.1)   Co. Rd. 87   0.7 (1.1)
                   West Lake Rd./Co. Rd. 97/24

↺ Continue traveling North on West Lake Rd./CR 97/24.

↺ ↷ Figure 8ers continue traveling South on West Lake Rd./CR 97/24.

10.7 (17.2)   NY 230   0.0 (0.0)
                   @ Co. Rd. 97/24/West Lake Rd.

↺ Back to the starting point.

↷ Figure 8 riders will turn South on to CR 97/24/West Lake Rd.

🚲 ⇔ Turn West on to NY 230 to return to the Keuka Lake Circumnavigation Route.

TRAVELER'S NOTE

There are no services past the intersection of Tyrone Hamlet or NY 226 @ Co. Rd. 23. Be prepared.

Clockwise   **WANETA - LAMOKA FIGURE 8**   Counterclockwise
Read ↓   **WANETA LAKE CIRCUMNAVIGATION**   Read up ↑

Clockwise	**WANETA - LAMOKA FIGURE 8**	Counterclockwise
Read ↓	**LAMOKA LAKE CIRCUMNAVIGATION**	Read up ↑

TRAVELER'S NOTE
Unlike the Waneta Lake Circumnavigation Route, Lamoka Lake is considerably hillier. Be prepared! There are very few services around either Lake.

0.0 (0.0)   Co. Rd. 25 @ Co. Rd. 23   12.1 (19.5)
↻ ♋ Travel East on Co. Rd. 23 circumnavigate Lamoka Lake and to do the bottom ½ of the figure 8. CR 23 will take you to the Lamoka Lake Circumnavigation Route, going clockwise 'round that Lake.
↻ WANETA LAKE CIRCUMNAVIGATION, turn West on to NY 23 to complete the circumnavigation of Waneta Lake.
⇔ SENECA LAKE TO KEUKA LAKE: SOUTHERN CONNECTING ROUTE uses CR 23.

0.5 (0.8)   Lamuka Lake Rd. @ Co. Rd. 23   11.6 (18.7)
↻ ♋ Turn South on to Lamuka Lake Rd. to circumnavigate Lamoka Lake.
⇔ Continue traveling E. on CR 23 to go to Watkins Glen.
↺ Counterclockwise travelers circumnavigating Lamoka Lake will turn West here to return to West Lake Rd.

1.7 (2.7)   Cemetery Rd. @ Lamoka Lake Rd.   10.4 (16.7)
Turn/continue traveling South on Lamoka Lake Rd.

2.5 (4.0)   NY 226 @ Lamoka Lake Rd.   9.6 (6.0)
↻ ↺ Turn South on to NY 226.
↺ Counterclockwise travelers: turn West on to Lamoka
Lake Rd.

6.2 (10.0)   Yawger Hill Rd. @ NY 226   5.9 (9.5)
↻ ↺ Turn West on to Yawger Hill Rd.
↺ Counterclockwise travelers, turn North on NY 226.

6.7 (10.8)   West Lake Rd.@ Yawger Hill Rd.   5.4 (8.7)
↻ ↺ Turn North on to West Lake Rd.
↺ Counterclockwise travelers: turn Southeast on to
Yawger Hill Rd.

11.4 (18.3)   West Lake Rd. @ Co. Rd. 23   0.7 (1.1)
↻ ↺ Turn East on to CR 23.
↺ Counterclockwise travelers, turn South on to West Lake
Rd. to go around Lamoka Lake.
Go due North across NY 23, on to West Lake Rd. and the
Waneta Lake Circumnavigation Route.
⇔ SENECA LAKE TO KEUKA LAKE: SOUTHERN
CONNECTING ROUTE, turn West on to CR 23 to go to
Hammondsport. Turn East on to CR 23 to go to Watkins
Glen and the southern end of Seneca Lake.

12.1 (19.5)   Co. Rd. 23 @ Co. Rd. 25   0.0 (0.0)
You've done it! 'Rounded Lamoka Lake!

TRAVELER'S NOTE
Unlike the Waneta Lake Circumnavigation Route, Lamoka
Lake is considerably hillier. Be prepared! There are no
services going around either Lake.

| Clockwise | **WANETA - LAMOKA FIGURE 8** | Counterclockwise |
| Read ↓ | **LAMOKA LAKE CIRCUMNAVIGATION** | Read up ↑ |

Read ↓	**SENECA LAKE TO KEUKA LAKE**	Read up ↑
E to W	**SOUTHERN CONNECTING ROUTE**	W to E

0.0 (0.0)   NY 414 Jct. NY 409   21.5 (34.6)
                   @ Franklin St.
That is: Fourth St. Jct. Upper Glen St. @ Franklin St.
Travel West on to NY 409. The sign will state: *To NY 23/28,
Hammondsport NY.*
WATKINS GLEN information is in the Seneca Lake
Circumnavigation Route.

0.5 (0.8)   Co. Rd. 28   21.0 (33.8)
                   @ NY 409/Upper Glen St.
Turn North on to Co. Rd. 28.

1.7 (2.7)   Co. Rd. 28 Jct. Co. Rd. 23   19.8 (31.9)
Bear/Turn Northwest on to CR 23/Hammondsport Rd.
You're climbin'!
🚲 ⇔ CR 28 goes North to NY 14A. NY 14A can be used to
go to Dundee and the Seneca Lake to Keuka Lake: Middle
Connecting Route.

5.4 (8.7)   Co. Rd. 27   16.1 (25.9)
                   @ Co. Rd.. 23/Hammondsport Rd.
Continue traveling West on CR 23/Hammondsport Rd.
🚲 Going North on to CR 27 will bring you to Dundee & the
Middle Connecting Route between Seneca & Keuka Lakes.
CHAPMAN CORNERS: No services.

6.9 (11.1)   Co. Rd. 21 @ Co. Rd. 23   14.6 (23.5)
Continue traveling West on Co. Rd. 23/Hammondsport Rd.
To enter Sugar Hill St. Rec. Area turn South on to Co. Rd.
21. 1 mi. (1.6 km.) on Co. Rd. 21 is Tower Rd., a dirt road.
Turn on to Tower Rd. to climb the Fire Tower! Camping
(primitive, no facilities) is possible in the Rec. Area.

10.6 (17.1)   NY 226   10.9 (17.5)
                   @ Co. Rd. 23/Hammondsport Rd.
Continue traveling West on Co. Rd. 23/Hammondsport Rd.
Follow the *To Tyrone NY 23* signs to cross NY 226.
Use extreme caution from the Tyrone Post Office on CR 23
to just past Tyrone Village. You will be climbing a fairly
steep hill (up going West) on a very narrow shoulderless
roadway. Most motorists accelerate as they climb the hill.
Those going down the hill tend travel fast. Overhanging
trees make it very shady. Make certain that your clothing

makes you stand out under shady conditions and put both your front and rear lights on.

11.1 (17.9)   Tyrone Village   10.4 (16.7)
                   @ Co. Rd. 23/Hammondsport Rd.
Continue traveling West on CR 23/Hammondsport Rd.
TYRONE: Local grocery/convenience store/gas station. If you are planning to circumnavigate either Waneta Lake or Lamoka Lake then I suggest you stop here to get a few supplies.

12.4 (20.0)   Co. Rd. 25 @ Co. Rd. 23   9.1 (14.6)
Continue traveling West on CR 23 to go to Hammondsport.
⇥ CR 25 will take you on the East side of Waneta Lake and meets NY 230 ~4 mi. (1.2 km.) North of this intersection. At NY 230, turn West for 1 mi. (1.6 km.) to bump into NY 54 and the Keuka Lake Circumnavigation Route.

13.5 (21.7)   West Lake Rd.   8.0 (12.9)
                   @ Co. Rd. 23/Hammondsport Rd.
Continue traveling on Co. Rd. 23.
Hey, West Rd. goes North to West Lake Rd. Using West Lake Rd., NY 230, CR 25, and CR 23, you can circumnavigate Waneta Lake! West Lake Rd. North of CR 23 is Steuben CR 97. There is no street sign for this road on the northern side of CR 23; but it is the first street after CR 25 going westward on CR 23.

13.8 (22.2)   Co. Rd. 114/96/Birdseye Rd.   7.7 (12.4)
                   @ Co. Rd. 23
Y intersection. Bear on to the North Fork, Birdseye Rd. (you can also take the southern fork). Signs will direct you to Hammondsport. Follow them!
Schuyler Co.-Steuben County Border. This means the numbers of all roads change! Fun and games! For instance CR 23 becomes CR 114 and then becomes CR 96.   Just ride West!

13.7 (22.0)   Rd. 87/Hammondsport-Wayne Rd.   4.2 (6.8)
                   @ Birdseye Rd./ Co. Rd. 96
Turn South on to CR 87/Hammondsport-Wayne Rd.

19.3 (31.1)   NY 54   2.2 (3.5)
                   @ Co. Rd. 87/Hammondsport-Wayne Rd.
↺ KEUKA LAKE CIRCUMNAVIGATION Route, turn South on to NY 54 to go to Hammondsport and 'round Keuka Lake in a clockwise direction.

↺ KEUKA LAKE CIRCUMNAVIGATION Route, turn North on to NY 54 to go to Penn Yan and around Keuka Lake in a counterclockwise direction.

20.5 (33.0)   NY 54 @ Main St.   1.0 (1.6)
Turn West on to Main St.
HAMMONDSPORT: Refer to the Keuka Lake Circumnavigation Route for information.
You're probably going to stop in HammondspoNY The following directions are simply to get you around downtown HammondspoNY It is pretty obvious which way to go to NY 54A and the West side of Keuka Lake.

HAMMONDSPORT STREETS
20.7 (33.3)   Lake St. @ Main St.   0.8 (1.3)
Continue traveling West on Main St. to go around Keuka Lake clockwise.
20.9 (33.6)   Sheather St. @ Main St.   0.6 (1.0)
Turn North on to Sheather St.
Sheather St. is the central shopping street.
21.2 (34.1)   Mechanic St. @ Sheather St.   0.3 (0.5)
Turn West on to Mechanic St.
21.4 (34.4)   William St. @ Mechanic St.   0.1 (0.2)
Turn North on to William St.
21.5 (34.6)   NY 54A @ William St.   0.0 (0.0)
↺ Bear North on to NY 54A to go clockwise around Keuka Lake.
HAMMONDSPORT STREETS

Read ↓	**SENECA LAKE TO KEUKA LAKE**	Read up ↑
E to W	**SOUTHERN CONNECTING ROUTE**	W to E

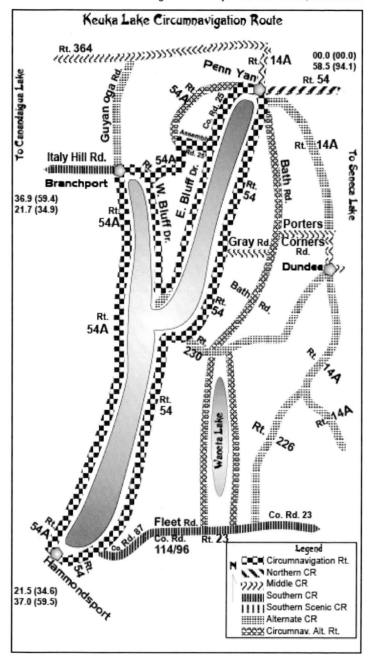

Moo and Yum

Most people associate New York State with New York City. There is no doubt that *The City* is important to the economic, social and political structure of the State. Few people realize that New York State's second largest industry is agriculture.

The peneplain which formed the original land form was itself a series of sedimentary layers of eroded materials rich with minerals. Glacial erosion not only carved the landscape to its current configuration it also brought soil and mineral nutrients from the Adirondacks and ancient Lake Iroquois. Add to this base a climate which encouraged the growth of forests and the result is layers of humus waiting for agricultural development.

For a good part of the 19th the Finger Lakes Region functioned as America's *bread basket*. To transport the agricultural largess of the Region to the population centers of the East Coast an extensive system of canals were developed by private entrepreneurs which linked the Lakes with the Erie Canal. The Seneca-Cayuga Canal is the sole remaining functioning canal connecting those Lakes to *The City* as well as to the Mid West markets. Railroads and eventually trucks supplanted the canals as primary transport mediums. What remains is a region dotted with abandoned canal and railroad beds which are now being converted for recreational uses - off road bicycling and hiking trails.

The geography of the Finger Lakes Region is not conducive to large scale grazing of beef cattle or vast flat farms growing one cash grain or corn crop. Yes, there are large commercial style farms of thousands of acres. In the Finger Lakes large scale farms are family owned and operated rather than owned by non-resident corporations and operated by employees as in the farms on the Great Plains. Most of the family farms in the area are based on only 500-1000 acres. Dairy cows, sheep, poultry, wheat, buckwheat, corn, vegetables, orchard fruits, grapes and timber are the mainstay of the area's agricultural economy. The bounty of raising dairy animals - cows and goats - are processed locally into milk, cheese and ice cream. Most of the world's buckwheat, normally a grain associated with central Europe, is processed in Penn Yan. The harvested timber goes both to the construction industry and to the area's furniture factories.

The most celebrated agricultural product of the Finger Lakes area is wine. The New York State Agricultural Experimental Station in Geneva develops new varieties of grapes and other fruits (among its other research activities) specifically to create new varietal wines. The Experimental Station and the Finger Lakes vintners have been immensely successful in producing exceptional white wines and sparkling (champagne) wines. Small and medium sized family owned and estate bottled wineries coexist with huge factory type wine production facilities. Almost all wineries in the Region have tasting rooms and most will give you a tour of the pressing and bottling facilities as well as the vineyards themselves. During the summer the vines are nurtured with weeding, pruning, and grafting. Grape arbor activities are labor intensive and demand a high degree of skill from the vintner to obtain high quality grapes to produce fine wine. Taste the wines as you travel along the Lakes.

It is in September when the grape and fruit harvests are in full swing that the Finger Lakes come alive with fresh baked fruit pies with the regional specialty being grape pies and tarts.

Keep in mind that BWI, bicycling while intoxicated is treated the same as driving while intoxicated. Take the bottle of wine back to your campsite or lodging. Purchase some local cheese and fresh baked bread. As the setting sun's rays glisten off the sailboats and water enjoy the bounties of the land.

Read ↓ **KEUKA LAKE CIRCUMNAVIGATION** Read up ↑
Clockwise   Counterclockwise

0.0 (0.0)   NY 54A/Elm St.   44.6 (71.8)
                 @ NY 14A & NY 54 South/Liberty St.
Turn South on to NY 14A/54 South
↺ Keuka Lake counterclockwise circumnavigators turn South on to NY 54A.
⇔ KEUKA LAKE TO CANANDAIGUA LAKE: ROLLIN' HILLS CONNECTING ROUTE.
⇔ SENECA LAKE TO KEUKA LAKE: CONNECTING ROUTES.

PENN YAN

Info.: Penn Yan CofC, 2375 Rte. 14A, Penn Yan 14527, 315 536-3111, 800 686-9283/315 536-3111; Finger Lakes Tourism Alliance, 309 Lake St., 800 548-4386/315 536-7488; NY Wine & Grape Found., 350 Elm St., Penn Yan 14527, 315 536-7442. AC 315. ZC: 14527.

Bike Info.: Weaver's Bicycle Shop, 1220 NY 14A, 536-3012. Keuka Lake Outlet Trail, trailhead at 104 Lake St. in Penn Yan, see the Seneca to Keuka Lake: Outlet Trail Connecting Route.

Services: All, hospital.

Lodging: Motels. B&Bs: Adda Trimmer House, 145 East Main St., 536-8304; Finton's Landing, 661 East Lake Rd., 536-3146; Fox Inn, 158 Main St., 536-3101; Los Gatos, 1491 NY 14A, 536-0686; Merritt Hill Manor, 2756 Coates Rd., 536-7682; Robertson House, 107 Court St., 536-9273; Top O' the Lake, 128 South Ave., 536-4940; Tudor Hall, 762 E. Bluff Dr., 536-9962; Wagener Estate, 351 Elm St., 536-4591.

Attractions: Agricultural Memories Mus., 1110 Townline Rd., 536-1206; Oliver House Mus., 300 Main St., 536-7318; Keuka Lake Outlet Trail,; Birkett Buckwheat Mills, 163 Main St., 536-3311. Many places to purchase buckwheat hull filled pillows and other buckwheat hull filled items.

Wine: Anthony Road Wine Cellars, 1225 Anthony Rd., 536-2182; Barrington Cellars, 2690 Gray Rd., 536-9686; Keuka Spring Vineyards, 273 E. Lake Rd., 536-3147; Rooster Hill Vineyards, 489 NY 54 S., 536-4773.

0.2 (0.3)   NY 54/Lake St.   44.4 (71.5)
                   @ NY 14A/Liberty St.
Turn South on to NY 54/Lake St.

1.8 (2.9)   Co. Rd. 17/Bath Rd. @ NY 54   0.0 (0.0)
Continue traveling South on NY 54
⇔ ↺ ↻ BATH RD RAMBLE PARALLEL ROUTE If
you really dislike the glassy smooth surface of NY 54
then turn South on to Co. Rd. 17/Bath Rd.

Crystal Clear Air, Azure Lake,
Verdant Green Trees with a Touch of Fall Color.

TRAVELER'S NOTE
The primary Keuka Lake Circumnavigation Route continues immediately after the Bath Rd Ramble Parallel Route.

Read ↓	**KEUKA LAKE CIRCUMNAVIGATION**	Read up ↑
Clockwise	**PRIMARY ROUTE CONTINUED**	Counterclockwise

0.0 (0.0)   Bath Rd./Co. Rd. 17 @ NY 54   15.0 (24.1)
Travel South on Bath Rd./Co. Rd. 17
Counterclockwise travelers: Turn North on to NY 54.

6.8 (10.9)   Gray Rd. @ Bath Rd.   8.2 (13.2)
Continue South on Bath Rd.
↰ ↻ ↺ Turn West on to Gray Rd. to return to the main
Keuka Lake Circumnavigation Route. Then go back to
Penn Yan on NY 54 to form a 18.6 mi. (30.0 km.) loop.
Or continue clockwise around the Lake on NY 54.

12.2 (19.6)   Wayne Rd. Jct. Bath Rd.   2.8 (4.5)
                     Co. Rd. 17 Jct. Co. Rd. 26
Continue traveling South on Co. Rd. 26/Wayne Rd.
Yup! You've crossed into Schuyler County & the road
number & name changed.

13.2 (21.2)   NY 230 @ Co. Rd. 26/Wayne Rd.   1.8 (2.9)
                     Co. Rd. 87 @ Co. Rd. 26/Wayne Rd.
↰ ↻ ↺ Turn West on to NY 230 to return to the main
Keuka Lake Circumnavigation Route.
↰ ⇔ ↺ Alternatively, continue traveling South on Co. Rd.
87 to go to Hammondsport on the southern end of Keuka
Lake via Seneca Lake to Keuka Lake: Southern
Connecting Route which intersects Co. Rd. 87 in 2.3 mi.
(3.7 km.).
WAYNE

15.0 (24.1)   NY 54 @ NY 230   0.0 (0.0)
↺ ↻ KEUKA LAKE CIRCUMNAVIGATION Route.
↺ Turn South on to NY 54 to go to Hammondsport and the
southern end of Keuka Lake.
↻ Turn North on to NY 54 to go to Penn Yan and the
northern end of the East Branch of Keuka Lake.

Read ↓   **KEUKA LAKE CIRCUMNAVIGATION**   Read up ↑
Clockwise   **PRIMARY ROUTE CONTINUED**   Counterclockwise

TRAVELER'S NOTE
The primary Keuka Lake Circumnavigation Route continues immediately after the Bath Rd Ramble Parallel Route.

3.8 (6.1)   East Lake Rd. (N. entrance)   40.8 (65.7)
                   @ NY 54
Turn South on to East Lake Rd. to go close to the shore. The shore is lined with cottages and East Lake Rd. is narrow but delightful.
It is the same distance whether you use NY 54 or East Lake Rd.

8.0 (12.9)   NY 54 @ East Lake Rd. @ Gray Rd.   36.6 (59.0)
Turn South on to NY 54 to continue 'rounding Keuka Lake.
⇔ SENECA LAKE TO KEUKA LAKE: MIDDLE CONNECTING ROUTE, turn East on to Gray Rd. to go to Dundee and Seneca Lake.

12.8 (20.6)   NY 230 @ NY 54   31.8 (51.2)
Continue traveling South on NY 54.
🚲 ⇔ ↺ KEUKA LAKE CIRCUMNAVIGATION: BATH RD RAMBLE ROUTE. **Counterclockwise travelers** can use NY 230, going East, to connect with the Ramble Route.

20.3 (32.7)   NY 87/Hammondsport-Wayne Rd.   24.3 (39.1)
                     @ NY 54
Continue traveling South on NY 54 to go to the southern end of Keuka Lake.
⇔ SENECA LAKE TO KEUKA LAKE: SOUTHERN CONNECTING ROUTE, turn East on to Co. Rd. 87 to go Watkins Glen and Seneca Lake.
⇔ ↺ KEUKA LAKE CIRCUMNAVIGATION: BATH RD RAMBLE ROUTE, **Counterclockwise travelers** NY 87, North connects with the Ramble Route.

21.5 (34.6)   Main St. @ NY 54   23.1 (37.2)
Turn West on to Main St.

HAMMONDSPORT

Info.: Hammondsport CofC, Box 539, Main St., Hammondsport 14840, 800 538-5228/607 569-2989. AC: 607. ZC. 14840.

Services: All, pharmacy, no hospital.

Lodging: Motels. B&Bs: 18 Vine Inn, 18 Vine St., 569-3039; Abundant Grace, 14498 NY 54, 292-3148; Amity Rose, 8264 Main St., 569-3402; Berry Basket, 8260 Main St. Ext., 569-2984; Blushing Rose, 11 William St., 569-2687; Captain's Cottage, 69 Shather St., 569-2157; Elm Croft Manor, 8361 Pleasant Valley Rd., 569-3071; Fine Thread, 38 Liberty St., 569-2093; J. S. Hubbs, 17 Shethar St., 569-2440; Park Inn Hotel, 37 Shathar St., 569-9387; Pleasant Valley Inn, 7979 NY 54, 569-2282; Village Inn, Village Sq., 569-2528. Camping: Donameer Cpgd., 7417 Smallige Rd., 569-2115.

Attractions: Glenn H. Curtiss Mus., 8419 NY 54, 569-2160; Greyton H. Taylor Wine Mus., 868-3610; Keuka Maid Dinner Boat, PO Box 648, 569-2628. Wineries: Bully Hill Vineyards, 8843 Greyton H. Taylor Mem. Dr., 868-3610; Dr. Konstantin Frank's Vinifera Wine Cellars, 9749 Middle Rd., 800 320-0735; Heron Hill Winery, 9301 CR 76, 800 441-4241; Pleasant Valley Wine Co., 8260 Pleasant Valley Rd., 569-6133; Ravines Wine Cellars, 14110 NY 54, 292-7007.

↓ HAMMONDSPORT VILLAGE STREETS ↓

21.7 (34.9)   Lake St. @ Main St.   22.9 (36.9)
> Continue West on Main St. to go around Keuka Lake clockwise.
> Turn South on Lake St. to go to Taylor Wine Co.

21.9 (35.2)   Sheather St. @ Main St.   22.7 (36.5)
> Turn North on to Sheather St.
> Sheather St. is the central shopping street.

22.2 (35.7)   Mechanic St. @ Sheather St.   22.4 (36.0)
> Turn West on to Mechanic St.

22.3 (36.0)   Mechanic St. @ William St.   22.3 (35.9)
> Turn North on to William St.

22.4 (35.7)   NY 54A @ William St.   22.2 (35.7)
> Bear North on to NY 54A to go clockwise around Keuka Lake.

↑ HAMMONDSPORT VILLAGE STREETS ↑

23.3 (37.5)   G. H. Taylor Mem. Dr. @ NY 54A   21.3 (34.3)
> Continue traveling North on NY 54A.
> Turn on to G. H. Taylor Mem. Dr. to use the Inland Route on the West side of Keuka Lake.

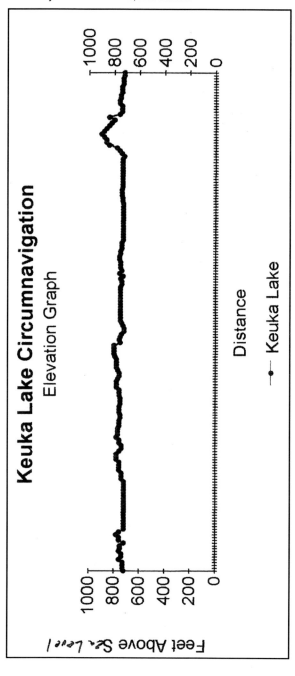

Keuka Lake Circumnavigation
Elevation Graph

Feet Above Sea Level

Distance

Keuka Lake

26.5 (42.6)   Urbana Rd. @ NY 54A   18.1 (29.1)
Continue traveling North on NY 54A.
URBANA: No services.

36.9 (59.4)   Italy Hill Rd./Guyanoga Rd.   7.7 (12.4)
                   @ NY 54A
Continue traveling North on NY 54A (actually you'll be
making a eastward turn at this intersection) to
circumnavigate Keuka Lake or go to Penn Yan.
⇔ KEUKA LAKE TO CANANDAIGUA LAKE: SOUTHERN
CONNECTING ROUTE, turn West on to CR 32/Italy Hill
Rd. to go to Canandaigua Lake & Naples.
⇔ KEUKA LAKE TO CANANDAIGUA LAKE: ROLLIN'
HILLS CONNECTING ROUTE, turn North on to CR 29/
Guyanoga Rd. to go to the middle of Canandaigua Lake.

BRANCHPORT
Info.: See Penn Yan information. AC: 607. ZC: 14418.
Services: Local convenience store, restaurant.
Lodging: Motel. B&Bs: 10,000 Delights, 252 W. Lake Rd.,
868-3731; Country Comforts, 2915 East Valley Rd. 595-
2532; Gone with the Wind, 453 W. Lake Rd., 868-4603.
Camping: Keuka Lake St. Pk., 3370 Pepper Rd., Bluff Pt.
14478, 315 536-3666; Wigwam Keuka Lake Campground,
3324 Esperanza Rd., 315 536-6352.
Attractions: Hunt Country Vineyard, 4021 Italy Hill Rd.,
315 595-2812.

38.1 (61.3)   Pepper Rd. @ NY 54A   6.5 (10.5)
Continue traveling North on NY 54A to return to Penn Yan.
⇔ ↻ KEUKA LAKE CIRCUMNAVIGATION: THE V OF
THE Y ROUTE, turn South on to Pepper Rd. to go into the
V of the Y of Keuka Lake! The sign will direct you to Keuka
Lake St. Pk.

ESPERANZA HAMLET
Lodging: B&B: Esperanza Mansion, 3456 NY 54A, Bluff
Pt. 14478, 315 252-1283. Camping: Keuka Lake St. Pk.,
3370 Pepper Rd., Bluff Pt. 14478, 315 536-3666; Wigwam
Keuka Lake Campground, 3324 Esperanza Rd., 315 536-
6352.
Attractions: Esperanza Mansion, 3456 NY 54A, Bluff Pt.
14478, 315 252-1283.

TRAVELER'S NOTE
THE V OF THE Y
The V of the Y on Keuka Lake begins at this point. The V

OF THE Y ROUTE directions immediately follow the Keuka
Lake Circumnavigation Route. The roads along the V are
not conducive to bicycle touring, especially loaded touring.
Before proceeding into the V read the entire V OF THE Y
ROUTE directions to determine if you want go into the V.
The views of Keuka Lake along both West and East Bluff
Rd. are very fine.

40.1 (64.5)   Co. Rd. 25/Assembly Rd.   4.5 (7.2)
                 @ NY 54A
Turn East on to CR 25/Assembly Rd. to go to Old West
Lake Rd. and East Bluff Rd., both are along the shore line.
Old West Lake Rd. goes North to Penn Yan. East Bluff Rd.
goes South into the V. The direction signs point to Keuka
College too!
The fast (non-scenic) way to go to Penn Yan is to continue
traveling North on NY 54A. We're using the scenic route.
BLUFF POINT: AC: 315. ZC: 14478. Cottages. Motel.
Camping: Wig Wam Harbor Cpgd., 3324 Esperanza Rd
(NY 54A), 536-6352; Keuka Lake St. Pk., 3370 Pepper Rd.,
536-3666.

40.6 (65.3)   Co. Rd. 25/Assembly Rd.   4.0 (6.4)
                 @ East Bluff Dr.
Turn North on to CR 25/Old W. Lake Rd. to go to Penn
Yan. Keuka College is at your front wheel. Of course all the
street signs say W. Lake Rd. NY 54A is now termed W.
Lake Rd. and the original road along the shore is now *Old
W. Lake Rd.*
To go into the V: Before following these directions read the
Traveler's Note at the beginning of the V of the Y Route.
Turn South on to East Bluff Dr. to go to the tip of the V of
the Y! 8.2 mi. (13.2 km.) along the shore, East Bluff Dr.
stops at a barrier. You will go on a dirt road for 2.3 mi. (3.7
km.) before reaching West Bluff Dr. &
and its narrow 1 lane road. However, all is not lost, go
around the barrier, ride and then walk along the E. Bluff Dr.
Ext. to the tip of the V (about 1.5 mi. (2.4 km.) to the tip).

41.2 (66.3)   Co. Rd. 21/Central Ave.   3.4 (5.5)
                 @ Co. Rd. 25
Continue traveling North along the shore on CR 21/Old
West Lake Rd. There are several motels, B&Bs, and
cottages to rent along Old W. Lake Rd. Some signs state
that this is CR 21 and some state that this is CR 25. It is
Old West Lake Rd. *Along the Shore Rd.* to me. And it
sounds more exclusive.

If you're tired of narrow 2 lane Old W. Lake Rd. then turn West on to Central Ave. and roll your wheels for .2 mi. (.3 km.) and your wheel will hit the asphalt of NY 54A. A sign even points to NY 54A!

42.9 (69.0)   NY 54A/West Lake Rd.   1.7 (2.7)
                    @ Old W. Lake Rd./Co. Rd. 21/25
↺ Turn North on to NY 54 to go to Penn Yan.
↺ Turn South on to NY 54A to go to Branchport & the West Branch of Keuka Lake.
Funny thing, the County Rd. sign on NY 54A points to Old West Lake Rd./CR 2<u>5</u>.

44.6 (71.8)   NY 14A @ NY 54A   0.0 (0.0)
You're in Penn Yan! Turn South on NY 14A and you can go around Keuka Lake again!
↺ ↻ KEUKA LAKE CIRCUMNAVIGATION Route.
⇔ KEUKA LAKE TO CANANDAIGUA LAKE: ROLLIN' HILLS CONNECTING ROUTE.
⇔ SENECA LAKE TO KEUKA LAKE: CONNECTING ROUTES.

Read ↓   **KEUKA LAKE CIRCUMNAVIGATION**   Read up ↑
Clockwise   Counterclockwise

Read ↓	**KEUKA LAKE CIRCUMNAVIGATION**	Read up ↑
Clockwise	**THE V OF THE Y**	Counterclockwise

TRAVELER'S NOTE

It is a very demanding route to the center of the V from the West Branch and out of the V along the East Branch of Keuka Lake. You will be traveling on a one lane chip sealed road. For 1.5 mi. (2.4 km.) at the bottom of the V the chip seal becomes dirt. The inclines/declines are not particularly severe but do not attempt to traverse the V as a loaded cyclotourist.

0.0 (0.0)   West Bluff Dr. @ Pepper Rd.   18.7 (30.2)
Turn West on to West Bluff Dr.
↺ ↻ KEUKA LAKE CIRCUMNAVIGATION Route, Turn North on Pepper Dr. to go to NY 54 A.

1.1 (1.7)   Keuka Lake @ West Bluff Dr.   17.6 (28.4)
You're at the Park's border. Go South!

5.2 (8.3)   Dirt Rd. on West Bluff Dr.   13.5 (21.7)
West Bluff Dr. becomes a dirt road and you're descending. But you'll climb up to the center of the V very shortly.

6.3 (10.1)   East Bluff Dr. Jct. West Bluff Dr.   12.4 (20.0)
The only way to go is North! And you'll be descending once again! You'll hardly notice this junction. But don't turn on to Skyline Dr., the road which goes due North up the center of the V.

7.5 (12.1)   E. Bluff Dr. Ext. @ East Bluff Dr.   11.2 (18.0)
Continue traveling North on East Bluff Dr. Asphalt again! A barrier & *Dead End* sign blocks your way on to E. Bluff Dr. Ext. If you want to go to the tip of the V then go around the barrier, ride and then walk along the E. Bluff Dr. Ext. to its logical conclusion at the point of the V, ~1.5 mi./2.4 km.

14.8 (23.8)   Co. Rd. 25/Central Ave.   3.9 (6.3)
                     @ East Bluff Dr.
Continue North on to CR 25/Central Ave. to go to Penn Yan and the East Branch of Keuka Lake. Just follow the Lake shore North!
East Bluff Dr. South of this point, really degenerates.
Keuka College.
⇔ Turn West on to CR 25/Assembly Rd. to go to NY 54A. Use NY 54A southbound to go to the West Branch of

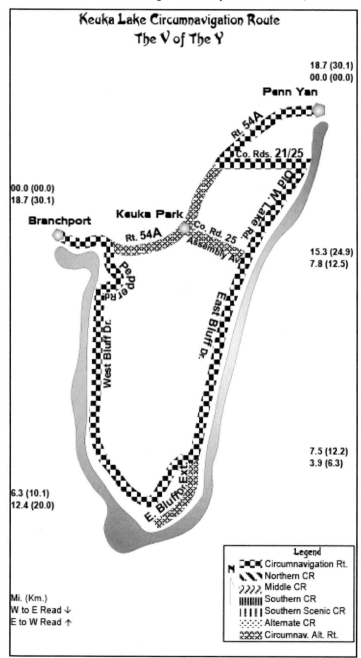

Keuka Lake Circumnavigation Route
The V of The Y

18.7 (30.1)
00.0 (00.0)

Penn Yan

Rt. 54A

Co. Rds. 21/25

Old W. Lake Rd.

00.0 (00.0)
18.7 (30.1)

Branchport

Keuka Park

Rt. 54A

Co. Rd. 25

Assembly Av.

15.3 (24.9)
7.8 (12.5)

Pepper Rd.

West Bluff Dr.

East Bluff Dr.

7.5 (12.2)
3.9 (6.3)

E. Bluff Dr. Ext.

6.3 (10.1)
12.4 (20.0)

Mi. (Km.)
W to E Read ↓
E to W Read ↑

Legend

N
▨▨▨ Circumnavigation Rt.
◥◥◥ Northern CR
⟩⟩⟩⟩ Middle CR
||||||| Southern CR
| | | | | Southern Scenic CR
⋯⋯⋯ Alternate CR
⨯⨯⨯⨯ Circumnav. Alt. Rt.

Keuka Lake & Branchport, 3.9 mi. (6.2 km.). Use NY 54A
northbound to go to Penn Yan. Intersection with the Keuka
Lake Circumnavigation Route.

15.3 (24.8)   Co. Rd. 21/ OldWest Lake Rd.   3.4 (5.4)
                   @ Co. Rd. 25
Continue North on CR 21/Old West Lake Rd. Same road,
different name, keep ridin' North on the road closest to the
Lake.

17.0 (27.4)   NY 54A   1.7 (2.7)
                   @ Co. Rd. 21/Old West Lake Rd.
⇔ KEUKA LAKE CIRCUMNAVIGATION ROUTE:
↻ Turn North on NY 54A to go to Penn Yan and the
circumnavigation start point.
↺ Turn South on to NY 54A to go to Branchport and coun-
terclockwise around Keuka Lake.

18.7 (30.1)   NY 14A @ NY 54A   0.0 (0.0)
PENN YAN: Refer to the Keuka Lake Circumnavigation
Route for information.
↺ Keuka Lake counterclockwise circumnavigators turn
South on to NY 54A.
⇔ KEUKA LAKE TO CANANDAIGUA LAKE:
CONNECTING ROUTES.
⇔ SENECA LAKE TO KEUKA LAKE: CONNECTING
ROUTES.

Read ↓   **KEUKA LAKE CIRCUMNAVIGATION**   Read up ↑
Clockwise   **V OF THE V**   Counterclockwise

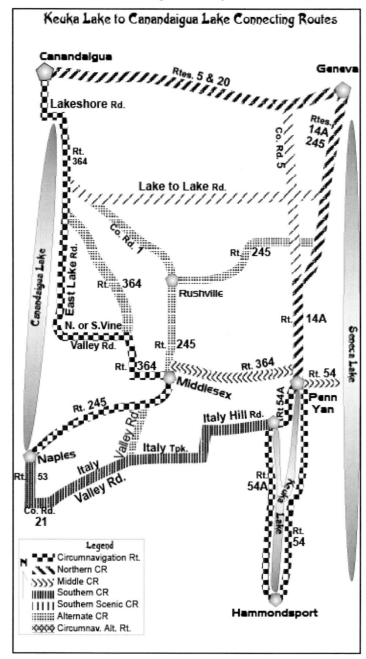

Keuka Lake to Canandaigua Lake Connecting Routes

TRAVELER'S NOTE
The hills on this Route don't scrape the sky but they can be intimidating because they sometimes occur in rapid succession. You'll be traveling through prime agricultural areas. Penn Yan, the northern most city on Keuka Lake is approximately at the same latitude as Naples, the southern most city on Canandaigua Lake.

0.0 (0.0)   NY 54A @ NY 14A   26.5 (42.6)
Turn North on to NY 14A.
PENN YAN: Refer to the Keuka Lake Circumnavigation Route for information.
↻ ↻ KEUKA LAKE CIRCUMNAVIGATION ROUTE
⇔ KEUKA LAKE TO CANANDAIGUA LAKE: CONNECTING ROUTES.
⇔ SENECA LAKE TO KEUKA LAKE: CONNECTING ROUTES.

0.7 (1.1)   NY 364 @ NY 14A   25.8(41.5)
Continue traveling North on NY 14A.
PENN YAN: Refer to the Keuka Lake Circumnavigation Route for information.
⇔ KEUKA LAKE: MIDDLE CONNECTING ROUTE, turn West on to NY 364 to use the Middle Connecting Route.

9.4 (15.1)   Post Rd./Co. Rd. 5 Jct. 14A   17.1 (27.5)
Continue traveling due North on to Post Rd./Co. Rd. 5. NY 14A bears Northeast at this intersection.
⇔ SENECA LAKE TO KEUKA LAKE: NORTHERN CONNECTING ROUTE, travel Northeast on NY 14A to go to Geneva and Seneca Lake.
Ontario County - Yates County border.

10.8 (17.4)   Lake to Lake Rd. @ Post Rd.   15.7 (25.3)
Turn West on to Lake to Lake Rd.
⇔ SENECA LAKE TO KEUKA LAKE: NORTHERN CONNECTING ROUTE: Travel East on Lake to Lake Rd., for about .5 mi. (.8 km.) to go to Geneva and Seneca Lake & you'll bump into NY 14A. Then follow the Northern Connecting Route directions.

20.6 (33.2)   Co. Rd. 1@ Lake to Lake Rd.   5.9 (9.5)
Turn Northwest on to CR 1.
⇔ KEUKA LAKE TO CANANDAIGUA LAKE: MIDDLE &
SOUTHERN CONNECTING ROUTES, turn South on to
CR 1. CR 1 intersects with NY 247 and NY 245, 4.6 mi.
(7.4 km.) South at Rushville (local convenience store/gas
station). Both 247 & 245 go South to NY 364, the Middle
Connecting Route. To go to Penn Yan & Keuka Lake, use
247. To go to the Southern end of Canandaigua Lake use
NY 245, which will take you directly into Naples at
Canandaigua Lake's southern end.

21.2 (34.1)   NY 364/East Lake Rd. @ Co. Rd. 1   5.3 (8.5)
↺ Turn North on to NY 364/E. Lake Rd. to go to
Canandaigua and the northern end of Canandaigua Lake.
↻ Turn South on to NY 364/East Lake Rd. to go to Naples
and the southern end of Canandaigua Lake.

25.3 (40.7)   Lake Shore Dr.   1.2 (1.9)
                   @ NY 364/East Lake Rd.
Turn West on to Lake Shore Dr.

26.5 (42.6)   Main St. & Rtes. 5&20   0.0 (0.0)
                   @ Lakeshore Dr.
The hills aren't really very big on this route. Actually they
are long gentle climbs for the most paNY
↻ ↺ CANANDAIGUA LAKE CIRCUMNAVIGATION Route.
⇔ CANANDAIGUA LAKE TO HONEOYE LAKE & other
Finger Lakes west of Canandaigua.
⇔ KEUKA LAKE TO CANANDAIGUA LAKE:
CONNECTING ROUTES.
CANANDAIGUA: Refer to the Canandaigua Lake
Circumnavigation Route for information.

Read ↓   **KEUKA LAKE TO CANANDAIGUA LAKE**   Read up ↑
E to W   **ROLLIN' HILLS CONNECTING ROUTE**   W to E

| Read ↓ | **KEUKA LAKE TO CANANDAIGUA LAKE** | Read up ↑ |
| E to W | **MIDDLE CONNECTING ROUTE** | W to E |

TRAVELER'S NOTE

This is a demanding route with a number of severe inclines/ declines and hairpin turns. The scenery is superb, roads used are excellent with wide shoulders and little traffic.

0.0 (0.0)   NY 54A @ NY 14A   35.3 (56.8)
Turn North on to NY 14A.
PENN YAN: Refer to the Keuka Lake Circumnavigation Route for information.
↺ ↻ KEUKA LAKE CIRCUMNAVIGATION ROUTE.
⇔ KEUKA LAKE TO CANANDAIGUA LAKE: CONNECTING ROUTES.
⇔ SENECA LAKE TO KEUKA LAKE: CONNECTING ROUTES.

0.7 (1.1)   NY 364 @ NY 14A   34.6 (55.7)
Turn West on to NY 364 to go to Canandaigua Lake.

8.9 (14.3)   Co. NY 29/Guyanoga Rd.   26.4 (42.5)
          @ NY 364
Continue cycling West on NY 364.
🚲 ⇔ KEUKA LAKE TO CANANDAIGUA LAKE: SOUTHERN CONNECTING ROUTE, turn South on to Guyanoga Rd./CR 29 and ride for 7.2 mi. (11.6 km.) to go to Branchport, From Branchport you can go to Naples & the southern end of Canandaigua Lake using the Keuka Lake to Canandaigua Lake: Southern Connecting Route. Branchport is the northern most village on Keuka Lake's West Branch & it is on the Keuka Lake Circumnavigation Route.

12.3 (19.8)   Rd. 18/Italy Valley Rd. @ NY 364   23.0 (37.0)
Continue traveling Northwest on NY 364, to *Potter*.
🚲 ⇔ KEUKA LAKE TO CANANDAIGUA LAKE: SOUTHERN CONNECTING ROUTE. It you suddenly have a change of heart and want to go to the Naples and the southern end of Canandaigua Lake, turn South on to CR 18/Italy Valley Rd. Follow CR18 southward for 9.5 mi. (15.3 km.) to CR 34/Italy Tpk. Use the directions in the Keuka Lake to Canandaigua Lake: Southern Connecting Route from that intersection.

14.2 (22.9)   NY 247 @ NY 364   21.1 (34.0)
Continue traveling West on NY 364.
ꗷ ꗄ NY 247 goes to Rushville. From Rushville you would
travel due North up the *hill* on to CR 1 which intersects with
E. Lake Rd. on Canandaigua Lake. E. Lake Rd. is on the
Canandaigua Lake Circumnavigation Route. This is a more
direct route to the North End of Canandaigua Lake but it is
up hill, going east to west, for about 2.0 mi. (3.2 km.). It is
one of my favorite routes, traveling light.

17.6 (28.3)   NY 364 @ NY 245   17.7 (28.5)
Continue traveling West on NY 364 to go to the East side of
Canandaigua Lake.
ꗷ ꗄ Turn South on to NY 245 to go to Naples, at the
southern end of Canandaigua Lake. This is the most direct
route to Naples. It is 9.1 mi. (14.7 km.) to Naples from this
intersection, mostly down hill!
MIDDLESEX: Flint Creek Campsites, 1455 Phelps Rd. (off
CR 18 S. of Potter), 800 914-3550.

20.4 (32.8)   Co. Rd. 10/North Vine Valley Rd.   14.9 (24.0)
                     @ NY 364
Either turn West on to Co. Rd. 10/North Vine Valley Rd.
ꗷ ꗄ OR continue due North on NY 364 [shorter than
turning West on CR 10 route by about 3 mi. (5 km.)] to go
northward towards Canandaigua on the East side of
Canandaigua Lake. Using CR 10 and then CR 39 will bring
you closer to the Lake but NY 364 is a wider road.

23.0 (37.0)   North Vine Valley Rd.   12.3 (19.8)
                     @ East Lake Rd.
Turn North on to CR 39/East Lake Rd.
There are a number of local convenience stores along E.
Lake Rd. **VINE VALLEY**

26.0 (41.8)   Co. Rd. 39 Jct. Co. Rd. 11   9.3 (15.0)
Continue traveling North on East Lake Rd.
The road name East Lake Rd. and asphalt's the same, only
the Co. Rd. number has changed. Why? You ask? You've
entered another County and to confuse the traveler the
number changes. Yates County - Ontario County border.

29.9 (48.1)   Co. Rd. 11/East Lake Rd.   5.4 (8.7)
                     Jct. NY 364
Continue traveling North on NY 364 which is now named
East Lake Rd. Folks who took NY 364 northward at
Middlesex join us here.

31.1 (50.1)   Co. Rd. 1 @ NY 364/E. Lake Rd.   4.2 (6.8)
Continue traveling North to go to Canandaigua and the
North end of the Lake.
⇔ KEUKA LAKE TO CANANDAIGUA LAKE: ROLLIN'
HILLS CONNECTING ROUTE. Turn East on to Co. Rd. 1
to return to Penn Yan! Ha!

34.0 (54.7)   Lake Shore Dr.   1.3 (2.1)
                 @ NY 364/East Lake Rd.
Turn West on to Lake Shore Dr.

35.3 (56.8)   Rtes. 5&20   0.0 (0.0)
                 @ Lake Shore Dr./Main St.
Quite a day's worth of wonderful bicycling!
↻ ↺ CANANDAIGUA LAKE CIRCUMNAVIGATION Route.
⇔ CANANDAIGUA LAKE TO HONEOYE LAKE & other
Finger Lakes west of Canandaigua.
⇔ KEUKA LAKE TO CANANDAIGUA LAKE:
CONNECTING ROUTES.
CANANDAIGUA: Refer to the Canandaigua Lake
Circumnavigation Route for information.

Read ↓   **CANANDAIGUA LAKE TO KEUKA LAKE**   Read up ↑
E to W   **MIDDLE HILLS CONNECTING ROUTE**   W to E

KEUKA LAKE TO CANANDAIGUA LAKE
SOUTHERN CONNECTING ROUTES
HAMMONDSPORT TO NAPLES

There two major ways to go from Hammondsport at the southern end of Keuka Lake to Naples at the southern end of Canandaigua Lake. The routes can involve fairly strenuous cycling over hilly terrain. This is the longer but less strenuous route.

0.0 (0.0)   NY 54 A @ CR 88   22.2 (36.0)
    Travel Southwest on CR 88.

1.6 (2.6)   CR 88 @ CR 89   20.6 (33.4)
    Travel west on CR 89/Mitchellville-Pleasant Valley Rd.

3.3 (5.3)   CR 13 @ CR 89   18.9 (30.6)
    Follow CR 13/Mitchellsville Rd. northwest to NY 53.

5.9 (9.6)   NY 53 @ CR 13   16.3 (26.4)
    Turn northwest on to NY 53.

12.0 (19.4)   CR 72 @ NY 53   10.2 (16.5)
    Continue traveling north west on NY 53.
    PRATTSBURGH: Lodging: B&Bs: Rider's Rest, 6154 NY 53 N (Naples-Prattsburg Rd.) at Nickles Rd., 522-6100; Taylor Farms, 6554 Cook School Rd., 522-5155; Feather Tick 'N Thyme B&B, 7661 Tuttle Rd., 522-4113. Camping: Taylor Farms, 6554 Cook School Rd., 522-5155.

22.2 (36.0)   NY 53 @ NY 21   0.0 (0.0)
    NAPLES: See Canandaigua Lake circumnavigation for Information.

KEUKA LAKE TO CANANDAIGUA LAKE
SOUTHERN CONNECTING ROUTES
HAMMONDSPORT TO NAPLES

Read ↓   **KEUKA LAKE TO CANANDAIGUA LAKE**   Read up ↑
E to W   **SOUTHERN CONNECTING ROUTE**   W to E
                       PENN YAN TO NAPLES

0.0 (0.0)   NY 14A @ NY 54A   22.9 (36.9)
Turn West on to NY 54A.
PENN YAN: Refer to the Keuka Lake Circumnavigation
Route for information.
↻ ↺ KEUKA LAKE CIRCUMNAVIGATION ROUTE.
⇔ KEUKA LAKE TO CANANDAIGUA LAKE:
CONNECTING ROUTES.
⇔ SENECA LAKE TO KEUKA LAKE: CONNECTING
ROUTES.

1.7 (2.7)   Co. Rd. 25/Old West Lake Rd.   21.2 (34.1)
                   @ NY 54A/West Lake Rd.
Continue traveling South on NY 54A.
If you want a small diversion use Old West Lake Rd. to Co.
Rd. 25/Assembly Rd. then turn West on to Assembly Rd. to
go back to NY 54A The distance is about the same.

4.5 (7.2)   Co. Rd. 25/Assembly Rd.   18.4 (29.6)
                   @ NY 54A
Continue traveling South of NY 54A.
Diversionary travelers rejoin us here. A few travelers who
conquered the V of the Y of Keuka Lake might tell you a
tale or two if you meet them.
⇔ ↻ KEUKA LAKE CIRCUMNAVIGATION: THE V OF
THE Y ROUTE

7.1 (11.4)   Pepper Rd. @ NY 54A   15.8 (25.4)
Continue traveling Southwest on NY 54A.
⇔ ↺ KEUKA LAKE CIRCUMNAVIGATION: THE V OF
THE Y ROUTE. Keuka Lake St. Pk.

8.4 (13.5)   Co. Rd. 32 & Co. Rd. 29   14.5 (23.3)
                   @ NY 54A
Travel West on to Co. Rd. 32/Italy Hill Rd.
🚲 ⇔ KEUKA LAKE TO CANANDAIGUA LAKE: MIDDLE
CONNECTING ROUTE. If you change your mind and
decide to go to the North end of Canandaigua Lake (shorter
route). Turn North on to CR 29/Guyanoga Rd. and ride for
7.2 mi. (11.6 km.) Where CR 29/Guyanoga Rd. intersects
NY 364 begin to follow the directions in the Keuka Lake to
Canandaigua Lake: Middle Connecting Route
↺ KEUKA LAKE CIRCUMNAVIGATION Route. Continue

traveling South on NY 54A to go around Keuka Lake coun-
terclockwise.
BRANCHPORT: Refer to the Keuka Lake
Circumnavigation Route for information.

13.3 (21.4)   Co. Rd. 35/Italy Friend Rd.   9.6 (15.4)
                     Jct. Co. Rd. 32/Italy Hill Rd.
Turn South on to Co. Rds. 32 & 35/Italy Friend Rd.

13.8 (22.2)   Co. Rd. 34/Italy Tpk.   9.1 (14.6)
                     @. Co. Rd. 35/Italy Friend Rd.
Turn West on to Co. Rd. 34/Italy Tpk.
ITALY HILL: No services.

17.0 (27.4)   Co. Rd. 18/Italy Valley Rd.   5.9 (9.5)
                     @ Co. Rd. 34/Italy Tpk.
Turn South on to Co. Rd. 18/Italy Valley Rd. to go to
Naples and the southern end of Canandaigua Lake.
🚲 ⇔ KEUKA LAKE TO CANANDAIGUA LAKE: MIDDLE
CONNECTING ROUTE. It you suddenly have a change of
heart and want to go to the northern end of Canandaigua
Lake, turn North on to CR 18/Italy Valley Rd. Follow Co.
Rd. 18 northward for 9.5 mi. (15.3 km.) to NY 364. Use the
directions in the Keuka Lake to Canandaigua Lake: Middle
Connecting Route from that intersection.
ITALY: And you didn't even have to cross the Atlantic to go
to Italy only the Yates County - Ontario County - Yates
County border is almost at the rubber on your tire.

20.5 (33.0)   Co. Rd. 21 @ Italy Valley Rd.   2.4 (3.9)
Bear and continue traveling West on to Co. Rd. 21.

22.7 (36.5)   NY 53 @ Co. Rd. 21.   0.2 (0.3)
Turn North on to NY 53.

22.9 (36.9)   St. NY 21 @ NY 53   0.0 (0.0)
NAPLES: Refer to the Canandaigua Lake
Circumnavigation Route for information.

Read ↓   **CANANDAIGUA LAKE TO KEUKA LAKE**   Read up ↑
E to W   **SOUTHERN CONNECTING ROUTE**   W to E
                              NAPLES TO PENN YAN

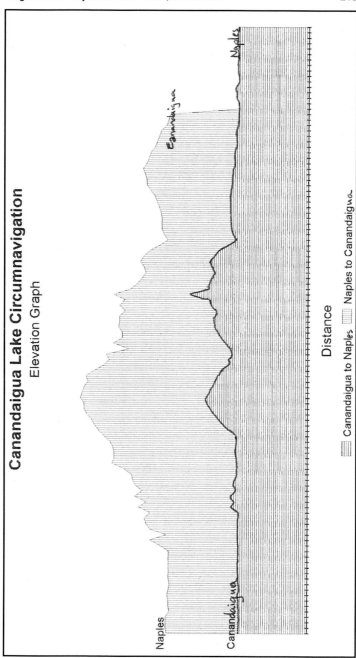

Canandaigua Lake Circumnavigation
Elevation Graph

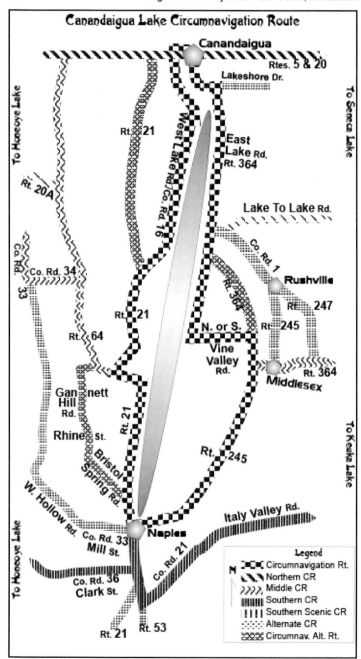

Canandaigua Lake Circumnavigation Route

Politics

The Finger Lakes Region was inhabited by citizens of the Iroquois Confederation long before Europeans even thought of the Western Hemisphere. Today, it is hard to visualize that the Iroquois Nations occupied land extending from near the Hudson River to near the Niagara River; and from the Adirondack Mts. to the Susquehanna River. The Mohawk, Oneida, Onondaga, Cayuga and Seneca Nations individually consolidated political and economic authority in their own areas prior to joining together to form the Confederation.

All the Iroquois Nations had complex social, economic and political structures. The Iroquois are particularly differentiated from other Native American Nations by their matrilineal social structure. Women participated in clan and family political decision making as essentially equals.

The popular Euro-American conception of the Iroquois as primarily nomadic hunters and gatherers is a simplification of their economic activities. Throughout the Mohawk River Valley and the Finger Lakes region the Iroquois established permanent settlements. Economic activities in these principal *villages* were based on hunting/gathering and agricultural products, trade and the influx of people to speak with political leaders; Not unlike any other culture's activities during the 12th - 14th centuries. The early Euro-American chroniclers of Iroquois reported seeing well maintained villages, pottery with a definite style, and pictographs.

A clear indication of how far South some Iroquois traveled and probably traded, prior to the arrival of Europeans on the continent, were Iroquois *explorers'* drawings, paintings and pictographs of alligators.

This freedom to *explore* other areas of North America by Iroquois citizens might have been driven by the need to determine possible areas in which to expand or to conquer. Native American Nations which had been vanquished by one or several Iroquois Nations told the European *explorers* stories of the ferocity and brutality of Iroquois warriors. In comparison to the European wars of the period and World War II, ferocity and brutality can be considered as relative terms used by the vanquished to regain their political position and land. The previous statements not withstanding the Iroquois were noted for being skillful warriors with well organized and led armies; and did, generally, follow a policy of annihilating their enemies.

The Iroquois Confederation was a reaction to the European invasion of Iroquois land. It was also a result of the political astuteness of Iroquois leaders. By uniting together, the five Nations could align with either the French or British to protect their lands from Euro-American settlement. A Confederation rather than a empire with a single all powerful monarch was a logical extension of the Iroquois Nations' political system which relied on discussion, mediation and consensus decision making. Not quite democracy but clearly not a totalitarian form of government.

| Read ↓ | **CANANDAIGUA LAKE** | Read up ↑ |
| Clockwise | **CIRCUMNAVIGATION** | Counterclockwise |

0.0 (0.0)   NY 332/Main St. @ Rtes. 5&20   51.8 (83.4)
Travel South on Main St. towards the Lake.
There is a bike shop in Parkway Plaza which is just East of this intersection on Rtes. 5&20. Groceries and other shops are along the 5&20 strip as well as along Main St.
⇔ KEUKA LAKE TO CANANDAIGUA LAKE: CONNECTING ROUTES.
⇔ CANANDAIGUA LAKE TO HONEOYE LAKE: CONNECTING ROUTES.
🛉 ⇔ CANANDAIGUA LAKE TO THE LAKES WEST OF CANANDAIGUA.
🛉 ⇔ CANANDAIGUA LAKE TO ROCHESTER:
A bit of elocution. All of us locals term route NY 5 and US 20 as one entity, *5&20*. Usually it is said very rapidly and most of the time used as a singular noun.

CANANDAIGUA
Info.: Ontario Co. Tourism, 25 Gorham St.., Canandaigua NY 14424, 585 394-3915. AC: 585. ZC: 14424.
Bike Info.: No bike shop. The Rochester Bicycling Club has many rides which begin in Canandaigua. Rochester Bicycling Club; PO Box 10100, Rochester 14610. Ride Hotline: 888 857-8198. www.rochesterbicyclingclub.org
Services: All, hospital, groceries, small boutiques, discount stores. Trailways/Greyhound service to Rochester and Binghamton. CATS buses connect with Rochester Transit Service buses at Victor/Eastview Mall. CATS buses do not have bike carriage facilities.
Lodging: Motels & cottages. B&Bs: 1795 Acorn Inn, 4508 Rt. 64S, 229-2834; 1840 Inn On The Main, 176 N. Main St., 394-0139; 1885 Sutherland House, 3179 NY 21S, 396-0375; Thendara Inn, 4356 E. Lake Rd., 394-4868; Oliver Phelps, 252 N. Main

St., 396-1650; Chambery Cottage, 6104 Monks Rd., 393-1405; Chosen Spot, 5395 Rts. 5&20, 393-9604; Filigree Inn, 5406 Bristol Valley Rd. NY 64, 229-5460; Habersham Country Inn, 6124 Rts. 5&20, 394-1510; Morgan Samuels Inn, 2920 Smith Rd., 394-9232; Farm House B&B, 1862 Rt. 5&20, 526-5420, Flint (~5 mi. (8 km.) West). Camping: Canandaigua KOA, 5374 Farmington Townline Rd., Farmington, 398-3582, ~5 mi. (~8 km.) North off NY 322; Camp in the Woods (adults only), 3770 Lake-to-Lake Rd., 554-6996, Flint (~5 mi. West). There are additional camping areas on the West side of the Lake.

Attractions: Finger Lakes Performing Arts Ctr., Lincoln Hill Rd. @ E. Lake Rd., 222-5000; See Naples for theater.
Sonnenberg Mansion & Gardens St. Hist. Pk., 151 Charlotte St., 394-4922; Granger Homestead, 295 N. Main St., 394-1472; Ontario Co. Hist. Soc., 55 N. Main St., 394-4975;
Capt. Gray's Boat Tours, 115 Howell St., 394-5270; Canandaigua Lady, 169 Lakeshore Dr., 685-8500. Amberg Wine Cellars, 2200 Rtes. 5&20, Flint, 526-6742; Finger Lakes Race Track, 5857 Rte. 96, Farmington 924-3232.

0.2 (0.3)   Lake Shore Dr. @ Main St.   51.6 (83.0)
Turn East on to Lake Shore Dr.
The small streets, Muar St. & Booth St., leading North from Lake Shore Dr. go to the "strip" along Rtes. 5&20.

1.5 (2.4)   NY 364/East Lake Rd.   50.3 (80.9)
                   @ Lake Shore Dr.
Turn South on to NY 364/East Lake Rd.

5.5 (8.9)   Co. Rd. 1 @ NY 364/E. Lake Rd.   46.3 (74.5)
Continue traveling South on NY 364.
↰ ⇔ KEUKA LAKE TO CANANDAIGUA LAKE: ROLLING

HILLS CONNECTING ROUTE. Turn East on to CRd. 1 to go to Seneca Lake & Keuka Lake using the least Hilly Connecting Route.

6.7 (10.8)   East Lake Rd./CR 11 Jct. NY 364   45.1 (72.6)
Either bear southwest on to East Lake Rd./CR 11 or continue traveling South on NY 364.

↬ ↺ **Clockwise travelers:** You're *gonna* have to make a decision. Essentially the mileage is the same either way you go South. East Lake Rd./CR 11 hugs the shore; NY 364 goes a bit inland at this point.

East Lake Rd. is a narrow road with "cottage" bound travelers. NY 364 is a typical wide State Rd. with a shoulder. Personally I like the shore. Thus these directions. But we'll rejoin those of you who use NY 364 at the intersection of North Vine Valley Rd., 9 mi. (14 km.) down the pike!

As you cross into Yates Co. from Ontario Co. East Lake Rd. will have a new numerical designation, Yates CR 39. It is still East Lake Rd.

13.0 (20.9)   East Lake Rd.   38.8 (62.4)
                        @ North (CR 10) or South Vine Valley Rd.
Turn East on to CR 10/North Vine Valley Rd.
VINE VALLEY: No services except for a small store/restaurant/bar 1 mi. (1.6 km.) down a hill on North or South Vine Valley Rds.at the Town beach on the Lake.

15.6 (25.1)   NY 364   36.2 (58.3)
                        @ CR 10/North Vine Valley Rd.
                        or @ South Vine Valley Rd.
Turn South on to NY 364.

↬ ↺ Counterclockwise **travelers:** You can either continue North on NY 364 to go to Canandaigua and the North end of the Lake; or you can turn West on to North Vine Valley Rd. and follow the described route. NY 364 is a typical wide State Rd. with a shoulder. The distance is about the same. NY 364 intersects with the described route 9 mi. (14 km.) northward. East Lake Rd. hugs the shore while NY 364 runs a bit inland at this point.

18.4 (29.6)   NY 245 @ NY 364   33.4 (53.8)
↺ Turn South on to NY 245 to go to the southern end of Canandaigua Lake and Naples.

↬ ⇔ KEUKA LAKE TO CANANDAIGUA LAKE: MIDDLE CONNECTING ROUTE, turn West on to NY 364 to go to Keuka Lake and Penn Yan.

MIDDLESEX: convenience store. Camping: Flint Creek Campsites, 1455 Phelps Rd., 800 914-3550.

27.6 (44.4)   NY 21/Main St. @ NY 245   24.2 (38.9)
You are now at the northern end of Naples. Your route choices are as follows:

↻ **Clockwise travelers:** CANANDAIGUA LAKE CIRCUMNAVIGATION Route, turn North on to NY 21.

↻ ⇔ GANNETT HILL ROUTE description follows the Canandaigua Lake Circumnavigation Route.

↺ Counterclockwise **travelers:** CANANDAIGUA LAKE CIRCUMNAVIGATION Route, turn North on to NY 245.

⇔ KEUKA LAKE TO CANANDAIGUA LAKE: SOUTHERN CONNECTING ROUTE, travel South on NY 21/Main St. to NY 53 at the southern end of Naples.

⇔ CANANDAIGUA LAKE TO HONEOYE LAKE: MIDDLE CONNECTING ROUTE and CROSS COUNTRY CONNECTING ROUTE, use the Circumnavigation Route to the intersection of NY 21/64 and then follow the Connecting Route directions.

⇔ CANANDAIGUA LAKE TO HONEOYE LAKE: SOUTHERN CONNECTING ROUTE.

NAPLES

Info.: Naples Visitors Booth, 196 N. Main St., Naples 14512, 585 374-2435. South Bristol Twn., 6500 Gannett Hill Rd., Naples 14512, 585 374-6341. AC: 585. ZC: 14512. Note that lodging & attractions may involve climbing out of the *Valley.*

Services: restaurants, grocery, other stores; roadside stands.

Lodging: Motels & cottages. B&Bs: Bristol Views, 6932 CR 12, 374-8875; Cheshire Inn, 6004 Rt. 21S, 396-2383; Grapevine Inn, 182 N. Main St., 374-9298; Inn at Reservoir Creek, 8623 Cohocton St. NY 21, 374-8010; Maxfield Inn, 105 N. Main St., 374-2510; Monier Manor, 154 N. Main St., 374-6719; Naples Valley, 7161 CR 12, 374-6397; Vagabond Inn, 330 Sliter Rd., 554-5371; Naples Hotel, 111 S. Main St., 374-5630. Camping: Ontario Co. Pk. at Gannett Hill, 6475 Gannett Hill Rd., Naples 14512, 716 374-6250. Also see the Bristol listing.

Attractions: Bristol Valley Theater, 151 S. Main St., 374-6318; Cummings Nature Ctr., Gulick Rd., 374-6160; Hi Tor Wildlife Mgt. Area, NY 245 (hiking & MTB trails), 226-2466. Finger Lakes Trail (hiking only). Wine: Arbor Hill, 6461 NY 64, Bristol Springs, 374-2870; Widmer's Wine Cellars, 1 Lake Niagara Ln., Naples, 14512, 800 836-5253. Grape Festival in Sep't. or Oct.

28.3 (45.5)   CR 12/Bristol Spring Rd. @ NY 21   23.5(37.8)
Continue traveling North on NY 21.

🚲 ↺ ⇔ GANNETT HILL ROUTE. Turn North on to CR 12/
Bristol Spring Rd. to go along a ridge above the Lake on
the Gannett Hill Road Route. Be forwarded getting up to
the ridge is a climb. Once you're up there, it is basically a
rolling hills type of route with no severe inclines/declines
until the northern end.

BRISTOL

Info.: Bristol Twn., 6740 Co. Rd. 32, Canandaigua 14424,
585 229-2400. AC: 585.

Also see: Canandaigua, Naples, Honeoye and Bloomfield.

Services: Along NY 21/64 and CR 12 there are some small
convenience & other stores. Many roadside stands

Lodging: Cottages, condo rental; Camping: Ontario
County Pk, Gannett Hill Rd. off Rt. 64, 374-6250; Bristol
Woodlands, 4835 S. Hill Rd., 229-2290.

Attractions: Bristol Hist. Soc., CR 3, 229-5613. Mt. Biking:
Bristol Mt. Ski Resort, 5662 NY 64, 374-6000; Stid Hill St.
Rec. Area, NY 64. CEK Mees Observatory (telescope),
University of Rochester, Friday and Saturday night tours,
rain or shine, call for reservations, 585 275-4385.

35.1 (56.5)   NY 64 @ NY 21   16.7 (26.9)
Continue traveling North on NY 21.
Read the next paragraph since you are already half way up
to the ridge why not go all the way!

⇔ CANANDAIGUA LAKE TO HONEOYE LAKE: MIDDLE
CONNECTING ROUTE.

⇔ CANANDAIGUA LAKE TO HONEOYE LAKE: CROSS
COUNTRY CONNECTING ROUTE.

↺ ⇔ **Counterclockwise travelers:** GANNETT HILL
ROUTE, turn on to NY 64 to go on the *ridge* above the
Lake route; the Ontario Co. Pk..

CLOCKWISE TRAVELER'S NOTE

The route directions for the primary Canandaigua Lake
Circumnavigation immediately follow the Gannett Hill Route.

CANANDAIGUA LAKE CIRCUMNAVIGATION

Read ↓   **PRIMARY ROUTE CONTINUED**   Read up ↑
Clockwise   Counterclockwise

Read ↓   **CANANDAIGUA LAKE CIRCUMNAVIGATION**   Read up ↑
Clockwise   **GANNETT HILL ROUTE**   Counterclockwise

TRAVELER'S NOTE

It is a steep climb to the which Gannett Hill Rd. ridge. Gannett Hill Rd. is a *rolling hills* road. As a friend who lives in Naples says, "You have to climb the hills to leave Naples."

0.0 (0.0)   NY 245 @ NY 21/Main St.   10.0 (16.1)
Travel North on NY 21.

0.7 (1.1)   Bristol Spring Rd. @ NY 21   9.3 (15.0)
Turn Northwest on to Co. Rd. 12/Bristol Spring Rd.

2.2 (3.5)   Rhine Rd. @ CR 12/Bristol Spring Rd.   7.8 (12.6)
Turn Northwest on to Rhine Rd.
Sign: *To Gannett Hill Rd. & Co. Park.*

3.8 (6.1)   Gannett Hill Rd. Jct. Rhine Rd.   6.2 (10.0)
                  @ Oakley Rd.
Continue traveling North on Gannett Hill Rd.
CEK Mees Observatory (telescope), reserv. 585 275-4385.

8.4 (13.5)   Ontario Co. Pk. Rd. @ Gannett Hill Rd.   1.6 (2.6)
Turn East on to Gannett Hill Rd. Confused? Gannett Hill Rd. makes a right angle turn here. The descent/assent from the Park to NY 64 is severe.
Go into the Park! The view is stupendous! You will have to climb a bit more. Ontario Co. Pk., camping, 585 374-6250.

9.8 (15.8)   Gannett Hill Rd. @ NY 64   0.2 (0.3)
↻ If you are 'rounding Canandaigua Lake, clockwise, continue traveling East on Gannett Hill Rd. to NY 21.
⇔ CANANDAIGUA LAKE TO HONEOYE LAKE: MIDDLE CONNECTING ROUTE: & the CROSS COUNTRY CONNECTING ROUTE:

10.0 (16.1)   NY 21 @ Gannett Hill Rd.   0.0 (0.0)
↻ Turn North on to NY 21 to complete the circumnavigation of Canandaigua Lake from begin from clockwise 35.1 mi. (56.5 km.).
↺ **Counterclockwise** Canandaigua Lake start here.

Read ↓   **CANANDAIGUA LAKE CIRCUMNAVIGATION**   Read up ↑
Clockwise   **GANNETT HILL ROUTE**   Counterclockwise

Read ↓   **CANANDAIGUA LAKE CIRCUMNAVIGATION**   Read up ↑
Clockwise   **PRIMARY ROUTE CON'T**   Counterclockwise

COUNTERCLOCKWISE TRAVELER'S NOTE
the primary Canandaigua Lake Circumnavigation route immediately follows the Gannett Hill Route.

35.1 (56.5)   NY 64 @ NY 21   16.7 (26.9)
Continue traveling North on NY 21.
Read the next paragraph since you are already half way up to the ridge why not go all the way! The view from Ontario County Pk. is spectacular.
⇔ CANANDAIGUA LAKE TO HONEOYE LAKE: MIDDLE CONNECTING RTE & CROSS COUNTRY CONNECTING RTE.
↻ ⇔ **Counterclockwise travelers:** GANNETT HILL ROUTE, turn on to NY 64 to go on this "ridge above the Lake" route; the Ontario Co. Park (camping); and Mees Observatory (reservations necessary).

40.6 (65.3)   CR 16/West Lake Rd. @ NY 21   11.2 (18.0)
Turn on to Co. Rd. 16/West Lake Rd.
⑃ Decisions! Yeah, you can continue traveling North on NY 21 to head into Canandaigua. It's broad and has a nice shoulder but it takes you away from the shore. We'll go a more scenic route via Co. Rd. 16/West Lake Rd.
The distance is about the same.
⑃ NY 21 travelers should note that they can turn West on to Rtes. 5&20 near end of this route just outside of Canandaigua; or they can continue to Main St., Canandaigua. Then the NY 21 traveler simply has to turn South on Main St. to make the ellipse complete.

51.1 (82.2)   Parrish St. @ CR 16/West Lake Rd.   0.7 (1.1)
Turn East on to Parrish St.

51.5 (82.9)   NY 332/Main St. @ Parrish St.   0.3 (0.5)
Turn South on to NY 332/Main St.

51.8 (83.4)   Lake Shore Dr. @ Main St.   0.0 (0.0)
    CANANDAIGUA

Clockwise   **CANANDAIGUA LAKE**   Counterclockwise
Read ↓   **CIRCUMNAVIGATION**   Read up ↑

Notes

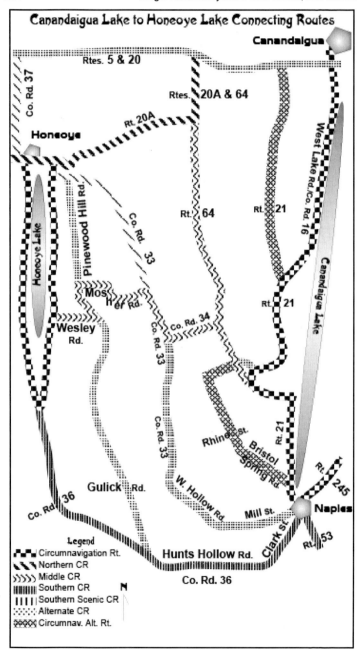

Canandaigua Lake to Honeoye Lake Connecting Routes

Legend
Circumnavigation Rt.
Northern CR
Middle CR
Southern CR
Southern Scenic CR
Alternate CR
Circumnav. Alt. Rt.

0.0 (0.0)   Rtes. 5&20 @ Main St.   19.8 (31.9)
Turn West on to Rtes. 5&20. Canandaigua.

2.2 (3.5)   NY 21 @ Rtes. 5&20   17.6 (28.3)
Travel West on Rtes. 5&20 to go to Honeoye Lake.
↺ CANANDAIGUA LAKE CIRCUMNAVIGATION Route,
turn South on to NY 21 to go counterclockwise.

7.1 (11.4)   Rtes. 64 & 20A @ Rtes. 5&20   12.7 (20.4)
Turn South on to Rtes. 64 & 20A.

11.9 (19.2)   NY 20A @. NY 64   7.9 (12.7)
Turn West on to NY 20A to go to Honeoye Lake &
Honeoye.
⇔ Travel South on NY 64 for 8.3 mi. (13.4 km.) to the
intersection of NY 21 @ NY 64. At that intersection you can
make connections with various Canandaigua Lake Routes.

18.9 (30.4)   East Lake Rd. @ NY 20A   0.9 (1.4)
Continue traveling West to go into Honeoye Village.
↻ Turn South on to East Lake Rd. to 'round Honeoye Lake
    clockwise.

19.8 (31.9)   Co. Rd. 36/West Lake Rd.   0.0 (0.0)
                    @ NY 20A
↺ HONEOYE LAKE CIRCUMNAVIGATION Route: Turn
South on to Co. Rd. 36 to 'round Honeoye Lake counter-
clockwise.
⇔ HONEOYE LAKE TO CANADICE LAKE: NORTHERN
CONNECTING ROUTE.
⇔ HONEOYE LAKE TO HEMLOCK LAKE: NORTHERN
CONNECTING ROUTE.
HONEOYE: Refer to the Honeoye Lake Circumnavigation
Route for information.

E to W   **CANANDAIGUA LAKE TO HONEOYE LAKE**   W to E
Read ↓   **MIDDLE CONNECTING ROUTE**   Read up ↑

TRAVELER'S NOTE
This route begins at the following intersection on the Canandaigua Lake Circumnavigation Route:

35.1 (56.5)   NY 64 @ NY 21   16.7 (26.9)

It also intersects the northern end of the Gannett Hill Route; the southern end of the Cross Country Route and part of it (NY 20A) is used in the Canandaigua Lake to Honeoye Lake Northern Connecting Route. It is a relatively straight forward route to Honeoye Lake using the smoothed out hills on State highways. It is very scenic. Loaded bicycle tourists should use this Route rather than the Canandaigua Lake to Honeoye Lake Cross Country Route.

0.0 (0.0)   NY 64 @ NY 21   19.4 (31.2)
Turn North on to NY 64.
⇔ CANANDAIGUA LAKE TO HONEOYE LAKE: CROSS COUNTRY CONNECTING ROUTE.
↻ ↻ CANANDAIGUA LAKE CIRCUMNAVIGATION Route
↻ ⇔ Counterclockwise: GANNETT HILL ROUTE.

0.4 (0.6)   Gannett Hill Rd. @ NY 64   19.0 (30.6)
Continue traveling North on NY 64 to go to Honeoye Lake
& Honeoye Village.
⇔ GANNETT HILL ROUTE, turn West on to Gannett Hill
Rd. to climb the hill to the County Park (camping) and
Gannett Hill. A beautiful view of the Lake; hiking (ONLY) on
the Finger Lakes Trail; seeing the stars from the CEK Mees
Observatory (reservations necessary); or going "overland
along the ridge" to Naples at the Southern end of
Canandaigua Lake awaits you if you climb this hill!

2.3 (3.7)   Co. Rd. 34 @ NY 64   17.1 (27.5)
Continue traveling North on NY 64.
⇔ CANANDAIGUA LAKE TO HONEOYE LAKE: CROSS
COUNTRY CONNECTING ROUTE.

10.6 (17.1)   NY 20A @ NY 64   8.8 (14.2)
Turn West on to NY 20A; and follow it for 7.9 mi. (12.7
km.) to go Honeoye Village. Rtes. 5&20 are 8.3 mi. (13.4
km.) North of this intersection.

18.5 (29.8)   E. Lake Rd. @ NY 20A   .9 (1.4)
Continue traveling West to go to Honeoye Village.
↺ HONEOYE LAKE CIRCUMNAVIGATION ROUTE.

19.4 (31.2)   Co. Rd. 36/West Lake Rd.   0.0 (0.0)
                  @ NY 20A
↺ HONEOYE LAKE CIRCUMNAVIGATION Route: Turn
South on to Co. Rd. 36 to 'round Honeoye Lake counter-
clockwise.
⇔ HONEOYE LAKE TO CANADICE LAKE: NORTHERN
CONNECTING ROUTE.
⇔ HONEOYE LAKE TO HEMLOCK LAKE: NORTHERN
CONNECTING ROUTE.
HONEOYE: Refer to the Honeoye Lake Circumnavigation
Route for information.

E to W   **CANANDAIGUA LAKE TO HONEOYE LAKE**   W to E
Read ↓   **MIDDLE CONNECTING ROUTE**   Read up ↑

E to W   **CANANDAIGUA LAKE TO HONEOYE LAKE**   W to E
Read ↓   **CROSS COUNTRY CONNECTING ROUTE**   Read up ↑

TRAVELER'S NOTE

This is a very strenuous and demanding cross country route. There are many inclines/declines with little room for gaining sufficient momentum to go completely up hill. Fair warning. But it is beautiful and fun. The Middle Connecting Route is just as beautiful and certainly less hilly than this route. Loaded bicycle tourists should not use this Route.

0.0 (0.0)   NY 21 @ NY 64   10.5 (16.9)
Turn North on to NY 64.
↻ ↺ CANANDAIGUA CIRCUMNAVIGATION ROUTE
⇔ GANNETT HILL ROUTE.
⇔ CANANDAIGUA LAKE TO HONEOYE LAKE: MIDDLE CONNECTING ROUTE
Note: NY 21 is the main road between Naples at the southern end and Canandaigua at the northern end of Canandaigua Lake. This intersection is at clockwise distance 35.1 mi. (56.5 km.) on the Canandaigua Lake Circumnavigation Route. And it is the last north bound entry on the Gannett Hill Route.

0.4 (0.6)   Gannett Hill Rd. @ NY 64   10.1 (16.3)
Continue traveling North on NY 64 to go to Honeoye Lake & Honeoye Village.
⇔ GANNETT HILL ROUTE, turn West on to Gannett Hill Rd. to climb the hill to the County Park (camping) and Gannett Hill. A beautiful view of the Lake; hiking (ONLY) on the Finger Lakes Trail; seeing the stars from the CEK Mees Observatory (reservations necessary); or going "overland along the ridge" to Naples at the Southern end of Canandaigua Lake awaits you if you climb this hill!

2.3 (3.7)   Co. Rd. 34 @ NY 64   8.2 (13.2)
Turn West on to Co. Rd. 34.
🚲 ⇔ CANANDAIGUA LAKE TO HONEOYE LAKE: <u>MIDDLE</u> CONNECTING ROUTE, continue traveling on NY 64 for a relatively non-hilly route to Honeoye Lake using NY 20A. NY 20A is 8.3 mi. (13.4 km.) North of this intersection. Turn West on to NY 20A; and follow it for 7.9 mi. (12.7 km.) to go Honeoye Village.
Going to Honeoye Lake along NY 20A is just as beautiful a ride as using this Cross Country Route and it is on wide

shouldered NY 20A with its relatively flattened hills. Loaded tourists should use NY 20A!

3.9 (6.3)   Co. Rd. 33 @ Co. Rd. 34   6.6 (10.6)
Turn North on to Co. Rd. 33 to go to Honeoye Lake.
🖬 Turn South on to Co. Rd. 33 to go to Naples and the southern end of Canandaigua Lake. Co. Rd. 33 is termed W. Hollow Rd. when it enters Naples Township and Clark St. in Naples itself! Ah, politics! Just follow it South for 8.3 mi. (13.4 km.) and you'll find yourself in Naples.

8.9 (14.3)   East Lake Rd. @ Co. Rd. 33   1.6 (2.6)
Turn North on to East Lake Rd. to go to Honeoye Village.
↻ HONEOYE LAKE CIRCUMNAVIGATION Route: Turn South on East Lake Rd. to 'round Honeoye Lake, clockwise.

9.5 (15.3)   NY 20A @ East Lake Rd.   1.0 (1.6)
Turn West on to NY 20A.

10.5 (16.9)   Co. Rd. 36 @ NY 20A   0.0 (0.0)
↺ HONEOYE LAKE CIRCUMNAVIGATION Route: Turn South on to Co. Rd. 36 to 'round Honeoye Lake counter-clockwise.
⇔ HONEOYE LAKE TO CANADICE LAKE: NORTHERN CONNECTING ROUTE.
⇔ HONEOYE LAKE TO HEMLOCK LAKE: NORTHERN CONNECTING ROUTE.
HONEOYE: Refer to the Honeoye Lake Circumnavigation Route for information.

E to W	**CANANDAIGUA LAKE TO HONEOYE LAKE**	W to E
Read ↓	**CROSS COUNTRY CONNECTING ROUTE**	Read up ↑

0.0 (0.0)   NY 21/Main St. @ NY 245   17.9 (28.8)
Travel South on NY 21/Main St.
↻ ↺ CANANDAIGUA CIRCUMNAVIGATION Route.
⇔ GANNETT HILL ROUTE.
⇔ CANANDAIGUA LAKE TO HONEOYE LAKE: MIDDLE
CONNECTING ROUTE & CROSS COUNTRY ROUTE.
Note: NY 21 is the main road between Naples at the
southern end and Canandaigua at the northern end of
Canandaigua Lake.

1.1 (1.8)   Co. Rd. 36/Clark St./   16.8 (27.0)
                   Hunts Hollow Rd.
                   @ NY 21/Main St.
Turn West on to Clark St. which is really Co. Rd. 36 by a
pseudonym. CR 36 is also termed *Hunts Hollow Rd.* for
part of its traverse. For ease we'll use, CR 36.

7.9 (12.7)   East Lake Rd. @ Co. Rd. 36   10.0 (16.1)
Continue traveling North on Co. Rd. 36 (W. Lake Rd.)
↻ ↺ HONEOYE LAKE CIRCUMNAVIGATION Route.
Counterclockwise travelers: You can turn on to East
Lake Rd. to go counterclockwise around Honeoye Lake.

17.9 (28.8)   Co. Rd. 36 @ NY 20A   0.0 (0.0)
↻ ↺ HONEOYE LAKE CIRCUMNAVIGATION Route:
⇔ CONNECTING ROUTES:
HONEOYE LAKE TO CANADICE LAKE.
HONEOYE LAKE TO HEMLOCK LAKE.
HONEOYE LAKE TO CANANDAIGUA LAKE.
HONEOYE: Refer to the Honeoye Lake Circumnavigation
Route for information.

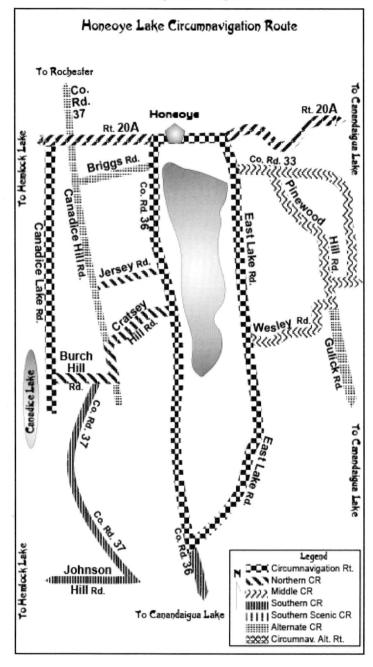

Honeoye Lake Circumnavigation Route

Conquest & Settlement

As you wander through the Finger Lakes you'll notice large and small plaques denoting places of historical significance. Some of these plaques are themselves part of history, being erected during the 20ᵗʰ century Depression as a Works Progress Administration program. Town fathers and mothers are noted; village founding dates; Iroquois Nations settlements; other significant and not so significant events in the history of the Region.

Plaques noting the Sullivan-Clinton Campaign during the Revolutionary War appear in the greatest number. Rarely remembered and rarely discussed, even in New York schools, this Campaign solidified the area for the colonists.

For Euro-Americans living on the Atlantic coast, the Finger Lakes Region was the American frontier. Only a few hearty woodsmen, traders, farmers and missionaries had made their way into the area. These emigrants bought/leased land or were permitted to stay in the area by an individual Iroquois Nation or clan. The Euro-American's descriptions of the area's lumbering potential, waterfalls and rich soil stimulated interest in the Finger Lakes area before the Revolutionary War. With the cities of the Atlantic coast experiencing an influx of immigrants in search of land and *freedom* from social and political structures more Euro-Americans began to come to the area. British policy essentially limited colonial expansion into the area by supporting Iroquois claims to sovereignty over Central and Western New York. The Revolutionary War changed everything!

The Iroquois Confederation was allied with the British. As more and more emigrants from the coast and the Hudson Valley moved to the frontier the Iroquois became more aggressive in asserting their sovereignty. The British, wanting to placate and keep their alliance with the Iroquois intact; wanting to maintain the Iroquois logistical support of food supplies (corn, grains, vegetables, meat and fish) and lumber (primarily for boats and troop housing) supported Iroquois claims to the Region. The new émigrés viewed the Native Americans as a nuisance and in many cases refused to honor agreements for leasing/ purchasing land or paying for trading rights. The Iroquois reacted by raiding the isolated interloping Euro-American settlers farms and villages. In doing so the Iroquois furnished the British with a second (third?) front to distract the American revolutionaries.

General Washington seeing the potential threat of a British invasion

from Canada after the defeat of Burgoyne at Saratoga in 1777;
the logistical importance of Iroquois supplies for the British; and
the potential economic/political benefits of the Finger Lakes
Region in the future Nation decided to solidify American claims
to Western New York.. An army of ~6300 men was assembled
at four locations - Fort Schuyler on the Upper Mohawk River
which joined a force at Canajoharie; Fort Pitt (Pittsburgh) in
Pennsylvania; and at Easton, Pennsylvania. Under Generals
John Sullivan and James Clinton these forces began a punitive
action against the Iroquois. Complete villages with their corn
fields, vegetable gardens, orchards, and domestic animals were
destroyed in slash and burn actions. Understandably, the
Iroquois fled; the settlers secured; and the new nations claims
to the American *West* would be clearly stated at the Peace
Treaty conferences.

The Iroquois who survived fled to the protection of British forts and
areas of influence. Many stayed in the Region and simply
disappeared into the forests. The Cayugas and Senecas were
particularly impacted by the Sullivan-Clinton Campaign. The
hegemony of the Iroquois Confederation was essentially over.
Thus opening the way for Revolutionary War veterans and folks
seeking land to safely come to the United States frontier.

The Iroquois leaders eventually made peace with the new nation.
Even playing one State off another by demanding recognition
and payment for their claims to the Finger Lakes, Central and
Western New York.

| Read ↓ | **HONEOYE LAKE** | Read up ↑ |
| Clockwise | **CIRCUMNAVIGATION** | Counterclockwise |

TRAVELER'S NOTE
There are no services along East Lake Rd. or Co. Rd. 36
(West Lake Rd.). Make certain you have sufficient snacks,
water and repair equipment for this circumnavigation.

0.0 (0.0)   Co. Rd. 36 @ NY 20A   19.4 (31.2)
Travel East on NY 20A.
⇔ HONEOYE LAKE TO CANADICE LAKE: NORTHERN
CONNECTING ROUTE, travel West on NY 20A.
⇔ HONEOYE LAKE TO HEMLOCK LAKE: NORTHERN
CONNECTING ROUTE, travel West on NY 20A.
⇔ HONEOYE LAKE TO CANANDAIGUA LAKE
CONNECTING ROUTES.

HONEOYE

Info.:   Richmond Twn., 20 E. Main St., Honeoye, NY 14471, 585 229-5757. AC: 585. ZC: 14471.
Services: Convenience store, restaurants.
Lodging: Cottage rentals. B&B: Greenwoods Inn, 8136 Quayle Rd., Honeoye 14471, 229-2111.
Attractions: Honeoye Lake. Harriet Hollister Spencer Pk. (MTB ok), Canadice Hill Rd. (S. of the Lake), 335-8111; Honeoye Lake St. Marina Pk. (no camping, no H2O), East Lake Rd. (south end of Lake).

0.9 (1.4)   East Lake Rd. @ NY 20A   18.5 (29.8)
Turn South on to East Lake Rd.

1.5 (2.4)   Co. Rd. 33 @ East Lake Rd.   17.9 (28.8)
Continue traveling South on East Lake Rd.
⇔ HONEOYE LAKE TO CANANDAIGUA LAKE: CROSS COUNTRY CONNECTING ROUTE Going to Canandaigua Lake? Turn East on Co. Rd. 33. This is a very demanding Route, not suitable for loaded bicycle tourists.

5.7 (9.2)   Honeoye Lake St. Marine Park   13.7 (22.0)
                   @ East Lake Rd.
Day use only. Toilets. No water. Yeah! I know that sounds
      funny but it means no drinking water.

9.2 (14.9)   Dirt Road Section on E. Lake Rd.   10.4 (16.7)
It's dirt for about .7 mi. (1.1 km.) to Co. Rd. 36.

10.0 (16.1)   Co. Rd. 36 @ East Lake Rd.   9.4 (15.1)
Turn North on to CR 36.
⇔ HONEOYE LAKE TO CANANDAIGUA: SOUTHERN CONNECTING ROUTE.

16.2 (26.1)   Cratsley Hill Rd. @ Co. Rd. 36   3.2 (5.1)
Continue North on Co. Rd. 36 to complete the circumnavigation of Honeoye Lake.
⇔ HONEOYE LAKE TO CANADICE LAKE: MIDDLE CONNECTING ROUTE.

19.4 (31.2)   NY 20A @ Co. Rd. 36   0.0 (0.0)
HONEOYE

Read ↓	**HONEOYE LAKE**	Read up ↑
Clockwise	**CIRCUMNAVIGATION**	Counterclockwise

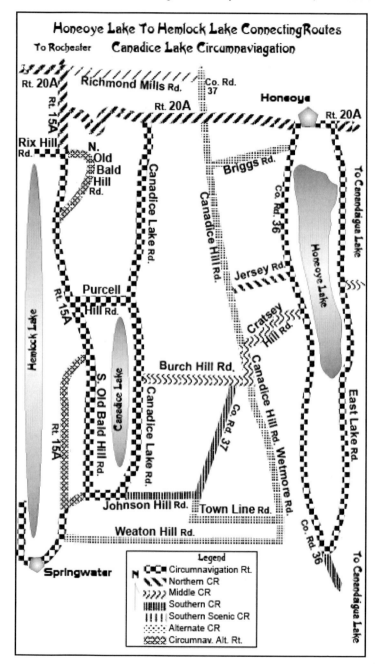

Honeoye Lake To Hemlock Lake ConnectingRoutes
Canadice Lake Circumnaviagation

Legend

- C C Circumnavigation Rt.
- Northern CR
- Middle CR
- Southern CR
- Southern Scenic CR
- Alternate CR
- Circumnav. Alt. Rt.

E to W	**HONEOYE LAKE TO CANADICE LAKE**	W to E
Read ↓	**NORTHERN CONNECTING ROUTE**	Read up ↑

TRAVELER'S NOTE

Honeoye Lake, Canadice Lake and Hemlock Lake are in close proximity to each other. Thus the use of a combined Connecting Route Map containing the Canadice Lake Circumnavigation Route.

Any way you go between Honeoye Lake and Canadice Lake you will be ascending/desending steeply sloped hills.

There is no easy way to go from the southern end of Honeoye Lake to the Southern End of Canadice Lake.

Canadice Lake and Hemlock Lake form the water shed and reservoirs for Rochester, NY. As such there are no services or cottages around either Lake. Be prepared to carry sufficient water, snacks and food when going around both Lakes.

0.0 (0.0)   Co. Rd. 36 @ NY 20A   7.8 (12.6)
Travel West on NY 20A.
⇔ HONEOYE LAKE TO HEMLOCK LAKE: NORTHERN CONNECTING ROUTE.
⇔ HONEOYE LAKE TO CANANDAIGUA LAKE CONNECTING ROUTES.
HONEOYE: Refer to the Honeoye Lake Circumnavigation Route for information.

3.6 (5.8)   Canadice Lake Rd.   4.2 (6.8)
                 @ NY 20A
This road is slightly obscure from NY 20A thus look for it! It is called Barnard Rd. on the North side of NY 20A. If you begin to descend to Hemlock on NY 20A you've missed Canadice Lake Rd.
Turn South on to Canadice Lake Rd.
⇔ HONEOYE LAKE TO HEMLOCK LAKE: NORTHERN CONNECTING ROUTE, continue traveling West on NY 20A to go to the northern end of Hemlock Lake.

4.3 (6.9)   Purcell Hill Rd.   0.0 (0.0)
                 @ Canadice Lake Rd.
Continue traveling South on Canadice Lake Rd.
Theoretically the northern end of Canadice Lake.
↻ ↺ CANADICE LAKE CIRCUMNAVIGATION Route.
⇔ CANADICE LAKE TO HEMLOCK LAKE NORTHERN CONNECTING ROUTE.

7.4 (11.9)   Boat launch @ Canadice Lake Rd.   0.4 (0.6)
Continue traveling South on Canadice Lake Rd.
The boat launch is barely discernible from the road.
Canadice Lake.

7.8 (12.6)   Burch Hill Rd.   0.8 (1.3)
          @ Canadice Lake Rd.
Wasn't that quick and easy! You're here at Canadice Lake.
⇔ HONEOYE LAKE TO CANADICE LAKE: MIDDLE
CONNECTING ROUTE. Turn East on to Burch Hill Rd. to
go to the middle of Honeoye Lake.

| E to W | **HONEOYE LAKE TO CANADICE LAKE** | W to E |
| Read ↓ | **NORTHERN CONNECTING ROUTE** | Read up ↑ |

TRAVELER'S NOTE

There is no direct southern route between Honeoye Lake and Canadice Lake. Use this Middle Connecting Route to go from the middle of the West side of Honeoye Lake to the North end of Canadice Lake.

You are pedaling up very steep slopes to the center of the ridge between Honeoye Lake and Canadice Lake. Then you are braking down the steep slope to Canadice Lake. The distances are not long but the slopes are severe. There are absolutely no services between the two Lakes. Make certain that you have water, snacks & repair supplies.

0.0 (0.0)   Cratsley Hill Rd. @ Co. Rd. 36   2.4 (3.9)
Turn West on to Cratsley Hill Rd.

1.2 (1.9)   CR 37/Canadice Hill Rd.   1.2 (1.9)
                   @ Cratsley Hill Rd.
Turn South on to Co. Rd. 37/Canadice Hill Rd.

1.6 (2.6)   Canadice Hill Rd.   0.8 (1.3)
                   Turns West
Turn West at the sign with big black letters on a white rectangular background hidden behind a tree with an arrow & stating: *Co. Rd. 37* →. Landmarks: Cemetery and Canadice Methodist Church.

1.8 (2.9)   Burch Hill Rd.   0.6 (1.0)
                   @ CR 37/Canadice Hill Rd.
Travel straight West on to Burch Hill Rd.
Co. Rd. 37/Canadice Hill Rd. bears South.
Use extreme care going down the slope on Burch Hill Rd.

2.4 (3.9)   Canadice Lake Rd.   0.0 (0.0)
                   @ Burch Hill Rd.
CANADICE LAKE! Interesting ride!
↻ ↻ CANADICE LAKE CIRCUMNAVIGATION Route.

Water

Contrast the purity of Canadice and Hemlock Lakes with the building laden shores of the other Lakes. Even Skaneateles Lake which serves as part of Syracuse's water supply has human habitation on its shores. The wilderness is preserved here with humankind's need for water.

Read ↓   **CANADICE LAKE CIRCUMNAVIGATION**   Read up ↑
Clockwise   Counterclockwise

TRAVELER'S NOTE

Canadice Lake and Hemlock Lake form the basis of Rochester's water supply. As such you can not swim in either Lake. Water supply reservoirs are also reservoirs of wilderness to some extent. There are no services at any point along the Canadice Circumnavigation Route. Be prepared and make certain that you have sufficient water, snacks and repair supplies before you use a Connecting Route from either Honeoye or Hemlock Lakes to Canadice Lake.

0.0 (0.0)   Purcell Hill Rd.   12.2 (19.6)
                   @ Canadice Lake Rd.
Travel South on Canadice Lake Rd.
⇔ CANADICE LAKE TO HEMLOCK LAKE: NORTHERN CONNECTING ROUTE

0.7 (1.1)   Boat launch   11.5 (18.5)
                   @ Canadice Lake Rd.
The boat launch is barely discernible from the road.

1.1 (1.8)   Burch Hill Rd.   11.1 (17.9)
                   @ Canadice Lake Rd.
Continue traveling South on Canadice Lake Rd. to circumnavigate the Lake.
⇔ HONEOYE LAKE TO CANADICE LAKE: MIDDLE CONNECTING ROUTE.

6.3 (10.1)   Johnson Hill Rd.   5.9 (9.5)
                   @ Canadice Lake Rd.
Turn West on to Johnson Hill Rd.
(A campground is 1 mi. (1.6 km.) South of this intersection on Wheaton Rd.

7.1 (11.4)   Bald Hill Rd. S. (S. entrance)   5.1 (8.2)
                  @ Johnson Hill Rd.
Turn North on Bald Hill Rd. S.
🚲 Alternatively you could continue traveling Southwest on
Johnson Hill Rd. for less than a pedal stroke to NY 15A.
Then turn North on NY 15A. The mileage and climb is
about the same using Bald Hill Rd. S. or NY 15A. NY 15A
has a 6 ft. (2 m.) shoulder and smooth asphalt but lots of
cars.

10.3 (16.6)   NY 15A   1.9 (3.1)
                  @ Bald Hill Rd. S. (N. entrance.)
Turn North on to NY 15A.

12.2 (19.6)   Purcell Hill Rd. @ NY 15A   0.0 (0.0)
Turn East on Purcell Hill Rd. to complete the
circumnavigation of Canadice Lake.
You have actually circumnavigated Canadice Lake.
However if you must go back to the starting point, go
ahead and turn East. It is a very steep climb to the center
of the ridge between Canadice and Hemlock Lakes. And
then a steep decent to the other Lake. You've just climbed
a mighty long steep hill, enjoy the decent!
⇔ CANADICE LAKE TO HEMLOCK LAKE: NORTHERN
CONNECTING ROUTE, using Purcell Hill Rd.
⇔ ↻ HEMLOCK LAKE CIRCUMNAVIGATION Route. NY
15A serves as both the road on the West side of Canadice
Lake and as the road on the East side of Hemlock Lake. A
2 for 1 lake road! Continue traveling North on NY 15A to
go to the Northern end of Hemlock Lake.

Read ↓   **CANADICE LAKE CIRCUMNAVIGATION**   Read up ↑
Clockwise   Counterclockwise

| E to W | **CANADICE LAKE TO HEMLOCK LAKE** | W to E |
| Read ↓ | **NORTHERN CONNECTING ROUTE** | Read up ↑ |

TRAVELER'S NOTE

We are pedaling steep climbs!

0.0 (0.0)   Purcell Hill Rd.   1.5 (2.4)
                   @ Canadice Lake Rd.
Travel West on Purcell Hill Rd.
You will be going up from Canadice Lake to the ridge between Canadice Lake at Lawrence Hill Rd. Then you make a steep decent from the ridge to Hemlock Lake.
↺ ↻ CANADICE LAKE CIRCUMNAVIGATION Route.

1.5 (2.4)   NY 15A @ Purcell Hill Rd.   0.0 (0.0)
Turn North on to NY 15A.
↺ ↻ HEMLOCK LAKE CIRCUMNAVIGATION Route.
Yup! 15A is the only road between Canadice Lake and Hemlock Lake at this point. It's a 2 lakes for 1 road goodie! If you call that hill a goodie!
You can go either way here. North or South. To avoid climbing up 15A again from the Northern end of Hemlock Lake, I suggest you begin your circumnavigation of Hemlock Lake from this point by going South. You are 3.6 mi. (5.8 km.) from the northern end of Hemlock Lake but it is a long climb up as you go North on NY 15A.

5.1 (8.2)   Rix Hill Rd. @ NY 15A   0.0 (0.0)
↺ ↻ HEMLOCK LAKE CIRCUMNAVIGATION Route.
Turn West on to Rix Hill Rd. A sign states that Hemlock Lake is the water supply for Rochester. You're at Hemlock Lake's northern end.

| E to W | **CANADICE LAKE TO HEMLOCK LAKE** | W to E |
| Read ↓ | **NORTHERN CONNECTING ROUTE** | Read up ↑ |

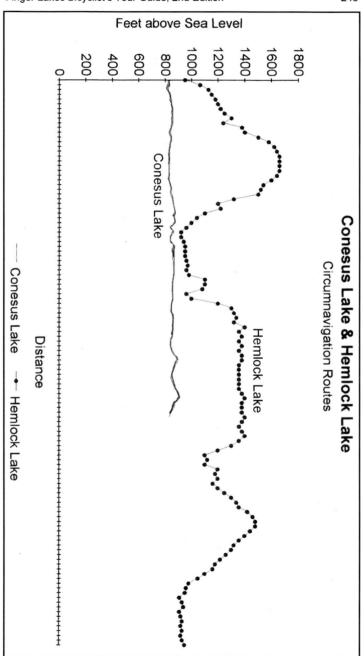

Conesus Lake & Hemlock Lake
Circumnavigation Routes

Feet above Sea Level

Conesus Lake

Hemlock Lake

Distance

—— Conesus Lake   —•— Hemlock Lake

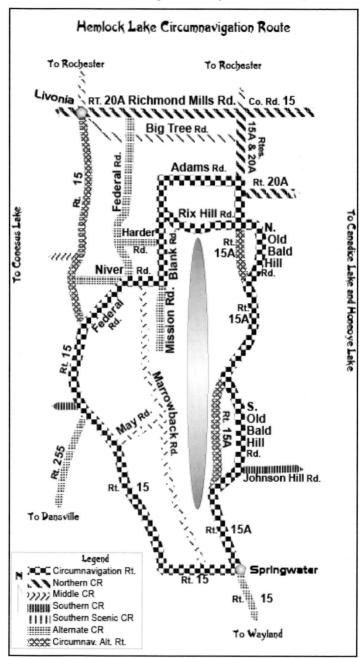

Hemlock Lake Circumnavigation Route

To Rochester   To Rochester

Livonia   RT. 20A Richmond Mills Rd.   Co. Rd. 15

Big Tree Rd.

Adams Rd.

Rt. 20A

Federal Rd.

Rt. 15

Rix Hill Rd.

Harder Rd.

N. Old Bald Hill Rd.

Blank Rd.

Rt. 15A

Niver Rd.

Federal Rd.

Mission Rd.

Rt. 15A

Rt. 15

Marrowback Rd.

May Rd.

S. Old Bald Hill Rd.

Rt. 15A

Rt. 255

Johnson Hill Rd.

Rt. 15

To Dansville

Rt. 15A

To Conesus Lake

To Canadice Lake and Honeoye Lake

Rt. 15   Springwater

Rt. 15

To Wayland

Legend

- Circumnavigation Rt.
- Northern CR
- Middle CR
- Southern CR
- Southern Scenic CR
- Alternate CR
- Circumnav. Alt. Rt.

Women

In 1848, 300 women met in Seneca Falls at the Northern end of Cayuga Lake. They discussed their condition as women in American society. In general the women who attended this conference were solidly middle class. Most were educated to the high school level. Almost all were married and had children. A few had careers as businesswomen, doctors and lawyers. A group of folks who lived a comfortable life style.

The Declaration of Sentiments proclaimed at that Convention began a civil rights movement for women which continues today. In the first quarter of the 20th century one of the most important goals of the Declaration was realized - voting rights for women. World War II enhanced women's economic power by opening employment opportunities as men left the labor market to become members of the armed forces.

Another period of *the comfortable life*, the 1950s and 60s, gave rise to a period of woman's rights activism from ~1970 until now. As the goals expressed by 300 women who issued the Declaration of Sentiments were accomplished, new economic and civil rights goals were established by other generation. Goals are funny things. Sometimes it is simply a passing of time for a goal to become a reality. Other goals need consistent lobbying and vigilance to be achieved. There is no denying that what began in Seneca Falls revolutionized politics in the United States.

Read ↓   **HEMLOCK LAKE CIRCUMNAVIGATION**   Read up ↑
Clockwise   Counterclockwise

TRAVELER'S NOTE
Please remember that this is "my" water supply. No swimming is allowed. Notice that there are no gas powered motor boats on the Lake. Only low powered electric motor, hand, and wind powered boats.

0.0 (0.0)   NY 15A @ NY 20A   1.0 (1.6)

⛟ You think I made a mistake! Nope! Folks who came to Hemlock Lake from Canadice Lake need to know where the nearest refueling depot is located. The convenience store at this intersection is the only store where you can obtain snacks, drinks etc. before you conquer Canadice Lake or the southern end of Honeoye Lake. Stock up here.

↺ From 15A @ 20A travel South on NY 15A to go to the northern end of Hemlock Lake and to circumnavigate Hemlock

Lake clockwise

↺ Travel North on NY 15A to circumnavigate Hemlock Lake counterclockwise.

⇔ CANADICE LAKE TO HEMLOCK LAKE: CONNECTING ROUTE, turn East on to NY 20A to go to the Northern end of Canadice Lake and the northern end of Honeoye Lake. Canadice Lake Rd., the turn off for Canadice Lake, is 1.7 mi. (2.7 km.) East of this intersection.

⇔ Honeoye Village and Honeoye Lake are 5.3 mi. (8.5 km.) from this intersection. As you go up the hill on NY 20A you will have a magnificent view of Hemlock Lake.

0.0 (0.0)   Rix Hill Rd./   29.7 (47.8)
                   Old Bald Hill Rd. **N.** (northern entrance)
                   Hemlock Lake Park
                   @ NY 15A

TRAVELER'S NOTE
Rix Hill Rd. at this intersection, is composed of large gravel. It always has been large gravel and I doubt if the City of Rochester, which owns Hemlock Lake, ever plans on paving or even chip sealing this section of the road. After ~100 ft. (34 m.) of gravel you can cut across the grass to asphalt. But to see Hemlock Lake in all its purity, you must first traverse the gravel.

Follow the directions to the registration tank! Sign the book. Take the permit. Keep it as a memento. Go to the Park and view the Lake. Look for the eagles! Follow the directions to the registration tank! Sign the book. Take the permit. Keep it as a memento. Go to the Park and view the Lake. Look

for the eagles!

There is a dirt road on the East side of the Lake, behind the water plant. I strongly suggest that you follow it to its end ~1 mi. (1.6 km.) and sit by the shore away from everything, for a while.

↻ **Turn** South on to NY 15A. NY 15A parallels Hemlock Lake for its entire length. You can use this highway to go all the way to Springwater at the southern end of the Lake.

🔄 OR cross 15A (very carefully) and use Old Bald Hill Rd. N. (northern entrance to Old Bald Hill Rd. N.) to go South. Old Bald Hill Rd. (N. & S.) parallels NY 15A, thus the mileage is the same using either road. It is a chip sealed rural road with a rolling hills character. NY 15A is a asphalt State Highway with a 6 ft. (2 m.) shoulder. Old Bald Hill is discontinuous and thus there are two sections, N. and S.

1.9 (3.1)	Old Bald Hill Rd. **N.** (southern entrance) @ NY 15A	27.8 (44.7)

Clockwise travelers: Turn on to (from Old Bald Hill Rd. N.) or continue traveling South on NY 15A.

Counterclockwise travelers: As an alternative to NY 15A you can turn North on to Old Bald Hill Rd. N. (southern entrance) and use it to go to the North end of the Lake. It is a chip sealed rural road with a rolling hills demeanor. Verses NY 15A's asphalt and straight up demeanor.

2.5 (4.0)	Purcell Hill Rd. @ NY 15A	27.2 (43.8)

Continue traveling South on NY 15A.

⇔ CANADICE LAKE TO HEMLOCK LAKE: NORTHERN CONNECTING ROUTE.

4.5 (7.2)	Old Bald Hill Rd. **S.** (northern entrance) @ NY 15A	25.2 (40.6)

Turn South on to Old Bald Hill Rd. S. (northern entrance). This section of Old Bald Hill Rd. is a bit nicer to bicycle upon. It also affords some beautiful views.

🔄 OR continue traveling South on NY 15A.

7.7 (12.4)	Old Bald Hill Rd. **S.** (southern entrance) @ NY 15A	22.0 (35.4)

Clockwise circumnavigators: Turn South from Old Bald Hill S. on to or continue traveling South on NY 15A.

Counterclockwise circumnavigators should turn on to Old Bald Hill S. (southern entrance). This road it is a more gentle climb above Hemlock Lake than NY 15A. The ascent elevation is the same but there are more flat spots on Old Bald Hill S. And there are real nice views of the Lake.

⇔ CANADICE CIRCUMNAVIGATION ROUTE: Clockwise and counterclockwise travelers who want to go to Canadice Lake's southern end should turn on to Old Bald Hill S. and then, almost immediately on to Johnson Hill Rd. From that point follow the Canadice Lake Circumnavigation Route, counterclockwise, northward on the East side of Canadice Lake.

11.0 (17.7)   NY 15/Springwater Rd. @ NY 15A   18.7 (30.1)
Turn North on to NY 15/Springwater Rd.

SPRINGWATER

Info.: Canadice Twn., 5949 Co. Rd. 37, Springwater 14580, 585 367-2050.

Serv.: Convenience store. 4 mi. (6.5 km.) S. of Springwater on NY 15 is Wayland. There is a grocery store; restaurants; and pharmacy in Wayland. Also NY 17, the Southern Tier Expressway for those arriving by auto.

Lodging: Camping: Holiday Hill Cpgd., 7818 Marvin Hill Rd., Springwater 14560, 585 669-2600.

Counterclockwise travelers: There are no services on the East side of Hemlock Lake. Circumnavigating Hemlock Lake involves ascending and descending a long steep hill on the East side of the Lake. Make certain that you have sufficient water, snacks and repair supplies. Make certain that your bicycle is in excellent condition.

11.5 (18.5)   Kellogg Rd./Marrowback Rd.   18.2 (29.3)
                   @ NY 15

Clockwise Circumnavigators: Continue traveling North on NY 15/Springwater Rd.

Counterclockwise Circumnavigators: Continue traveling South on NY 15/Springwater Rd.

Kellogg Rd. is a dirt road leading to Marrowback Rd. (also a dirt road). However, for the most insane of bicyclists who have a mountain bike and want to go up a 85 degree slope for 6 mi. (9.8 km.) this route is included. It is definitely <u>not</u> recommended to use this route and is included because all this cycling and keyboarding has made me a bit nuts!

0.0 (0.0)	Kellogg Rd. @ NY 15	11.9 (19.2)

Turn North on to Kellogg Rd.

.4 (.6)   Marrowback Rd. @ Kellogg Rd.   11.5 (18.5)
Turn North on to Marrowback Rd. Begin your assent up (no fooling it is an 85°+ slope).

3.2 (5.1)   White Rd. @ Marrowback Rd.   8.7 (14.0)
Had enough? Then turn West on to White Rd.. It is the only way off Marrowback Rd. and leads you to May St. and to NY 15 on the Hemlock Lake Circumnavigation Route.

8.0 (12.9)   Bishop Rd. @ Marrowback Rd.   3.9 (6.3)
Turn East on to Bishop Rd.

8.7 (14.0)   Mission Rd. @ Bishop Rd.   3.2 (5.1)
Turn North on to Mission Rd. Hey, Mission Rd. has a chip seal surface!

9.2 (14.8)   Vineyard Rd. @ Mission Rd.   2.7 (4.3)
              @ Mission Rd./Blank Rd.
Yes there is a winery! And you deserve to get drunk for using Marrowback Rd. Eagle Crest Vineyards, 7107 Vineyard Rd., 346-2321.
Half way between Vineyard Rd. & the next intersection Mission Rd. changes its name to Blank Rd.

11.1 (17.9)   Niver Rd. @ Blank Rd.   .8 (1.3)
Continue traveling North on Blank Rd. You'll hit a short .5 mi. (.8 km.) dirt section of Blank Rd.

11.9 (19.2)   Harder Rd. @ Blank Rd.   0.0 (0.0)
Follow the Hemlock Lake Circumnavigation Route from this intersection.
You're crazy! Absolutely crazy for using this Route. It's just as crazy to go down!

15.7 (25.3)   May Rd. @ NY 15   14.0 (22.5)
Continue traveling North on NY 15.
Marrowback Rd. crazies join us here.
WEBSTER CROSSING. No services.

19.7 (31.7)   NY 255 & Slicker Hill Rd. @ NY 15 10.0 (16.1)
Continue traveling North on NY 15.
⇔ HEMLOCK LAKE TO CONESUS LAKE: SOUTHERN CONNECTING ROUTE.

CONESUS

Services: Convenience store/gas station. There are a few seasonal convenience stores along Conesus Lake's East Lake Rd. Water & toilet at ball field. AC: 585. ZC: 14435.
Lodging: Cottages: B&Bs: East Lake, 5305 E. Lake Rd, 346-3350; Conesus Lake, 2388 East Lake Rd., 346-6526,

Camping: Conesus Lake Cpgd., 2202 E. Lake Rd., 346-5472; Southern Shores Cpgd., 5707 East Lake Rd, 346-5482.

Attraction: Eagle Crest Vineyards, 7107 Vineyard Rd., 346-2321, although Eagle Crest has a Conesus address, it is really located far above the Lake. It actually overlooks Hemlock Lake.

20.7 (33.3)   Co. Rd. 56/Federal Rd. @ NY 15   9.0 (14.5)
Bear Northeast on to Federal Rd.
You can continue traveling North on NY 15. NY 20A in Livonia is 6.7 mi. (10.8 km.) North on 15. At the intersection of NY 15 & NY 20A turn East for 3.1 mi. (4.9 km.) to the Jct. of Rtes. 20A & 15A. Turn South on to Rtes. 20A/15A and ride for 2.9 mi. (4.7 km.) and you'll be at Rix Hill Rd., the North end of Hemlock Lake

22.3 (35.9)   Cole Rd. @ Co. Rd. 56/Federal Rd.   7.4 (11.9)
Continue traveling North on Federal Rd.
If you don't like Federal Rd. you can turn Southeast on to Cole Rd. & return to NY 15.

23.6 (38.0)   Niver Rd.   6.1 (9.8)
                    @ Co. Rd. 56/Federal Rd.
Continue North on Federal Rd.
Turn East on to Niver Rd. to go Marrowback Rd. (only riders with loose spokes for brains will use Marrowback Rd.) and Mission Rd. The signs will direct you to the winery on Mission Rd. This is a chip sealed road route to the winery.

24.2 (38.9)   Harder Rd.   5.5 (8.9)
                    @ Co. Rd. 56/Federal Rd.
Turn East on to Harder Rd.

25.2 (40.6)   Blank Rd. @ Harder Rd.   4.5 (7.2)
Turn North on to Blank Rd.
Turning South on to Blank Rd. brings you to a short stretch of dirt road at Blank and Niver Rd. Ride South on the dirt for .5 mi. (.8 km.) to Mission Rd. & follow the winery signs. From the winery there is a beautiful view of the Lake.

26.0 (41.8)   Rix Hill Rd. @ Blank Rd.   3.7 (6.0)
Continue traveling North on Blank Rd.
Yes, you can use Rix Hill Rd. to go back to the North end of Hemlock Lake at Hemlock Park. It is partially a dirt road (solid pack clay) and going this way, that is, down the slope is very nice. Excellent view of the Lake. You will also

cut off miles (km.) from the distance by using Rix Hill Rd.
from this point. It is a very short but somewhat steep .5 mi.
(.8 km.) to the Valley floor.

27.0 (43.5)   Adams Rd. @ Blank Rd.   2.7 (4.3)
Turn East on to Adams Rd.

27.8 (44.7)   Rtes. 20A/15A @ Adams Rd.   1.9 (3.1)
Turn South on Rtes. 20A/15A.
⇔ HEMLOCK LAKE TO CONESUS LAKE: NORTHERN
CONNECTING ROUTE. You're already ½ way up the NY
15A hill in Hemlock. Keep going North.

28.7 (46.2)   Rte. 15A Jct. NY 20A   1.0 (1.6)
Continue traveling South on NY 15A to go to the North end
of Hemlock Lake.
⇔ HEMLOCK LAKE TO HONEOYE LAKE: NORTHERN
CONNECTING ROUTE. Turn East on NY 20A to go to
Honeoye Village and Honeoye Lake.

29.7 (47.8)   Rix Hill Rd. @ NY 15A   0.0 (0.0)
HEMLOCK LAKE northern end.

Read ↓   **HEMLOCK LAKE CIRCUMNAVIGATION**   Read up ↑
Clockwise   Counterclockwise

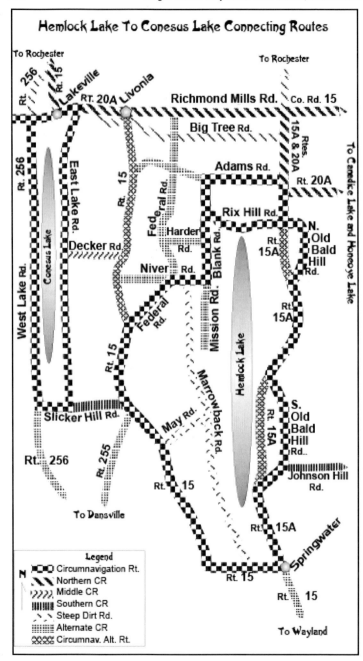

Hemlock Lake To Conesus Lake Connecting Routes

E to W Read ↓	**HEMLOCK LAKE TO CONESUS LAKE** **NORTHERN CONNECTING ROUTE**	W to E Read up ↑

0.0 (0.0)   Rix Hill Rd. @ NY 15A   9.1 (14.6)
Turn North on to NY 15A.

1.0 (1.6)   NY 20A Jct. NY 15A   8.1 (13.0)
Continue North on Rtes. 15A/20A.

2.2 (3.5)   Big Tree Rd. @ Rtes. 15A/20A   6.9 (11.1)
Continue traveling North on Rtes. 15A/20A.
⮌ Alternatively you can turn West on Big Tree Rd. Big Tree
Rd. ends on NY 20A in Livonia. The distance using Big
Tree Rd. or this route is about the same. But Big Tree Rd.
has more ups and downs.

3.3 (5.3)   NY 20A/Richmond Mills Rd.   5.8 (9.3)
                   Jct. NY 15A
Turn West on to NY 20A/Richmond Mills Rd.

6.4 (10.3)   NY 15 Jct. NY 20A   2.7 (4.3)
Continue traveling West on Rtes. 20A/15.
LIVONIA: See Conesus Lake Circumnavigation Route.

7.8 (12.6)   Co. Rd. 6/East Lake Rd.   1.3 (2.1)
                   @ Rtes. 20A/15
↺ CONESUS LAKE CIRCUMNAVIGATION Route, clockwise circliers turn South on to CR 6/East Lake Rd.

8.6 (13.8)   NY 20A Jct. NY 15   0.5 (0.8)
Continue traveling West on NY 20A.
LAKEVILLE: See Conesus Lake Circumnavigation Route.

9.1 (14.6)   NY 256/West Lake Rd. @ NY 20A   0.0 (0.0)
↺ Counterclockwise travelers turn South on to NY 256/
West Lake Rd. to go 'round the Lake.

E to W Read ↓	**CONESUS LAKE TO HEMLOCK LAKE** **NORTHERN CONNECTING ROUTE**	W to E Read up ↑

E to W Read ↓	**HEMLOCK LAKE TO CONESUS LAKE** **MIDDLE CONNECTING ROUTE**	W to E Read up ↑

0.0 (0.0)   Rix Hill Rd. @ NY 15A   10.7 (17.2)
Turn North on to NY 15A.

1.0 (1.6)   NY 20A Jct. NY 15A   9.7 (15.6)
Continue traveling North on Rtes. 15A/20A.

1.9 (3.1)   Adams Rd. @ Rtes. 20A/15A   8.8 (14.2)
Turn West on Adams Rd.

3.4 (5.5)   Blank Rd. @ Adams Rd.   7.3 (11.7)
Turn South on to Blank Rd.

5.2 (8.4)   Harder Rd. @ Blank Rd.   5.5 (8.9)
Turn West on to Harder Rd.

6.2 (10.0)   Co. Rd. 56/Federal Rd.   4.5 (7.2)
                          @ Harder Rd.
Turn North on to Co. Rd. 56/Federal Rd.

6.8 (10.9)   Coe Rd. @ Co. Rd. 56/Federal Rd.   3.9 (6.3)
Turn South on to Co. Rd. 56/Federal Rd.

8.3 (13.4)   NY 15 @ Coe Rd.   2.4 (3.9)
Turn South on to NY 15.

8.8 (14.2)   Decker Rd. @ NY 15   1.9 (3.1)
Turn West on to Decker Rd.

10.7 (17.2)   East Lake Rd. @ Decker Rd.   0.0 (0.0)
↻ Clockwise circumnavigators turn South on CR 6/East
Lake Rd.
↺ Counterclockwise 'round Lake Conesus travelers turn
North on to CR 6/East Lake Rd.

E to W Read ↓	**CONESUS LAKE TO HEMLOCK LAKE** **MIDDLE CONNECTING ROUTE**	W to E Read up ↑

| E to W | **HEMLOCK LAKE TO CONESUS LAKE** | W to E |
| Read ↓ | **SOUTHERN CONNECTING ROUTE** | Read up ↑ |

0.0 (0.0)   NY 15/Springwater Rd. @ NY 15A   9.0 (14.5)
Turn North on to NY 15/Springwater Rd.
SPRINGWATER: See Hemlock Lake Circumnavigation
Route for information.

0.5 (0.8)   Kellogg Rd./Marrowback Rd.   8.2 (13.2)
                    @ NY 15
Continue traveling North on NY 15/Springwater Rd.

4.7 (7.6)   May Rd. @ NY 15   4.0 (6.4)
Continue traveling North on NY 15
WEBSTER CROSSING

8.7 (14.0)   NY 255 & Slicker Hill Rd. @ NY 15   0.3 (.5)
Turn West on to Slicker Hill Rd.

9.0 (14.5)   East Lake Rd. @ Slicker Hill Rd.   0.0 (0.0)
Southern End of Conesus Lake. Clockwise travelers
continue West along Slicker Rd. to West Lake Rd. Counter-
clockwise travelers turn North on to East Lake Rd.
CONESUS: Refer to the Conesus Lake Circumnavigation
Route for information.

| E to W | **CONESUS LAKE TO HEMLOCK LAKE** | W to E |
| Read ↓ | **SOUTHERN CONNECTING ROUTE** | Read up ↑ |

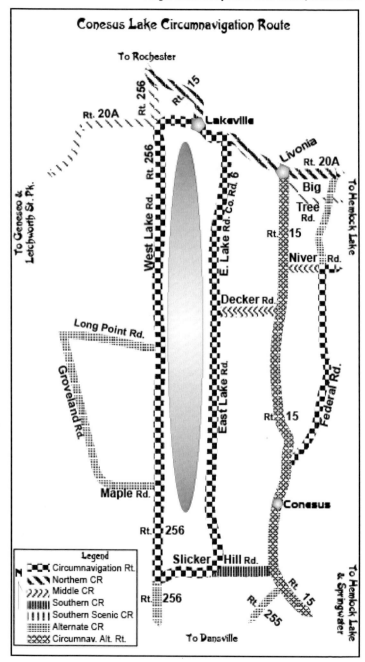

Conesus Lake Circumnavigation Route

Pristine and Not So Pristine

With the exception of a few small parks along its eastern and western shores and the marsh at its southern end, Conesus Lake epitomizes human habitation on the Finger Lakes. Its shores crowded with cottages large and small. Its rocky water line laden with boat lifts and docks. In summer its center is filled with fast moving skiffs and sleek sailboats. Laughter rings out from front yards facing the Lake. Splashing families play. Fish, at dawn and dusk, catch darning flies and mosquitoes. Birds swoop down for insects and fish as frogs croak incessantly on humid summer nights.

There is nothing wrong with what transpires on the Finger Lakes. It's simply ironic that folks who have cottages along the shores go there to escape the heat and crowded conditions in urban and suburban Rochester, Buffalo and Syracuse. To have a bit of private time with their families and friends; to entertain and provide a place for children and grandchildren to frolic. Yet they crowd themselves along the shore, cottage abutting cottage. For many the *cottage* started as a small non-nondescript building, a dream for summer delights. Over the years the cottage was enlarged and modern conveniences such as electricity and good water were installed. The septic system draining eventually into the lake replaced with connections to the town sanitary sewer system. More land was sold along the shores and more people came to enjoy the beauty of the lake. And then the original reason for building a lake shore cottage, the beauty of the lake and its surrounding hills, became obscured.

Gad! I want a lake shore cottage. But one with 40 acres, in all directions, between mine and my neighbor's cottage!

Read ↓	**CONESUS LAKE CIRCUMNAVIGATION**	Read up ↑
Clockwise		Counterclockwise

0.0 (0.0)   Co. Rd. 6/East Lake Rd.   18.6 (29.9)
                   @ Rtes. 20A/15
Turn South on Co. Rd. 6/East Lake Rd. to circumnavigate
Conesus Lake clockwise.

LAKEVILLE & LIVONIA

Info.: Livonia Area CofC, PO Box 571, Lakeville NY 14480.
Lakeville is about 1 mi. (1.6 km.) West of Livonia.
AC: 585. ZC: Lakeville, 14480; Livonia,

Biking Info.: Regional Transit Service (RTS), 654-0200. All RTS buses have bike racks (accommodating 2 bicycles). During the morning or evening rush hours, you can use a RTS bus & its bike rack to go to and return from the Lakeville Park & Ride Stop near the northern end of Conesus Lake. Park & Ride buses only operate during weekday rush hours. Nearest bike shop is in Geneseo, ~10 mi. (16 km.) West of Lakeville on NY 20A.

Services: Grocery, convenience store, restaurants, bank & laundromat.

Lodging: Rental cottages. B&Bs: MacPhail House, 5477 Lakeville Rd, Geneseo 14454, 346-5600; Stoney Grove, 5851 Barber Hill Rd, Geneseo 14454, 243-9629.

3.9 (6.3)   Decker Rd.   14.7 (23.7)
                   @ Co. Rd. 6/East Lake Rd.
Continue traveling South on Co. Rd. 6/East Lake Rd.
Turn East on to Decker Rd. to go to Hemlock Lake via the Middle Connecting Route.

CONESUS

Info.: Although not directly on East Lake Rd. the Village of Conesus is accessible via Decker Rd. @ NY 15. AC: 585. ZC: 14435.

Biking: H_2O and portapotty at ball field on NY 15A.

Services: convenience store on NY 15 and on E. Lake Rd.

Lodging: Cottage rentals; B&B: EastLake, 5305 E. Lake Rd, 346-3350; Conesus Lake, 2388 East Lake Rd., Conesus 14435, 346-6526, Conesus Lake Cpgd., 2202 E. Lake Rd., 346-5472; Southern Shores Cpgd., 5707 East Lake Rd, 346-5482.

Attraction: Eagle Crest Vineyards, 7107 Vineyard Rd., 346-2321, although Eagle Crest has a Conesus address, it is really located far above the Lake. It actually overlooks Hemlock Lake.

8.2 (13.2)   Sliker Hill Rd. @ East Lake Rd.   10.4 (16.7)
Turn West on to Sliker Hill Rd.

8.8 (14.2)   NY 256/West Lake Rd.   9.8 (15.8)
                   @ Sliker Hill Rd.
Turn North on to NY 256/West Lake Rd.

10.0 (16.1)   Beach Rd./Co. Rd. 45   8.6 (13.8)
                   @ NY256/West Lake Rd.
Continue traveling North on NY 256/West Lake Rd.
Use Beach Rd./CR 45 to go to Mt. Morris and Letchworth St. Pk. via the Finger Lakes to Chautauqua Lake Route.

13.6 (21.9)   Long Pt. Rd.   5.0 (8.0)
                    @ NY 256/West Lake Rd.
        Continue traveling North on NY 256/West Lake Rd.
        Long Pt. Co. Pk.: H_2O, beach, open shelter, toilets.

17.3 (27.8)   NY 256/West Lake Rd. @ NY 20A   1.3 (2.1)
        Turn East on to NY 20A to go to East Lake Rd. and the
        beginning of the Conesus Lake Circumnavigation Route.
        Use NY 20A West to go to Geneseo and eventually
        Chautauqua Lake

17.8 (28.6)   NY 15 Jct. NY 20A   0.8 (1.3)
        Continue traveling East to complete the ellipse.
        Use NY 15, northbound, to go to Rochester.

18.6 (29.9)   Co. Rd. 6/East Lake Rd.   0.0 (0.0)
                    @ Rtes. 20A/15
        LAKEVILLE

Read ↓   **CONESUS LAKE CIRCUMNAVIGATION**   Read up ↑
Clockwise   Counterclockwise

The Road Not Taken

Two roads diverged in a yellow wood,
And sorry I could not travel both
And be one traveler, long I stood.
And looked down one as far as I
    could
To where it bent in the undergrowth;

Then took the other, as just as fair,
And having perhaps the better claim,
Because it was grassy and wanted
    wear;
Though as for that the passing there
Had worn them really about the
    same,

And both that morning equally lay
In leaves no step had trodden black.
Oh, I kept the first for another day!
Yet knowing how way leads on to
    way,
I doubted if I should ever come back.

I shall be telling this with a sigh
Somewhere ages and ages hence:
Two roads diverged to a wood, and
    I—
I took the one less traveled by,
And that has made all the
    difference.

                    Robert Frost

Bibliography

Dennis, Matthew. *Cultivating A Landscape of Peace: Iroquois-European Encounters in Seventeenth-Century America.* Ithaca, NY: Cornell University Press and New York State Historial Association. 1993.

Doty, Lockwood, ed. *Boyd and Parker: Heroes of the American Revolution.* Geneseo, NY: Livingston County Historical Society. 1928.

Fairchild, Herman Le Roy. *Geologic Story of the Genesee Valley and Western New York.* Rochester, NY: The Author. 1928.

Flick, A. C. *The Sullivan-Clinton Campaign In 1779: Chronology and Selected Documents.* Albany, NY: The State Historian, Division of Archives and History, The University of the State of New York. 1929.

Isachsen, Y. W., et al. *Geology of New York: A Simplified Account.* Albany, NY: New York State Museum/Geological Survey. 1991.

Richter, Daniel K. *The Ordeal of the Longhouse: The Peoples of the Iroquois League in the Era of European Colonization.* Chapel Hill, NC: University of North Carolina Press. 1992.

Thompson, John H. *Geography of New York State.* Syracuse, NY: Syracuse University Press. 1977.

Van Diver, Bradford B. *Roadside Geology of New York.* Missoula, MT: Mountain Press Publishing Co. 1985.

von Engeln, O. D. *The Finger Lakes Region: Its Origin and Nature.* Ithaca, NY: Cornell University Press. 1964.

Acknowledgments

Family and friends are always important to acknowledge for they give the impetus and ask that very vital question, "What's your next book?" Bicyclists who used my other *Tour Guides* and write me kind words or not so kind words are very important. I wish I could include all these folks but alas, space is limited.

My father and mother Samuel and Lillian Botzman; my sister and brother in law Gail and Gerald; nieces and husbands Randi and Ron; Bonnie and Mark; great nephews Alex, Zachary and Jordan; uncles and aunts blood and not Avrum and Celia; Joe and Sylvia have all encouraged me to continue writing these guides.

Friends from teenage years, Larry, David, Barry and Ron; together with those from adulthood, Jeff, Judy, Ed, Martha, Jim, Becky, Pat, Laurie, Gervais, Mike, Bob, Ray, Leticia and Mary have all given me valuable encouragement and an occasional meal to sustain my efforts.

Administratiors and teachers in the Rochester City School District who have employed me as a substitute teacher.

Bicyclists from the Rochester Bicycling Club and the Finger Lakes Cycling Club who suggested alternate routes which cyclotourists could master deserve a hearty thanks.

Thank you all.

Harvey Botzman

April 1, 2005

Appendix

Contents

	Page
Chautauqua Lake	264
Equipment Lists	267
Order Form	270
Comment Form	271
Survey Form	273
Expense Logs	275

Chautauqua Lake

Not far from the Finger Lakes near the shores of Lake Erie is Chautauqua Lake. It is a two and a half day bicycle ride from the western most Finger Lake.

The route around Chautauqua Lake is included here simply because bicyclist who used the First Edition thought it would be a good addition to this *Tour Guide*.

Chautauqua is famous for its summer colony at the *Institution*. In the late 20th century the *Institution* presents more secular than religious programs. The programs belie the *Institution's* Methodist summer *camp* roots. This is a *high* culture haven for those on a vacation with a need to continually think.

Between the Pennsylvania border and Dunkirk/Fredonia is New York State's Lake Erie wine country. It is centered around Westfield but actually extends in a sweeping arc through Pennsylvania and into Ohio.

The USA's *North Coast* and Canada's *South Coast* is truly wonderous!

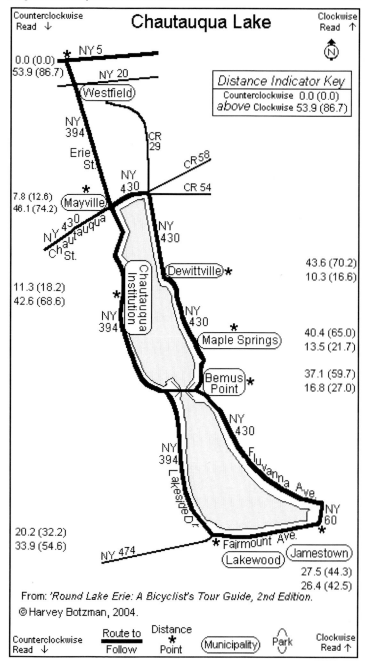

Chautauqua Lake

Counterclockwise
Read ↓

Clockwise
Read ↑

Ⓝ

NY 5

0.0 (0.0)
53.9 (86.7)

NY 20

Westfield

Distance Indicator Key

Counterclockwise 0.0 (0.0)
above Clockwise 53.9 (86.7)

NY
394

Erie
St.

CR
29

CR 58

NY
430

CR 54

7.8 (12.6)
46.1 (74.2)

Mayville

NY 430

Chautauqua

NY
430

Ch St.

Dewittville

43.6 (70.2)
10.3 (16.6)

11.3 (18.2)
42.6 (68.6)

Chautauqua Institution

NY
394

NY
430

Maple Springs

40.4 (65.0)
13.5 (21.7)

Bemus
Point

37.1 (59.7)
16.8 (27.0)

NY
430

NY
394

Fluvanna Ave.

Lakeside Dr.

NY
60

20.2 (32.2)
33.9 (54.6)

Fairmount Ave.

NY 474

Lakewood   Jamestown

27.5 (44.3)
26.4 (42.5)

From: *'Round Lake Erie: A Bicyclist's Tour Guide, 2nd Edition.*
© Harvey Botzman, 2004.

| Counterclockwise Read ↓ | **Route to Follow** | Distance * Point | Municipality | Park | Clockwise Read ↑ |

Equipment List

✓ Clothing
○ Cycling Short
○ Cycling Shorts
○ Cycling Shorts
○ Cycling Gloves
○ Off Cycling Shorts
○ Tee Shirts
○ Tee Shirts
○ Socks #_____
○ Short Socks #_____
○ Underwear
○ Jacket
○ Sweater/Fleece top
○ Dress pants
○ Long (thermal) Tights
○ Jeans
○ Rain Gear
○ Shoes
    ○ Cycling
    ○ Off-cycling
○ Dress
○ Blouse #_____
○ Shirt #_____
○ Wicking base layer
○ Bathing Suit
○ Scarf (*do rag*)
○ Belt
○ Clothes Pins
○ Sewing Kit
○ Hat

○ Other _____

○ Other _____

✓ Tools
○ Combination tool
○ Patch Kit
○ Screwdriver(s)
    ○ Philips
        ○ # 0
        ○ # 1
        ○ # 2
    ○ Flat
        ○ 5mm/ ^{3}/8 in
        ○ 8mm/ ^{5}/8 in
○ Wrenches
    Hex, Open, Box
    or Sockets
        ○ 4mm-H O B S
        ○ 5mm-H O B S
        ○ 6mm-H O B S
        ○ 8mm-H O B S
        ○ 9mm-H O B S
        ○ 10mm-H O B S
○ 11mm-H O B S
        ○ 12mm-H O B S
        ○ 13mm-H O B S
        ○ 14mm-H O B S
        ○ Other_____
○ Pliers
○ Vise Grips
    ○ 3in
    ○ 5in
○ Cone Wrenches
○ Screws
○ Freewheel Remover
○ Crank Remover
○ Electrical Tape

Equipment List

✓ Bicycle
○ Rear Rack
○ Front Rack
○ Low Riders
○ Rear Panniers
○ Handlebar Bag
○ Front Light
○ Rear Flashing Red
○ Light Other Color
○ Wiring for Lights
○ Generator
○ Batteries
○ Extra Batteries
○ Cables
   ○ Brake
   ○ Gears
○ Other_____
○ Special Screws
○ Special Screws
○ Cyclometer
○ Bungie Cords #_____
○ Other _____

○ _____

○ _____

○ _____

○ _____

○ _____

○ _____

○ _____

✓ Personal
○ Watch
○ Towel
○ Sunglasses
○ Helmet
○ First Aid Kit
○ Soap
○ Tooth Brush
○ Tooth Paste
○ Cosmetics
○ 2nd pair of
   Eyeglasses
○ Shaving
   Equipment
○ Medical
   Prescriptions
○ Eyeglass
   Prescription
○ Contact Lens
   Solutions
○ Journal
○ Citizenship ID
○ Pen
○ Stamps
○ Sun Screen
○ Medicine
○ Calculator
○ Flashlight
○ 25¢ (for phone)
○ Credit Cards
○ Passport & Visas
○ Tickets
○ Maps
○ Camera & Film
○ Photographs (self)

Equipment List

✓ Camping
- ○ Tent
  - ○ Tent stakes
  - ○ Tent Poles
  - ○ Ground cloth
- ○ Rope (3m/10ft)
- ○ Sleeping Bag
- ○ Mattress
- ○ Day pack
- ○ H$_2$0 Purifier/Filter
- ○ Toilet Paper
- ○ Candle
- ○ Flashlight
- ○ Other
- ○ _____
- ○ _____

✓ Food
- ○ Pasta
- ○ Cereal
- ○ Rice
- ○ Dried Milk
- ○ Fruit
- ○ Cookies
- ○ Snacks
- ○ Other _____
- ○ _____
- ○ _____

LESS IS MORE
LESS IS MORE

✓ Cooking
- ○ Cup
- ○ Pot (Cook Set)
- ○ Knife
- ○ Fork
- ○ Spoon
- ○ Can
- ○ Opener/Cork Screw
- ○ Stove
  - ○ Fuel Bottle
  - ○ Fuel
  - ○ Matches
  - ○ Pre-Starter
- ○ Stove Repair Kit
- ○ Swiss Army Knife
- ○ Wire (2m/2yds)
- ○ Other _____

- ○ Peanut Butter
- ○ Oil or fat
- ○ Vegetables _____
- ○ Vegetables _____
- ○ Vegetables _____
- ○ Other _____
- ○ _____
- ○ _____
- ○ _____

LESS IS MORE
LESS IS MORE

Order Form
Erie Canal Bicyclist & Hiker Tour Guide

The tow path along the historic Erie, Seneca/Cayuga, Lake Champlain, & Oswego Canals in New York State and the Chambly Canal in Quebec are being developed as a continuous off road bicyclist/hiker route. This Tour Guide also includes the Hudson River Valley bicycle routes to New York City from Albany, NY.

Have no fear road Cyclotourists! Your needs met! A scenic, historic and basically level cyclotouring route has been researched by the Author. A road route parallel to these Canals has been mapped & is described for your use when the tow path has a dirt or gravel surface most suitable for mt. bike bikepackers.

All B&Bs, campgrounds, attractions and information sources are listed in the text together with maps and pictures.

Please send me the books I have checked ✓.

○ Erie Canal Bicyclist & Hiker Tour Guide	us$24.95
○ 'Round Lake Erie: A Bicyclist's Tour Guide	us$24.95
○ 'Round Lake Ontario: A Bicyclist's Tour Guide	us$24.95
○ 'Round Lake Michigan: A Bicyclist's Tour Guide	us$24.95
○ 'Round Lake Huron: A Bicyclist's Tour Guide	us$24.95
○ 'Round Lake Superior: A Bicyclist's Tour Guide	us$24.95
○ Finger Lakes Bicyclist's Tour Guide	us$24.05
○ EDB Guides to the French Canal System	us$25.95
+ Shipping (to USA addresses)	us$ 5.00
TOTAL	us$

_____
YOUR NAME

_____
STREET

_____
CITY, STATE (PROVINCE), ZIP (POSTAL CODE)

Send your US funds
check or money order to:

Cyclotour Guide Books
PO Box 10585
Rochester, NY 14610

E-mail your order to:
Telephone/fax your order to:
Credit card orders:
Check out our web site:

cyclotour@cyclotour.com
585 244-6157
https://www.paypal.com
www.cyclotour.com

Comments

I appreciate your comments. Please feel free to add comments.

Dates you toured: _____

Which chapters or information did you find most useful in *Finger Lakes Bicyclist's Tour Guide, 2nd Ed.*

          ○ Tour Preparation
          ○ The Route
          ○ Distance Information
          ○ Lodging Information
          ○ Municipal Information
          ○ Other: _____

Lodging Recommendations

Attractions Recommendations

Restaurant/Bakery/Grocery Recommendations

Route Recommendations

Other Comments :

Optional Information:
Your Name: _____

Your Address: _____

City, State/Prov., Zip/PC: _____

E-mail: _____

The name of a friend who might be interested in receiving our
    brochure:

Name: _____

Address: _____

City, State/Prov., Zip/PC: _____

E-mail: _____

We do not sell or rent our mailing list.

Please return this Comment Form to:
Cyclotour Guide Books, PO Box 10585, Rochester, NY 14610

Thanks,
Harvey

Survey Form

One of the most significant problems facing bicycling advocates is the the lack of data on cyclotourism and cyclotourists. It is almost impossible to make a case for improving roadway and general bicycle touring conditions unless cycling advocates have data on bicycle tourists.

This Survey is anonymous. You do not have to provide your name, etc. and I will not compare this Form to the *Comment Form*. That's why there are two separate forms.

I have tried to make this Survey Form easy for you to complete. Check the boxes or fill in the spaces, almost all of which are on the right side of the page. Sorry lefties!

Tour of _____

How many people were in your touring party? _____

Demographic data of cyclotourists

Your age? _____ Sex? _____

Spouse's age? _____ Sex? _____

Child's age? _____ Sex? _____

Child's age? _____ Sex? _____

Friend's age? _____ Sex? _____

Friend's age? _____ Sex?_____

Friend's age? _____ Sex? _____

Your approximate per annum income range:

O US $ O CAN $ O EURO €   O Other _____

Teenager on allowance?   O

College Student?   O

Below US$20,000   O

US $20,001 - $30,000   O

US $30,001 - $40,000   O

US $40,001 - $50,000   O

US $50,001 +   O

Enough of this demographic stuff but It is important for presenting a case for better bicycling conditions.

What was the total distance you toured? _____ mi.

The average daily distance you traveled? _____ mi.

Did you tour in segments? _____ How many? _____

Average amount of money expended each day, per person?
In ○ US $ ○ CAN $ ○ EURO ∈   ○ Other _____

Less than US$10.00	○
US $10.01 - 15.00	○
US $15.01 - 25.00	○
US $25.01 - 35.00	○
US $35.01 - 45.00	○
US $45.01 - 55.00	○
US $55.01 - 65.00	○
US $65.01 - 75.00	○
US $75.01 - 85.00	○
Over US $85.01	○

What was the average amount of money you expended each day for these items? In US$___ CN$___ Euros___ Other ___

Amount	Lodging	Food, incl. snacks	Enterainment Attractions	Misc.
< $5.00				
$5.01-10.00				
$10.01-20.00				
$20.01-25.00				
$25.01 +				

How did you cyclotour? General description.

Loaded touring?	○
Camping & eating in restaurants?	○
Sagwagon camping?	○
○ B&Bs ○ Motels & preparing own meals?	○
○ B&Bs ○ Motels & eating in restaurants?	○
Other: _____	○

Feel free & you are encouraged to add other comments or data:

Please return this form to: Cyclotour Guide Books, PO Box, 10585, Rochester, NY 14610.
Thanks,
Harvey

Cyclotour Expense Log

Date	Odometer	Destination	Brkfast	Lunch	Dinner	Groceries	Snacks	Lodging	Bicycle	Misc.	Daily Total	Running Total
Total												

Cyclotour Expense Log

Date	Odometer	Destination	Brkfast	Lunch	Dinner	Groceries	Snacks	Lodging	Bicycle	Misc.	Daily Total	Running Total
Total												

Index

Street and Municipality Index

This index is keyed to the Maps.

Adams Rd.	244, 252	Co. Rd. 1	162, 206, 214
Assembly Rd.	202	Co. Rd. 2	148, 162
Auburn	80, 88, 94	Co. Rd. 4	148, 162
Aurora	94, 100, 112	Co. Rd. 5	148, 162, 206
Avon	56	Co. Rd. 5	156, 162
Bacon Hill Rd.	80	Co. Rd. 6	256
Bath Rd.	176, 190	Co. Rd. 15	236, 244
Becker Rd.	74	Co. Rd. 16	214, 224
Big Tree Rd.	244, 252ff	Co. Rd. 21	202
Birdseye Rd.	176, 190	Co. Rd. 23	176, 190
Blank Rd.	244, 252	Co. Rd. 25	176, 190, 202
Bloomfield	56	Co. Rd. 28	176
Borodino	74	Co. Rd. 33	214, 224, 232
Branchport	190, 204	Co. Rd. 34	214, 224
Brewerton Rd.	50	Co. Rd. 36	224, 232
Briggs Rd.	234, 236	Co. Rd. 37	214, 224, 232
Bristol Spring Rd.	214, 224	Co. Rd. 87	176, 190, 202
Burch Hill Rd.	234, 236	Co. Rd. 096	190
Burdett	148, 162	Co. Rd. 097	176
Burdock Rd.	80, 88	Co. Rd. 114	190
Burnet Ave.	50	Co. Rd. 129	148, 162
Calkins Rd.	56	Co. Rd. 131	148, 162
Camillus	50	Co. Rd. 131A	148, 162
Canadice Hill Rd.	234, 236	Co. Rd. 132	148, 162
Canadice Lake Rd.	234, 236	Coldbrook Rd.	74, 80
Canandaigua	56, 204, 214	Conesus	256
Canoga St.	148, 162	Coon Hill Rd.	74, 80
Cayuga Hts. Rd.	100, 112, 126	Court St.	112, 126
Cayuga St.	112, 126	Cratsey Hill Rd.	234, 236
Cayuga St.	112, 148	Creek Rd.	102, 112, 126
Cheese Factory Rd.	88	Decker Rd.	252, 256
Cherry Valley Tpk.	50, 74, 80	Dresden	162, 176, 190
Church St.	88	Dundee	162, 176, 190
Clark St.	214, 224	Dundee Starkey Rd.	176
Co. Line Rd.	176	E. Bluff Dr.	202

E. Bluff Dr. Ext.	202	Lake Rd.	80
E. Henrietta Rd.	56	Lake Ridge Rd.	112, 126
Earl's Hill Rd.	176	Lake to Lake Rd.	176, 204
East Lake Rd.	74, 80	Lakeshore Dr.	204, 214
Elbert Rd.	74, 80	Lakeville	56, 256
Erie Canal Tow Path	56	Lansing	112, 126
Federal Rd.	244, 252	Leader Rd.	148, 162
Fleet Rd.	190	Lehigh Sta. Rd.	56
Freese Rd.	112, 126	Lima	56
Freeville	100, 112	Linn St.	112, 126
Fulton Ave.	112	Livonia	56, 252, 256
Gannett Hill Rd.	214, 224	Locke	102, 112, 126
Geneva	148, 162, 176	Locke Rd.	102, 112, 126
Gilbert Rd.	148, 162	Lodi	112, 148
Glen Haven	80, 88	Long Point Rd.	256
Glen Haven Rd.	80	Manlius Ctr. Rd.	50
Gray Rd.	176, 190	Maple Rd.	256
Green St.	112, 126	Marcellus	50
Groton	100, 112	Marietta	50, 74, 80
Groveland Rd.	256	Marrowback Rd.	244, 252
Gulick Rd.	224, 232	May Rd.	244, 252
Guyanoga Rd.	190	Meadow St.	112, 126
Hammondsport	190	Mecklenburg Rd.	148, 162
Hanshaw Rd.	112, 126	Middle Rd.	56
Harter Rd.	244, 252	Middlesex	204, 214
Hector St.	148, 162	Mill St.	214, 224
Heifer Rd.	80, 88	Mission Rd.	244, 252
Honeoye	56, 226, 232	Montour Falls	162
Howe Rd.	70	Moon Hill Rd.	74
Hunts Hollow Rd.	204	Moravia	80, 88, 94
Interlaken	112, 148	Mosher Rd.	224, 232
Italy Hill Rd.	190, 204	N. Old Bald Hill Rd.	236, 244
Italy Tpk.	204	N. Vine Valley Rd.	204, 214
Italy Valley Rd.	204, 214	Naples	204, 214
Ithaca	94, 100, 112, 148	New Hope	80, 88
Jersey Rd.	234, 236	New Hope Rd.	80, 88
Johnson Hill Rd.	234, 236, 244	Niver Rd.	244, 252, 256
Jugg St.	88	North St.	112, 148
Kime Rd.	148, 162	Nunnery Rd.	74, 80

King Ferry	94, 100, 112, 148	NY 5	50ff
Lake Rd.	80	NY 11	50
Lake Ridge Rd.	112, 126	NY 13	112, 126
Lake to Lake Rd.	176, 204	NY 14	162, 176
Lakeshore Dr.	204, 214	NY 14A	162, 176, 190, 204
Lakeville	56, 256	NY 15	56, 244, 252, 256
Lansing	112, 126	NY 15A	56, 236, 244, 252
Leader Rd.	148, 162	NY 20	50ff, 70, 80
Lehigh Sta. Rd.	56	NY 20A	56, 214, 226, 232ff
Lima	56	NY 21	176, 214, 224
Linn St.	112, 126	NY 23	162, 176
Livonia	56, 252, 256	NY 28	162, 176
Locke	102, 112, 126	NY 34	102, 112, 126
Locke Rd.	102, 112, 126	NY 34A	100, 112
Lodi	112, 148	NY 34B	112, 126
Long Point Rd.	256	NY 38	100, 112
Manlius Ctr. Rd.	50	NY 38A	88
Maple Rd.	256	NY 41	74, 80, 88
Marcellus	50	NY 41A	80, 88
Marietta	50, 74, 80	NY 53	204, 214
Marrowback Rd.	244, 252	NY 54	162, 176, 190
May Rd.	244, 252	NY 54A	176, 190, 202, 204
Meadow St.	112, 126	NY 64	56, 214, 224
Mecklenburg Rd.	148, 162	NY 65	56
Middle Rd.	56	NY 79	112, 126, 148, 162
Middlesex	204, 214	NY 89	100, 112
Mill St.	214, 224	NY 90	102, 112, 126
Mission Rd.	244, 252	NY 96	112, 126, 148, 162
Montour Falls	162	NY 96A	112, 126, 148, 162
Moon Hill Rd.	74	NY 141	112, 148
Moravia	80, 88, 94	NY 174	50, 74, 80
Mosher Rd.	224, 232	NY 175	50, 74, 80
N. Old Bald Hill Rd.	236, 244	NY 226	176, 190
N. Vine Valley Rd.	204, 214	NY 230	176, 190
Naples	204, 214	NY 245	204, 214
New Hope	80, 88	NY 255	252, 256
New Hope Rd.	80, 88	NY 256	252, 256
Niver Rd.	244, 252, 256	NY 327	102, 112, 148
North St.	112, 148	NY 364	176, 190, 204, 214

NY 366	102, 112, 126	Springwater	236, 244
NY 409	162, 176	State St.	112
NY 414	148, 162	Sunset Rd.	112, 126
Old W. Lake Rd.	190, 204	39 Syracuse	50
Otisco Valley Rd.	70	Talmadge Rd.	112
Outlet Trail	162	Thurston St.	112, 126
Ovid	112, 148	Town Line Rd.	236
Park Rd.	112, 148	Triphammer Rd.	102, 112, 126
Park St.	50	Trumansburg	112, 148
Penn Yan,	176, 190, 204	Union Springs	112
Picnic Area Rd.	148, 162	University Ave.	112, 126
Pinewood Hill Rd.	224, 232	Upper Lake Rd.	148, 162
Pittsford	56	Vincent Hill Rd.	80
Porters Cors. Rd.	176, 190	W. Bluff Dr.	190, 204
Purcell Hill Rd.	236	W. Genesee St.	50
Remington St.	112, 126	W. Groton Rd.	102, 112, 126
Rhine St.	214, 224	W. Henrietta Rd.	56
Richmond Mills Rd.	236, 244	W. Hollow Rd.	214, 224
Ridge Rd.	176	W. Lake Rd.	80, 88,
Rix Hill Rd.	236, 244, 252		214, 224 252
Rochester	56	W. Salina St.	50
Rockefeller Rd.	88, 94	W. State St.	50
Rose Hill Rd.	74	W. Valley Rd.	70
Rtes. 5 & 20	56ff	Wait Ave.	112, 126
Rushville	204, 214	Waterloo	148
S. Old Bald Hill Rd.	236, 244	Watkins Glen	148, 162, 176
S. Vine Valley Rd.	204, 214	Wesley Rd.	224, 232
Sawmill Rd.	74	West Ave.	112, 126
Seneca Falls	94, 100, 148	West Lake Rd.	176
Seneca St.	112, 126, 148, 162	Weston Hill Rd.	236
Sherwood Rd.	94, 100, 112	Wetmore Rd.	236
Skaneateles	50, 74, 80	Willard St.	148, 162
Slicker Hill Rd.	252, 256	Willowdale Hill Rd.	70
South Bay Rd.	50	Willowdale Rd.	70
Spaffford	74, 80	Woodworth Rd.	80
		Yellow Tavern Rd.	148, 162

Notes